THE CITY AND THE VELD

THE CITY
AND THE VELD

The Fiction
of Doris Lessing

Mary Ann Singleton

Lewisburg
Bucknell University Press
London: Associated University Presses

©1977 by Associated University Presses, Inc.

Associated University Presses, Inc.
Cranbury, New Jersey 08512

Associated University Presses
Magdalen House
136-148 Tooley Street
London SE1 2TT, England

Library of Congress Cataloging in Publication Data

Singleton, Mary Ann.
    The city and the veld.

      Bibliography: p.
      Includes index.
      1. Lessing, Doris May, 1919–   —Criticism
and interpretation.   I. Title.
PR6023.E833Z89   823'.9'14   75-5145
ISBN 0-8387-1652-0

The author thanks:
    Doubleday & Company, Inc. for permission to quote from The Sufis,
    copyright 1964 by Idries Shah. Reprinted by permission of Double-
    day & Co., Inc.

    Simon & Schuster, Inc., for permission to quote from Doris Lessing,
    African Stories *(copyright © 1951, 1953, 1954, 1957, 1958,*
    1962, 1963, 1964, 1965 by Doris Lessing); Children of Violence
    vols. 1 and 2 (copyright © 1952, 1954, 1964 by Doris Lessing);
    Children of Violence *vols. 3 and 4 (copyright © 1970 by Doris*
    Lessing); The Golden Notebook *(copyright © 1962 by Doris*
    Lessing). All reprinted by permission of Simon and Schuster.

PRINTED IN THE UNITED STATES OF AMERICA

For my parents
RALPH and MERCEDES SINGLETON

Contents

Preface

Few people can read Doris Lessing and then just forget about her; she affects lives—the way people view themselves and their world. Too many of us can find ourselves somewhere among Lessing's characters—with Jack Orkney, Charles Watkins, or Kate Brown—beginning to perceive the superficiality of what they had considered exemplary lives; with Anna Wulf and Martha Quest struggling against the mental entrapment of traditional female roles; with the many characters who have been violated by an insane society. I know people who, having glimpsed themselves here, are then unable to remain fixed by the patterns of life and thought that Lessing exposes so artfully.

Yet to explicate Lessing's fiction would seem to do it violence; such an endeavor is of course reductive, and Lessing continually strikes out against the mental divisions that she believes distort the human spirit. Nevertheless, at the same time she does wish to be understood. This fact is clear, both in her novels and in the comments she makes about them in essays and interviews. Quite simply, she believes (with many others) that our civilization is slipping ever-faster toward the precipice. Almost from the beginning, her work has explored what in human nature is causing this catastrophe and what, if anything, can be done about it. I believe that no novelist writing today has treated these crucial issues with her art, perception, and persuasiveness.

Lessing's attention is always turned toward humanity's destructive weaknesses and potential strength, and it is essentially these that I have called the two *cities* and the *veld*. For Lessing, the African veld is the unconscious, physical world of nature that nourishes mankind with its unity but also inflicts its own mindless repetition and, in human terms, cruelty and indifference. The city is half-evolved consciousness, the destructive fragmentation of partial awareness. The ideal City is a hope for the future: the unified individual in a harmonious society. To impose such an intellectual scheme upon Lessing's work goes against its spirit; however, if it leads to increased understanding of her writing, perhaps to do so is forgivable.

It seems to me that the key issue here is the nature of understanding. In Lessing's story, "Report on the Threatened City," the inhabitants know intellectually that a major earthquake in their midst is predicted and is inevitable; nevertheless, they are unable to integrate that knowledge into their lives. They neither leave the city nor take precautions against the coming disaster. That is, their understanding has been superficial. The understanding that Lessing calls for is different, like that described by a yoga master I know who insists that true perception can not be separated from action: to see a tree about to fall across your path is to move out of its way. Or, as he puts it, "Seeing *is* movement." For Lessing, right action is possible only through true understanding, one of the characteristics of the City.

In describing Lessing's themes I have drawn many parallels to the work of Carl Jung. In doing so, my wish is not the sterile one of showing influences. Rather, some of his theories—especially that of the personal and mass shadow—illuminate Lessing's work. Jung outlined what he felt to be the chief illness of modern society, and Lessing has dramatized the same ideas. Since *Landlocked*, Sufism has been important to her work. Lessing has been a student of this transcendental psychology for a decade, and its effect on her perception has been profound, posing a special problem for the critic, as the main characteristic of Sufism is that it is inimical to analysis. As a result, I have chosen not to attempt a detailed discussion of it. Serious readers of Lessing should read the books of Idries Shah, especially *The Sufis*.

I am of course interested in Lessing as an artist, and I deal with her narrative technique, choice of images, and the structure of some novels. This part of the study is for specialists in literature who, like myself, enjoy understanding fiction from the formalist point of view. But artistry aside, I particularly wish to convey that Lessing is writing about the same matters as Jung, R. D. Laing, the later Aldous Huxley, the humanistic psychologists, and the exponents and explicators of traditional Eastern psychology and philosophy.

Like these others, Lessing lays bare the really important problems that face us today: survival, and beyond that, the potential of the human spirit. And while one can encounter ideas similar to hers in other places, she does what only the novelist can do—dramatize them and imbue them with the special reality of the artistic imagination. In doing so, her hope surely is to effect the kind of understanding that leads to movement instead of just discussion.

Acknowledgments

Grateful acknowledgment is made to those named below for permission to quote from the works as listed:

Aldus Books Limited, for permission to quote from Aniela Jaffé, "Symbolism in the Visual Arts;" Carl G. Jung, "Approaching the Unconscious;" and M.-L. von Franz, "The Process of Individuation," all from *Man and His Symbols*, edited by Carl G. Jung © 1964 Aldus Books Limited, London.

Curtis Brown Limited, for permission to quote from Doris Lessing, *African Stories* (1964); *Briefing for a Descent into Hell* (1971); the *Children of Violence* series (1952, 1954, 1958, 1965, 1969); *The Golden Notebook* (1962); "On *The Golden Notebook*," which first appeared in *Partisan Review* (Winter 1973); *The Summer Before the Dark* (1973); and *The Temptation of Jack Orkney and Other Stories* (1972).

John Cushman Associates, Inc., for permission to quote from Doris Lessing, *The Summer before the Dark* (Alfred A. Knopf, Inc., 1973) and *The Temptation of Jack Orkney and Other Stories* (Alfred A. Knopf, Inc., 1972). Reprinted by permission of John Cushman Associates, Inc.

Alfred A. Knopf, Inc., for permission to quote extensively without charge from Doris Lessing, *The Four-Gated City* (Copyright ©1969 by Doris Lessing Productions, Ltd.) and

THE CITY AND THE VELD

1

The City and the Veld

Yeats once said that "there is for every man some one scene, some one adventure . . . that is the image of his secret life."[1] Similarly, in the work of some writers is a scene, or a composite of several scenes, that crystallizes the essential problems from which most of the writing springs. For Hemingway there is Nick Adams in "Big Two-Hearted River," just back from war, meticulously carrying out the ritual of trout fishing, but carefully avoiding the dark areas of the swamp; for Yeats himself, perhaps a lonely poet in a tower, troops marching by in the street below, swans wheeling above. For Doris Lessing, too, there is such a scene: two cities on the African highveld. The veld itself appears stark and barren, but actually it teems with life. Sky and land meet in the brilliance of clear air. One city is all too recognizable in its division into slums and mansions and the unhappiness and strife of its citizens. Behind it, like a mirage, shimmers the image of another city that never was, except in the Utopian imagination. Martha describes it in *Martha Quest:*

> There arose, glimmering whitely over the harsh scrub and the stunted trees, a noble city, set foursquare and colonnaded along its falling, flower-bordered terraces. There were splashing fountains,

and the sound of flutes; and its citizens moved, grave and beautiful, black and white and brown together; and these groups of elders
paused, and smiled with pleasure at the sight of the children—the
blue-eyed, fair-skinned children of the North playing hand and
hand with the bronze-skinned, dark-eyed children of the South.
Yes, they smiled and approved these many-fathered children, running and playing among the flowers and the terraces, through the
white pillars and tall trees of this fabulous and ancient city.[2]

The ideal of the City stands behind everything Lessing has
written, an expression of her firm sense of purpose, put most
explicitly in an important essay, "The Small Personal Voice."
There she affirms a belief in "committed" literature, in which
the writer considers himself/herself "an instrument of change."
For if the ideal of the City stands in the background of Lessing's work, the Armageddon of technological disaster looms
there as well. In the same essay she states the alternatives as
she sees them:

There are only two choices: that we force ourselves into the effort
of imagination necessary to become what we are capable of being;
or that we submit to being ruled by the office boys of big business,
or the socialist bureaucrats who have forgotten that socialism means
a desire for goodness and compassion—and the end of submission
is that we blow ourselves up.

Lessing believes that mankind is at a crucial point in history
and that artists must paint the possible evil as well as
strengthen "a vision of good which may defeat the evil"[3]; that
is, art for society's sake. Lessing's criteria for art fit her own
work. Not simply an artist, she is also critic and prophet, dissect-
ing in minute detail the faults of a society "hypnotized by the
idea of Armageddon" and prophesying the calamitous results of
those faults. At the same time, she attempts to delineate possible solutions to the world's problems.

There are three main motifs in Lessing's work, which I have
called the two *cities* and the *veld*, and they are apparent in her

themes, imagery, and structures. The veld represents the unity of nature, whole and complete, but in which the individual counts for nothing. Before the birth of self-consciousness, as it is known today, mankind readily participated in this natural world and at times was scarcely differentiated from it; but the price of unity was to be caught in the ceaseless round of natural repetition, all instinct with no reason.

The city represents modern consciousness, expressed in a strife-torn society. Its origins are the loss of mythic consciousness that prevailed in early, simpler cultures; its power, the ability to use the tools of reason; its culmination, the achievements and excesses of the last two hundred years, when logic and reason have come to be valued by society as a whole almost to the exclusion of other modes of perception. Reason has the power to raise mankind above the brute, instinctual level, but in its present form it is partial, fragmented. This idea is expressed in a well-known fable about a group of blind men trying to describe an elephant. One says that it is long and soft and emits air. Another insists that it is massive, cylindrical, and hard. A third is sure that it is rough and scaly. Each has part of the whole truth, depending on whether he touched trunk, leg, or skin. According to Lessing, such fragmented perception is presently leading mankind to certain disaster—much like fire in the hands of a child—causing unbalanced, private lives and conflict in society. As citizens of the contemporary city, mankind is a victim of a second type of repetition, not of natural cycles this time, but the constant replaying of destructive patterns of behavior. Both here and in the veld he has no hope of change except from natural evolution, in which he is simply acted upon: Jude rather than Prometheus.

The third motif is the ideal City, a new and more unified form of consciousness, in which everyone can perceive the whole elephant, expressed as a harmonious society of unified citizens. The human imagination holds the key: "[we must]

force ourselves into the effort of imagination necessary to become what we are capable of being." Nature's harsh unity is no longer compatible with human self-consciousness and values. Partial truths have proved disastrous. The next step is to create new, whole forms that will somehow contain intuition along with reason, both myth and logic, with all the complexities the terms suggest. When—and if—this new unity is accomplished, the ideal City will be possible, the Golden Age finally at hand. The City in the veld is a man-made harmony—part of nature, yet at the same time separate from it, as consciousness is of and yet above nature.

Most of Lessing's fiction may be seen within this overall pattern. For the most part, Lessing depicts the psychically warped citizens of the city, all inexorably headed for disaster. The early *The Grass Is Singing* concerns Mary Turner's complete destruction by social and psychic forces of which she is not even aware, and many of the short stories dramatize the fragmented lives of people who have varying degrees of awareness. *Retreat to Innocence* shows Julia Barr's refusal to leave the superficial life of the city.

After *The Grass Is Singing*, Lessing's major protagonists and more visionary characters search for ways to integrate the city and the veld, even while they are inextricably caught in the tangles of the mass psyche and society. *The Golden Notebook* is an odyssey of the individual in search of wholeness, and while Anna Wulf's story is central, the reader sees beyond it to the society that conditions her and limits what she can be. *Children of Violence* is Lessing's most complete portrait of the fragmented city. Here, half a century passes before one's eyes, as Martha and her closest friends search in vain for inner and outer versions of the City, as society races with increasing speed toward its destruction. In *Children of Violence* Lessing comes closest to the first half of her criterion for the committed writer—to paint a vision of evil; her view of the good that may defeat it has evolved slowly and is therefore more clearly presented in the later works. *Briefing for a Descent into Hell* shows the richness of the intuitive, mythical world that is ignored by modern society as a whole; it focuses on the underside of the city, which needs to be integrated with consciousness. *The Summer before the Dark* and "The Temptation of Jack Orkney" show characters who are beginning to awaken to the inner space that lies on the other side of consciousness. It is in *Briefing, Summer,* and several stories in *The Temptation of Jack Orkney and Other Stories* that Lessing best portrays a saving vision of unity.

There is a substantial difference between Lessing's view of humanity's possibilities and the predominant attitude of most twentieth-century novels, in which the hero is perforce an antihero, stumbling gallantly through the world. Certainly Lessing's view of man in his present condition is bleak: in these lost generations, too, everyone is sick. Nevertheless, she extends a glimmer of hope that somewhere latent in man is, after all, the possibility of psychic health.

Like Lawrence, Yeats, and the later Aldous Huxley, Lessing looks back to the lost wisdom of philosophy and religion ignored by Western culture since the age of science. This is not to say that she settles into a hazy mysticism. As Margaret Drabble has justly said, "she is one of the very few novelists who have refused to believe that the world is too complicated to understand."[4] It is the combination of ancient wisdom with modern insistence to understand that stands at the heart of Lessing's work.

Lessing is a writer of great variety. Her short stories are usually economical and carefully crafted, while *Children of Violence* sprawls over five long novels, finally moving away almost entirely from customary narrative techniques. In structure and themes *The Golden Notebook* questions the value of the ordinary, realistic novel, while Lessing's recent *The Summer before the Dark* is quite traditional in form. *Briefing for a Descent into Hell*

takes place almost entirely in the private world of Charles Watkins's unconscious mind—paradoxically, where the mind loses
its uniqueness in the mass psyche—while most of Lessing's
work delineates with precision the nuances of personal relationships and the nature of the persona. But if her forms vary, her
metaphysic, which I have summed up in the images of the two
cities in the veld, remains essentially the same.

Three of Lessing's short stories, taken as a group, concisely
sum up this basic philosophy: "A Sunrise on the Veld,"
" 'Leopard' George," and "The Antheap." "A Sunrise on the
Veld" is one of Lessing's finest stories; in it the protagonist, an
adolescent boy, gets his first glimpse of what it means to be
human. He must face the knowledge that he is a dual
creature—part of nature and its blind fatality, but also (unlike
the wild creatures he lives among) a responsible being capable
of ethical judgments. This new awareness sends him spinning
out of the joyful garden of his childhood.

To summarize briefly, the boy rises early for a hunting ex-
pedition and, exhilarated by the morning and his freedom,
leaps joyfully through the bush "like a duiker." Momentarily it
occurs to him that he might break an ankle, but he discards the
thought quickly; it can not happen to him. Pure joy surges in
him, with feelings of power: "I contain the world. I can make
of it what I want. If I choose, I can change everything that is
going to happen: it depends on me, and what I decide now."
Then he is confronted by a horrifying scene: a young buck
being eaten alive by ants. Though sick and angry, he enjoys a
grim new stoicism brought on by his new perception of fatality:
"It was right and nothing could alter it."

And at that moment he could not have performed the smallest
action of mercy, knowing as he did, having lived on it all his life,
the vast unalterable, cruel veld, where at any moment one might
stumble over a skull or crush the skeleton of some small creature.

Then a new thought occurs to him; how did the buck get trapped by the ants? He examines the remains, already a cleanly picked skeleton, to discover a broken leg, undoubtedly injured by natives throwing stones at the animal. He remembers the many times he himself has taken a quick shot at a disappearing buck and failed to track it—leading it, perhaps, to a similar fate? "For a moment he would not face it. He was a small boy again, kicking sulkily at the skeleton, hanging his head, refusing to accept the responsibility."[5] But the thought remains with him, disturbingly, as something to be thought out.

The boy's kinship to the buck is apparent; he, too, could have broken a leg on that lonely veld. Like the buck, he is part of the "grim fatality" affecting all living things. He is not all-powerful, as it had seemed in his boyish exuberance, but neither is he merely a cog in the great machine. In some way he combines those two positions; though part of blind nature, he is responsible—but how?

This story charts the fall from a mythic unity of man and the universe to the fragmentation and responsibility of consciousness. As a child the boy is a joyful, unthinking part of a larger whole, although this is no harmonious Eden. Nor is it the beatific nature of Wordsworth and Coleridge; rather, it is "vast" and "cruel." But as an unconscious participant, the boy is not aware of such concepts as cruelty; he unknowingly contains them, part of nature. This is the state of wholeness, the veld, that with the growth of consciousness is lost, because when one knows, one knows responsibility: to commit cruelty and to do so knowingly are two different things.

The focus of "A Sunrise on the Veld" is the boy's revelation; the reader never knows how—or if—the boy works this knowledge into his life. In " 'Leopard' George" is a more complete view of a similar awakening. In this story George is forced to recognize his responsibility, but he refuses to face it squarely. The result is a complete distortion of his personality. This story is important because it clearly illustrates one of Lessing's basic tenets, well documented by twentieth-century psychology, that when one refuses to admit to elements in his own personalities, they take their own revenge, in their own way. A familiar example is the man who prides himself on his morality. Unable to see his own weaknesses, only those of others, he may become viciously intolerant, seriously immoral in a different way than he could imagine.

Lessing seems to share C. G. Jung's theory that a whole society may be similarly affected by mass suppression of psychic elements and that the Western tendency to rely on reason and logic at the expense of the unconscious, the failure to give the devil his due, puts society as a whole at the mercy of its "shadow." Thus "mankind always stands upon the verge of those actions that it performs itself but does not control. The whole world wants peace, and the whole world prepares for war, to give but one example."[6] "Modern man does not understand how much his 'rationalism' . . . has put him at the mercy of the psychic 'underworld.' "[7]

" 'Leopard' George" dramatizes the revenge of the unconscious when Eden is lost and the conscious mind refuses to accept the darker side of the psyche, leaving it free to develop and wield control. George, like the boy in "A Sunrise on the Veld," is very nearly at one with nature as the story begins. He buys a remote, barren farm and during weekdays rides there alone, avoiding all passersby, lapsing at times into an almost mystic absorption with his surroundings. One high point of land especially attracts him:

> He would stay there half the morning, with the crooning of the green-throated wood-pigeons in his ears, and when he rode back home for his meal, his eyes were heavy and veiled.

The whole farm is harmonious and natural. To the natives it is home. For the animals it is a preserve, for George will allow none shot. Though wifeless and somewhat remote from society, he is content: "for there are some people the word loneliness can never be made to fit. George was alone, and seemed not to know it." That is, he does not see himself as separate. He is part of a whole.

> Somewhere a dog was howling at the moon; all the sounds of the night rose from the bush, bird noises, insect noises, animal noises that could not be named: here was a vast protean life, and a cruel one. George . . . felt as he always did: it was the feeling which had brought him here many years before. It was as if, while he looked, he was flowing softly outwards, diffused into the bush and the moonlight. He knew no terror; he could not understand fear; he contained that cruelty within himself, shut safe in some deep place.

George is jolted from this unity when, without willing it, he nevertheless becomes indirectly responsible for the death of a young native woman by a leopard. He has unwittingly taken as a mistress the young wife of Old Smoke, his dignified old manager. When the woman persists in coming to George, he simply locks her out; when she returns to the compound late at night, she is killed. Once unconsciously containing nature and contained by it, George, like the boy in "A Sunrise on the Veld," becomes confronted by his own guilt, which he can not face. He suffers fragmentation, the curse of consciousness, and his whole universe rearranges itself:

> In the now strong sunlight he shivered again; and crossed his arms so that his hands cupped his shoulders: they felt oddly frail. Till lately they had included the pushing strength of mountains; till this morning his arms had been branches and the birds sang in them; within him had been that terror which now waited outside and which he must fight.[8]

Because George fails to meet the challenge of maturity through self-knowledge, he is doomed to play out the same drama again and again, killing leopards compulsively, even with his bare hands, trying to satisfy the strange new hunger that gnaws him. He can not see that his real enemy is within: the callousness that led to the young woman's death. Instead, he projects it outside, making leopards his antagonists, but since it is a shadow-enemy only, it can never be conquered by physical violence. The result is a life of fruitless repetition. George's plight is a paradigm of Lessing's view of what has gone wrong with society: when people mistake their enemies, projecting an inner weakness and turning it into a cause célèbre, the result is ever-repeating patterns of violence. Self-knowledge is the only solution.

Important to this story is the conflict between wholeness and social consciousness: the veld and the city. Until the native woman is killed, George could virtually ignore the society around him. The natives on his farm have been handled by Old Smoke, longtime friend of his father; love has been merely affectionate sex, without emotional ties or responsibility. Having no wife, George has not been drawn into the normal social life of the other farmers. Afterwards, everything is changed. Smoke leaves and George is then "in the position of his neighbors," with a tangle of native problems. Also, he marries. These events, along with his leopard mania, dramatize his passing from a state of unity to an ordinary part of society, but they also underline the chasm between these two states. Society— the city—unlike the veld, necessarily extends the challenge of responsibility.

This is not to say that George becomes a man of feeling. His earlier callousness to the native girls who were his lovers carries over into his new life; his wife, the reader is told, knew "what she could and could not do if she wished to remain mistress of Four Winds" (p. 224). For Lessing, true responsibility means to accept what one is and how one affects the welfare of others. So long as George was able to live in a natural, unified state, he could ignore such concerns; it was only when his first native woman made a public claim on him, appearing seductively in front of his guests, that he had to act with wisdom and compassion—which he failed to do, summarily sending her away to a certain life of prostitution in the city.

True responsibility implies both knowledge and right feeling. George fails because he neither understands himself nor extends his imagination far enough to have empathy for others. His story provides in cameo form Lessing's view of society's illness. Fragmented, people will not accept responsibility for their own nature, their own actions. As a result, they are incapable of healthy responses and are bound to endless automatic repetitions of behavior—often violent and unfeeling. In this way, right feeling becomes transmuted into such collective passions as race prejudice or religious intolerance. Or a person may become blocked to emotion altogether. In *The Golden Notebook* it is an inability to feel that takes Anna to a psychiatrist. Only when she has learned to know herself and is able to deal with her shadow is she cured and able once again to create. In "A Sunrise on the Veld" it was noted that the boy is capable of empathy for the most part; he is sick with horror at the misery of the buck—except for one moment, when he divorces himself from it because "that's life." Momentarily he becomes unfeeling, and sympathy does not return until he begins to accept responsibility for his part in the scheme of things. In Lessing's philosophy, if the City is ever to replace the fragmented city of today, it will be through knowledge and feeling, which lead inevitably to an acceptance of responsibility. These are ingredients of the healing imagination.

In "The Antheap," a story unusually optimistic for Lessing, Tommy Clarke recognizes his responsibility and acts on it, both consciously and unconsciously. That is, he confronts his problem with his entire being, through wholeness. So does his opposite, Dirk. The result is small but certain victory through a combination of knowledge, feeling, responsibility, and intuition—the fourth ingredient of the creative imagination.

In this story Tommy is raised as the only white boy at a remote gold mine owned by the unscrupulous Mr. Macintosh, who carelessly sacrifices the lives of his workers for high profits. The machinery of the mine stamps out the sound, "Gold, Gold, Gold," and the mine itself is like a huge antheap, a consistent symbol throughout Lessing's work of the steady natural forces that constantly and mindlessly destroy and rebuild, in endless repetition.[9] Tommy would seem to be headed toward the usual life of the white child raised in Africa. At a certain age he is sent to school to become prepared for a suitable career, and at the same time he is told that during his holidays it is no longer appropriate to play with his native friends, even his constant companion, the half-caste Dirk.

At first Tommy accepts the situation, but he has a moment of revelation that changes the course of his life when he finally sees that Dirk, half-white, must be the son of Mr. Macintosh, the mine owner. Mr. Macintosh has always treated Tommy like the son he claims he never had, leaving Dirk, the real son, to his fate—which is to be an outcast of both white *and* black society. The injustice of the situation never leaves Tommy. From that time he accepts responsibility for Dirk, giving him any spending money that comes from Mr. Macintosh and educating him during school holidays. The boys build a hut on a nearby antheap in which they study and where Tommy stores various carvings that he makes. Finally Tommy uses as a wedge Mr. Macintosh's love for him and respect for his artistic talent and persuades him to send Dirk to college along with himself. Dirk already seems to be headed toward a successful career in civil rights, while Tommy is by then an obviously gifted sculptor.

In this story the two boys, who are complete opposites, contribute to each other the wholeness that releases their creativity. Through Tommy's tutelage, Dirk soon becomes proficient in mathematics, history, and law, easily surpassing his young teacher, and is soon holding classes for the mine workers, teaching them about their rights. He becomes the reverse of the cruel little child of nature of his early years.

Tommy, on the other hand, child of a white society, born to education and expectations, rebels against his culture as Dirk does. Unlike Dirk, he does not want to "be" anything. Instead, his gift is intuitive—art. From earliest childhood he has shown genius, but only his encounters with Dirk have drawn it forth: his subjects have been the fawn that Dirk inadvertently killed by taking it too young from its mother, Dirk's family, and most important, Dirk himself. In every case it has been an emotional response that Tommy has transmuted into art. Toward the end, he sees that sculpture is not frivolous and gains "a new respect for it and for himself." His carving of Dirk, half tree and half man, becomes a powerful statement about the emerging black man.

Tommy and Dirk are opposites and as a result are able to help create each other. It is the dialectic of Hegel, the central principle of Coleridge; a tension of opposites leads to something new. Tommy gives intellect and conscience to the child of nature, and Dirk gives intuition and responsibility to the child of the ruling class. This dialectic is dramatized throughout the story in the boys' frequent fights. Brothers yet enemies, they fight viciously because of their differences, only to end each battle with a renewed and heightened feeling of kinship.

Fatality plays a part in this story, as it does in " 'Leopard' George" and "A Sunrise on the Veld." The fate of the buck and the death of the native girl are examples, but in both of these stories fatality occurs through a mixture of purely natural events and human intervention. Natural fatality exists, but mankind need not copy its blind and violent patterns. In "The Antheap" it is imaged by the ants chewing away at Tommy and Dirk's hut, to "make food for themselves," and to create "new material for their different forms of life."[10] The gold mine, a human antheap, shows how greed and callousness cause men simply to follow the patterns of nature, unenlightened by empathy and imagination. Tommy and Dirk's hut is built directly on the antheap, a steady reminder that they are part of relentless forces, both natural and human, that seem certain to send both their hopes crashing much as the ants destroy anything edible, whatever its value to human beings. Yet as both Tommy and Dirk lift themselves out of the grip of fatality by means of their intellect and imagination, the antheap provides a counterpoint to their achievement. By joining their disparate elements the two boys succeed in changing the shape of their lives. Through a mixture of intellect, intuition, feeling, and responsibility, both have a chance to be whole and creative and at least partially in control of events.

Lessing never lets one forget, however, that any gain toward harmony is minuscule in a society where the problems of fragmentation run broad and deep. Mr. Macintosh reminds the boys of the prejudice they will face at college; they will not dare even to be seen together. Similarly, in *The Golden Notebook* one understands that Anna's—or anyone's—difficult progress toward wholeness will have little effect in the world, where the forces of blind repetition are so overwhelming that individual effort, however heroic, can scarcely make any real advance against them. And in *Children of Violence* it appears that only a mutated race may be capable of the kind of consciousness that can save the world from never-ending violence. Nevertheless, Lessing gives a model of success. If harmony ever comes—if the City should ever be possible—it will be along these lines: through integration of the human imagination and intelligence.

The young Dirk, George, and the boy in "A Sunrise on the Veld," before their crises, illustrate the not-yet-socialized state in which they are still at one with their world. Although Lessing's nature is cruel, these still unconscious people are not bothered by such concepts as cruelty. Dirk, for example, without a twinge, can kill an antelope with a stone and allow its fawn to die; he has not felt himself to be separate from nature and in some way responsible for needless cruelty. These characters may be said to dramatize an evolution of consciousness similar to the evolution of humankind as a whole. In *The Origins and History of Consciousness* Erich Neumann has analyzed the emergence of consciousness from the paradisical unconscious state of nature in which there are "no doubts and no division of the world into two" to the differentiation of the ego with its attendant dangers. According to Neumann, this development is mirrored in each individual. Childhood is the golden age of unconsciousness, but with true maturity comes the challenge and the problems of the ego.

The state of unity experienced by Dirk, George, and the boy in "A Sunrise on the Veld" in the beginning of all three stories is that of the Great Mother, in which one is not separated from creation as a whole but takes part in the cyclical repetition of life and death. It is a "state of being contained in the whole, without responsibility or effort"[11] and is comparable to the unconscious collective state in a primitive society, to which Levy-Bruhl attached the term *participation mystique*. Jung describes this state as one in which a person senses no distinction between subject and object: "What happens outside also happens in him, and what happens in him also happens outside."[12] Meaning is not separate from word, and a part is also the whole, as one's shadow is not separate from self in the primitive mind. Unlike the analytical world of man-made concepts, the mythic perception does not admit distinctions; it is an "unbroken, continuous whole." And man is not alienated, possessing a separate ego; rather, he is moved by a "deep conviction of a fundamental and indelible solidarity of life that bridges over the multiplicity and variety of its various forms. He does not ascribe to himself a unique and privileged place in the scale of nature."[13]

This mythic state is the world of the veld, which human beings share insofar as they are the veld's unthinking inhabitants. The city comes into existence along with logical, discursive thought and language—and with them, the gradually maturing concept of *I*—which has shattered the unity. If the result is loss of Eden, it is the gain of full humanity with consciousness and, its corollary, responsibility. It is Milton's Adam and Eve leaving the Garden. But in addition, discursive thought brings with it the possibility of control. Humankind is then in the position of creating a reality of its own, for "Whatever has been fixed by a name, henceforth is not only real, but is Reality." Experience can then be manipulated in a logical manner. This new kind of thinking frees people from their environment, allowing their minds free play over the new world of ideas and concepts, but the necessary penalty is to lose touch with experience. While in myth "only the tangible reality exists," in theoretical thinking the word stands apart from experience, and therefore it can move freely.[14] Whether one approves or not, there is no reversing the process:

> Man cannot escape from his own achievement. He cannot but adopt the conditions of his own life. No longer in a merely physical universe, man lives in a symbolic universe. . . . No longer can man confront reality immediately; he cannot see it, as it were, face to face. He has so enveloped himself in linguistic forms, in artistic images, in mythical symbols and religious rites that he cannot see or know anything except by the interposition of this artificial medium. . . . Hence, instead of defining man as an *animal rationale,* we should define him as an *animal symbolicum.*[15]

Furthermore, once a myth or linguistic form—a symbol—is created, it begins to take on a life of its own. Once a god is named, says Cassirer, instead of merely representing a power, that god begins to take on personality and "continues to develop by a law of its own."[16] That is, symbolic creations become autonomous. Finally man loses control and ends by responding compulsively to the symbols of his own creation. He begins by celebrating the power of fruition and ends by obeying Ceres.

Thus, it is this that George responds to: the demon he has created in the leopard, which arouses in him an automatic, emotional response and depends for its power on his unconscious reactions. A major theme in Lessing's work is this autonomous power of man's symbols, which enthrall her characters. Similarly, A. N. Whitehead has noted the ways a symbol will affect people in contemporary society, causing direct action that bypasses the actual thing symbolized: "Its insistence plays the part of hypnotizing the individual to complete the specific action associated with the symbol."[17] In *Martha Quest*, for example, Martha gets ready for a party, virtually hypnotized by her romantic vision of a first dance and dressing for a man. She acts "under that power of a compulsion that seemed to come from outside" (p. 108). Indeed, the first three volumes of *Children of Violence* are predominantly a sequence of Martha's submission to and escape from such symbols. On the highest level, society as a whole is an autonomous monster-symbol, an "organism which above all is unable to think . . . to diagnose its own condition." Like a sea creature with poisonous tentacles, it takes anything new and stuns it into immobility or distorts it though attaching a label: "Communism, traitor, espionage, homosexuality, teen-age violence—for instance. Or anger, or commitment, or satire."[18] The upshot is that man does indeed create his own reality but is then forced to live in it on its own terms. In the words of Joseph Campbell, "For the human mind . . . is the ultimate mythogenetic zone—the creator and destroyer, the slave and yet the master, of all the gods."[19] The task at hand is to become more master, less slave.

Most of Lessing's fiction deals with the need to join the mythic and discursive, the veld and the city—to be in touch with the mythic state, unified and close to experience, yet without losing the uniquely human values of ego-consciousness and logic. It is to be a hard-won wholeness based on a joining of reason and myth: something new. This is the unity suggested by the image of the City in the veld. The ideal City represents a man-made achievement, a triumph of consciousness and mental and physical harmony, standing apart from and yet integral to the cruel, unconscious, yet harmonious veld.

Lessing has said that people must force themselves, through effort of imagination, to become what they are capable of being; her image of the City, superimposed upon her picture of fragmented and violent society is such an attempt, as are all descriptions of Utopia. As Cassirer has said, such an image is "a symbolic construct designed to portray and to bring into being a new future of mankind. . . . It is symbolic thought which overcomes the natural inertia of man and endows him with a new ability, the ability constantly to reshape his human universe."[20]

It will be readily apparent that Lessing is scarcely unique in this wish to recover wholeness. If analytic thought is man's crowning achievement, it is also the "single vision" blasted by William Blake over a century ago. The main aim of Coleridge's philosophy was to substitute "life and intelligence . . . for the philosophy of mechanism, which, in everything most worthy of the human intellect, strikes Death."[21] Elizabeth Sewell in *The Orphic Voice* traces a tradition throughout human history dedicated to wholeness of human experience running counter to modern "division of it into mind and body" that is "the result of overemphasis on logic and intellect in near isolation which has led us into so one-sided a view of the activity of thought, so gross an underestimation of the body's forms of thought and knowledge."[22] And of course it is now a truism that forms, concepts, and abstractions are suspect. No one needs to be reminded that this is one of the primary tenets of twentieth-century existentialism. Frederic Henry finally found the words "honor" and "in vain" meaningless next to the reality of war, and each person today can find his own examples. As reasoning beings, humankind must have symbols, but Lessing above all is aware that the times demand new ones, as well as a return to ancient symbols, made more powerful with the light of modern consciousness.

In searching for a reconciliation between the intellect and intuition, Lessing is working within a strong contemporary movement. Tindall has suggested that one major stream of twentieth-century literature has been the reunion of matter and spirit, the conscious and unconscious, the self and the world.[23] Certainly T. S. Eliot's recognition of "dissociation of sensibility" is based on such a split, and his own imagery an attempt to defeat it. Charles Feidelson has pointed out that philosophy in this modern time appears to be heading toward a solution to the Cartesian split "that has dogged our thinking since the seventeenth century" and "divides not only reality but [also] the very act of knowing."[24]

Many Westerners are turning to the East, where many of the religious traditions are based on a belief in unity of consciousness through mysticism—Sufism, Hinduism, Buddhism, and yoga, for example. Such a movement is readily apparent in popular culture, but it also appears at the highest intellectual levels. For example, at the Research Institute for Eastern Wisdom and Western Science in Starnberg, Germany, C. F. von Weizacker, the eminent German physicist, has brought together a group of scientists to work with himself and Gopi Krishna, master of Kundalini Yoga. Weizacker has come to believe that the physical-psychic energy called *prana* is a "moving potency" and not incompatible with the term *probability amplitude* designated by the quantum theory.[25] He and Gopi Krishna believe that the West has much to learn from the Eastern religious traditions.

Also significant is the work of Robert Ornstein, a research psychologist who has worked with the recent findings that the two sides of the human brain have different functions. The left side is analytical, rational, and verbal and has been favored in the West for the past several hundred years. The right side is holistic, intuitive, and spatial and has been most highly developed within the mystical traditions. Such research gives biological basis for ideas once considered to be solely in the domain of religion and philosophy. Says Ornstein concerning present trends:

> Current psychology is undergoing the first stirrings of a synthesis of the two modes. These may form the beginnings of a more complete science of human consciousness, with an extended conception of our own capabilities. This "new" conception of possibility is the ancient one of the traditional, esoteric psychologies, but it is beginning to be combined with the methods and technology of contemporary science.[26]

Werner Heisenberg has expressed a similar idea in his belief, despite his own lifelong contributions to natural science, that science has for the moment gone as far as it can go and is about to be supplanted by the study of consciousness. Moreover, "The space in which man as a spiritual being is developing has more dimensions that the one within which he has moved forward in the preceding centuries."[27]

Heisenberg's famous "uncertainty principle" showed that it is impossible to observe elementary particles without influencing their action and that it is therefore meaningless to talk about them except in relation to man and his instruments. As a result, Heisenberg came to believe that the central fact of twentieth-century man is that the world is a product of his own ingenuity and technology: "for the first time in the course of history, man on earth faces only himself . . . he finds no longer any other partner or foe."[28] Cassirer has the identical thought: "Instead of dealing with the things themselves, man is in a sense constantly conversing with himself."[29]

It is this revelation that finally comes to Martha during her last appearance in *The Four-Gated City*, and these words crown the long exploration that has been her life:

> She thought, with the dove's voices of her solitude: Where? But *where*. How? Who? No, but *where*, where. . . . Then silence and the birth of a repetition: *Where?* Here. Here?
>
> Here, where else, you fool, you poor fool, where else has it been, ever. (p. 559)

In these ideas the argument has come full circle. In the primitive mind, man and world also are one, but only because consciousness has not yet differentiated between the two. In some of the most sophisticated twentieth-century philosophies, man and world are again one, but this time through the nature and power of consciousness. "The individual is the only reality."[30]

Lessing, then, is moving with a widespread philosophical trend in her belief in a new unity of consciousness that would amount to a willed change in human nature. In "The Temptation of Jack Orkney," Orkney describes it; he would like to explain to the young

> that the survival of the world depended on them, that they had the chance to break this cycle of having to repeat and repeat experience: they could be the first generation to consciously take a decision to look at history, to absorb it, and in one bound to transcend it. It would be like a willed mutation.[31]

If this view seems the stuff of fiction only, it is interesting to compare it to Gopi Krishna on the men and the new possibilities he believes can result from a union of Western science and Eastern wisdom:

> To the share of this lofty class of men, adorned with the knowledge of inner and outer worlds, will face the Herculean task of educating humanity in the essentials of the almighty spiritual Law to guide the race to the glorious estate ordained for it.[32]

If Lessing shares in this Utopian dream, she usually describes the world of here and now, trying to analyze what is going wrong. As a result, she seems to combine two extreme views of man. On the one hand, like Jude or Tess, mankind seems always to be a victim of "grim fatality." From this point of view, if a finer consciousness should arise, willed human creativity will have no hand in it: at the end of *The Four-Gated City* Martha writes of the new children who are mutations, affected by the radiation of the catastrophe. Their consciousness is a product of natural evolution, comparable to the first sea creatures who crept up to land. On the other hand, Lessing's work never quite relinquishes the possibility that a "willed mutation" will be possible, that through new modes of perception men and women have the power to catapult themselves back to the top of the great chain of being; this time even higher than the angels and perhaps on a godly level themselves, as their own creators.

2
Imagery and Narrative Technique

Images of Fragmentation: The City

Although Lessing constantly holds up the utopian City as a glimmering ideal, an elusive possibility, most of her work dramatizes the world everyone knows in which men and women are trapped by the rigid patterns they—and society— have constructed. "Leopard" George creates a symbol, the leopard, that to him appears as an evil outside himself, but is actually his own destructive force. Because George does not see the leopard for what it is, he will never claim responsibility for his own actions and is doomed to repetitive, violent behavior in response to a demon of his own creation. In "A Sunrise on the Veld" the boy fashions for himself an image of fatality. ("It was right and nothing could alter it.") Had he retained it, like the leopard, it would be only a partial truth, not allowing perception of his own responsibility for others' suffering.

Alfred North Whitehead has pointed out that society operates through a "vast system of inherited symbolism," in some cases visual and direct like great men or national flags, in others amorphous and subtle like rules of behavior and canons of art.

[39]

According to Whitehead, a healthy society will constantly re-
vise its symbolic code. Otherwise, it "must ultimately decay
from anarchy, or from the slow atrophy of a life stifled by
useless shadows."[1] (It will be evident that this concept is entirely different from literary symbolism, in which an artistic
image suggests meanings beyond its strictly mimetic denota-
tions.) In Lessing's fiction, society for the most part is indeed a
system of worn-out symbols, which entrap the vision of most of
the characters. One such image is the traditional, idealistic view
of marriage and motherhood, in which two people live happily
ever after and the wife selflessly nurtures her responsive children. Some others are views of communism either as fearsome
threat or world-saving ideal; the simplistic labeling of other
people according to a physical, ideological, or personal trait;
words themselves with their power to deflect one from experience and limit vision. These social symbols (as opposed to
literary symbols) become part of Lessing's subject matter,
examples of fragmentation or false unity.[2] They tend to fall into
two groups: symbols that like the leopard embody disowned
psychic elements, comparable to the Jungian shadow, and
those that convey an illusory sense of wholeness, such as the
image of fatality that momentarily comforts the boy in "A Sunrise on the Veld." Both kinds are merely unsuccessful substi-
tutes for the vision of wholeness that would be the result of true
unity of the self.

Symbols of the fragmented city, such as those listed above,
are related to discursive thinking and represent only partial
truths because they channel and limit vision. As a result, they
also affect action. Yet it is unrealistic to suggest that a person
must break out of all constricting images and see things as they
"really are." Humans require constructs; without them the
world would be the nauseous blur that Roquentin slips into in
Sartre's *Nausea* or the untenable state of Anna's madness in *The
Golden Notebook*. The solution is not to sweep away all symbols

but to introduce new ones that are more complex and admit a larger share of experience.

The formation of such an image is seen in "The Old Chief Mshlanga," when the young protagonist's view of the natives, and finally the whole surrounding African landscape, changes and expands. In the beginning, this young (unnamed) girl of English parents, growing up—like Lessing—on an African farm, superimposes on her world the images from English fairy tales. The veld scarcely exists for her; replacing it in her mind's eye are lush English scenes of oak, ash, and sleepy rivers. Northern witches inhabit the mealie fields. She "could not see a masasa tree, or the thorn, for what they were."[3] Because only her private scenes are real, the natives, too, are remote, "an amorphous black mass, mingling and thinning and massing like tadpoles, faceless, who existed merely to say, 'Yes, Baas,' take their money and go" (p. 50). Later they take a new, equally unreal shape, signified by the European label of contempt, "Kaffir." The native-as-Kaffir is to be ridiculed, hounded, and unconsciously feared. It is only when the girl recognizes the dignity and humanity of the Old Chief that her image of the natives enlarges to encompass their complexity as men. Her whole relationship to the land changes as a result:

> and slowly that other landscape in my mind faded, and my feet struck directly on the African soil, and I saw the shapes of tree and hill clearly. (p. 53)

At this point she begins to see her valley in a new way, as "the Old Chief's country," rather than by the name attached to it by white settlers "which held no implication of usurped ownership" (p. 52). Ironically, the land seems to step back from her in a new way even as she finally sees it clearly: "it was as if I stood aside to watch a slow intimate dance of landscape and men, a very old dance, whose steps I could not learn" (p. 53).

The reason is simple. Being white, she shares the guilt of the usurpers, and as a result, the country seems to reject her.

This story illustrates the double-bind caused by a confining symbol shared with society as a whole. The issue here is the need for harmony and unity with one's surroundings. At first the girl is separated from the land and its people by the literary symbols of fairy tales and then, more destructively, the social symbol "Kaffir," a view of the natives that provides the basis for an entire social system of callousness and repression. The girl breaks through that constricting vision to recognize the rights and dignity of the old chief and his people, leading to a new, whole perception of Africa. But the land then eludes her in a different way when she perceives herself, inevitably, as an intruder. There is only one way to close this new chasm: the complete breakdown of the symbol of "Kaffir" and the social structure based on it.

Here is seen one of the basic dilemmas of Lessing's characters. Even when they are able to break out of the acquired, confining symbols of the culture to form more complex symbols of knowledge and responsibility, they are still trapped by the pressures around them. *Going Home,* Lessing's autobiographical study of Rhodesia in 1957, shows the only routes possible for someone who has reached the final vision of the girl in "The Old Chief Mshlanga," and neither is satisfactory. In this narrative Lessing recounts some of her many interviews with conscientious teachers and social workers who are striving to right some of the social wrongs in their country. Aware of the inequities, they try in small ways to improve the lot of the natives, but their work is unendurably frustrating because it can accomplish so little. On the other hand, anyone in a position to make real changes through political activity or perhaps through publishing accounts of injustice will simply be exiled—as Lessing herself was at the end of the visit to Rhodesia, after which *Going Home* was written.

The world Lessing shows is in a state of atrophy, tied to its old symbols instead of moving forward to a new, more complex view of experience. For example, in *The Golden Notebook* Anna joins the Communist Party from "a need for wholeness, for an end to the split, divided, unsatisfactory way we all live."[4] Later she sees that communism has its own oversimplified images. Martha's final opinion of the Communist Party is true for Anna as well. After visiting a meeting of "second generation" communists, Martha sees that it is all hopeless, because of the unreal symbols involved:

> And keeping your minds firmly on the vision, as if it were an entity, a thing, quite separate from the minds and personalities which created it, you overlook the lies, the exaggeration, and the sheer damned lunacy.[5]

Anna is finally driven to say, "sometimes I think the one form of experience people are incapable of learning from is political experience" (*The Golden Notebook*, p. 384). Pessimism about political action is most extreme in "The Temptation of Jack Orkney." In this novella the characters are not idealistic communists, who must somehow work around the knowledge of Stalin's excesses, but the most generous and forward-looking progressives of the 1970s. Orkney realizes that all of their labor will accomplish nothing.

> What he could not endure was that his son, all of them, would have to make the identical journey he and his contemporaries had made, to learn lessons exactly as if they had never been learned before. . . . That humanity was unable to learn from experience was written there for everyone to see, since the new generation of the intelligent and consciously active youth behaved identically with every generation before them.[6]

Humanity can not learn from experience because it veils the complexity of things with fragmentary images based on such words as *liberal, conservative, communist,* and *capitalist;* also, each new generation, full of ideals, sees itself springing "virginal and guiltless . . . out of its debased predecessors." Orkney recognizes that inevitably the result is "division, and self-righteousness and vituperation" instead of increasing social health (p. 276).

Individuals do not see one another but rather some personal symbol of their own devising. In *Landlocked* Thomas complains that his wife Rachel is not able to accept his crude, peasant side and therefore simply leaves seventy percent of him out of account: "she was quite prepared to like me, but she had to forget me to do it . . ." (p. 436). Martha's failure to see Douglas, substituting the image of a serious young man who reads *The New Republic*, allows her to make the mistake of marrying him. For both Martha and Rachel a private, partial image has replaced the complexity of the whole man.

In *The Four-Gated City* Lynda complains that psychiatrists do not recognize the complexity of their patients or see that illness may be the body's attempt toward a new sort of wholeness. Instead, they prefer to say that someone is "nothing-but" a schizophrenic or paranoic, as if that is all that needs to be known. Thus a patient is reduced to a label.[7]

Characters who appear to be whole generally are so because they settle for fragmentation. As Anna suggests to Mother Sugar, her analyst, neurosis is often a sign of being highly conscious and developed, while false wholeness comes from ignoring what can not easily be tolerated. "People stay sane by blocking off, by limiting themselves" (p. 402). In the novel *Free Women* within *The Golden Notebook*, Tommy's blindness, a result of his attempted suicide, is a symbol for this kind of self-limitation—Anna's fictional rendering of the "real" Tommy's settling for a shallow and unimaginative liberalism.

There is a group of "city" symbols related to these in which the mind grasps a piece of knowledge but fails to attach to it the necessary emotion that might be a spur to effective action. The result is not so much failure of perception as of feeling, another kind of knowing, related to intuition. As Brandon says in *The Four-Gated City*, "It seems as if there's always just enough energy to state the fact, the problem. And not much more. The stating of it exhausts the possibilities."[8]

"Report on the Threatened City" focuses on this failing. Everyone in the city knows that an earthquake is imminent, with great loss of life, but everyone goes on as if it would not happen, refusing to move and even continuing to build tall buildings on the fault line. The story is an accurate portrayal of the attitude of San Franciscans, but there is also an implicit analogy to a world that sees disaster coming and still does nothing to change course and avoid it. Jack Orkney's son Joseph agrees cheerfully that in twenty years he and his friends will be the "Old Guard," as his father's generation was at present. He even admits that they may all be dead by then. But he is unable to make the emotional connection between possible disaster and the way generations simply repeat. It is finally this paralysis that leads Jack Orkney to despair of the situation and give up any hope for real change.

The result of settling for fragmentation of any sort is the creation of "the monster repetition," a world of "doomed individuals carrying their doom inside them" *(A Proper Marriage*, p. 55). Because of it, people can seldom make real contact with one another and usually are forced to play and replay their own unconscious patterns. Worse, every generation repeats the mistakes of those who have gone before.

This distrust for the fragmentation of present forms of rational thought lies behind Doris Lessing's own gradual disillusionment with communism. In Africa, she became involved with radical politics because the communists there were for the most part idealistic, using pure Marxism for their guide. As Frederick McDowell has justly pointed out, "Mrs. Lessing's radicalism is indistinguishable from a humanism which men at either extreme violate."[9] That is, the leaders of the Communist Party treat men as objects who must conform to certain prescribed forms or be executed. At the other extreme, the McCarthy witch-hunts of the fifties were intolerably repressive. Beginning with *The Golden Notebook* Lessing's work shows her increasing disillusion not just with communism, but also with any political activity as an effective method for righting the world's wrongs. Rather, she begins to focus on a theme that has always been present in her work but is understated in the earlier novels—that effective change must come from a deep, intuitive, and personal source that is inimical to formed concepts of any kind.

In short, it is failure of imagination that leads to the narrow, repetitive behavior incurred by clinging to barren symbols. To avoid disaster, people must *see,* with complexity and right feeling. An incident exhibiting failure of imagination precipitates Jack Orkney's "temptation": a group of his son's friends nearly burn the house down with a can of paraffin placed carelessly near a flame. It is an act of thoughtlessness, failure to see what they were doing. On a large scale, this kind of failure is behind much of the brutality of the world. In *Landlocked* Martha considers the deaths of World War II: "Forty-odd million human beings had been murdered, deliberately or from carelessness, from lack of imagination . . ." (p. 463). In this novel Thomas describes how Sergeant Tressel has been in charge of the camp where he worked. Tressel allowed the Africans to be short of food and to live in filthy conditions not out of any particular ill will but because he could not be bothered. As Thomas describes it, "he was a bastard out of carelessness, out of sheer indifference—" (p. 409). Thomas is one of Lessing's visionary characters, like Saul in *The Golden Notebook*, and his assessment carries weight: "I tell you, it was Sergeant bloody Tressel that finally made me understand the world" (p. 410).

Thomas's experience also illustrates another type of city

symbol, in which personal psychic elements appear disastrously as outer symbols, as in " 'Leopard' George." Thomas's "leopard" is the cruel indifference of Tressel and of British soldiers who will kill Jewish refugees before letting them set foot in Israel. In an imaginary conversation in which Martha works out for herself what is happening to Thomas, she points out rationally to him that to go to Israel and kill young English soldiers will accomplish nothing, that it goes against everything he believes. He responds with irony: "So you don't believe in violence, Martha?" She then understands that it is meaningless to say that violence does no good, should not be used:

> Having lived through a war when half the human race was en-gaged in murdering the other half, murdering more vilely, sav-agely, cruelly, than ever in human history, what does it mean to say: I don't believe in violence. . . .
> Martha did not believe in violence.
> Martha was the essence of violence, she had been conceived, bred, fed and reared on violence. (p. 462)

Martha and Thomas are both part of "the soul of the human race," are held there "as frogspawn is held in jelly." Therefore, all violence in the world occurs also "in Martha's soul and in Thomas's, twisting and warping them" (p. 462).

Thomas, then, shares inevitably in the violence around him. Even though Martha sees him as a sturdy brown peasant who radiates warmth and energy, his own violence reveals itself for the first time in the movie theater. Martha and the others are shocked to see their first close view of an "enemy" face, a pathetic young German boy. But Thomas, whose family has been killed by the Germans, can only repeat, "The Bastards!"

> "All right, Martha, but I tell you, I'd torture everyone of them myself, with my own hands."
> She said, "Some of them looked about fifteen."
> "Well? They should simply be stamped out—they should be wiped out, like vermin." (pp. 323–24)

Later Martha will confront her own "shadow" in the self-hater, and she has a narrow escape back to sanity. Thomas is not so fortunate; he is totally absorbed by it. "But I feel as if I were under the sea, or dead—or something. I can't say anything I want to say. I hate myself all the time" (p. 443). After fighting in Israel, he tries to remove himself completely from white society, working with natives in the bush, but his "last testament" remains to show the final black vision he retains of the world and himself as part of it: "Vermin, vermin, . . . The world is a lump of filth crawling with vermin" (p. 535).

In *The Grass is Singing* Mary Turner is unconsciously drawn toward Moses, who represents the sensuality that her conscious mind has rejected. His killing her is an allegory for the way she has been destroyed by a fragmented personality, as Thomas is in *Landlocked*.

Moses and the leopard are symbols on two levels. Within the virtual world of the novel they are constricting symbols to the characters, like Whitehead's flag—structures that block wider vision. But, of course, they are also literary symbols through which Lessing conveys meaning. As such, Moses and the leopard suggest more than their easily stated significance to the characters; they provide a cluster of connotations, an aura of emotions. Moses represents not just Mary's repressed sensuality, but also its power and ambivalence. He suggests racism, as well, and the way it can result from lack of self-knowledge; and he dramatizes the violence and darkness that surrounds such repressions. And the leopard, more than an image of George's repressed violence, captures a sense of the instinctive violence in nature; as such it provides both a comparison and a contrast to George's cruelty.

Lessing uses various literary symbols and metaphors to suggest the fragmentation of her characters. Anna, and also Mark, in *The Four-Gated City*, both pin on the wall, layers of newspaper clippings describing violent or ominous world events: society's madness in a concise image. For Anna, the chaotic walls are also a sign of her own mental state, which in turn reflects the condition of the world. In *Landlocked* Martha's disjointed state of mind is compared to a house with no center but with only separate, unrelated rooms. Images of dryness are a consistent motif throughout *Children of Violence*. Typically, when Martha thinks about the brutality of war, she feels her blood flowing "as if ebbing out into dry sand" (*Landlocked*, p. 462).

In *The Golden Notebook* is a motif of the crocodile, an image for the destructiveness of partial vision. Martha dreams of a jeweled crocodile with a grinning, sardonic snout: She finds herself about to give to a group of people a precious object in a box. Suddenly she realizes that the men are businessmen and that in the box are fragments of objects that relate to violence: metal from a gun, flesh from people killed in war, a communist badge from someone who died in a Soviet prison. But when the box is opened, it contains a beautiful, jeweled crocodile. Later, awake, Martha recognizes its sardonic smile on her own face, and the connections become clear: the crocodile is the force of destruction that Anna believes is hidden in her writing but that delights the business world—presumably, because it sells.

This incident sheds light on the oddly powerful hallucinations of Charlie Themba, an African revolutionary who has gone mad. Writing to Anna in *Free Women*, he is convinced that he is being fed shreds of human flesh and crocodile meat: "The crocodile will have its revenge. At night I see its eyes shining at me, and its snout comes at me through the walls" (p. 442). In the golden notebook section, when Martha finally learns to deal with her own share of joy-in-destruction and to overcome her sardonic outlook, the crisis is described in a dream in which she flies up and out of crocodile-infested water.

Lessing's images of the city, then, convey the limiting mental constructs that cause violence, destructive repetition, and sterility. She opposes them with images of unity.

Images of Unity: The Veld

Looking at Lessing's work as a whole, it is possible to distinguish a consistent metaphysic. Human experience takes place on four levels and significant action must take all levels into account; fragmentation exists because most people fail to do so.

At the furthest reach of experience lies an area completely remote from human values and perceptions. A similar region exists in much twentieth-century literature. For example, in *A Passage to India*, E. M. Forster uses the Marabar Caves to symbolize the depths of existence beyond good and evil and all other human distinctions: no matter what one says there— poetry, mathematical propositions, or obscenity—the Caves turn it into "ou-boum." Mrs. Moore is so deeply affected by the caves that human values become irrelevant for her, and the profundity of her vision is suggested by the way she becomes a popular local saint. In Sartre's *Nausea* Roquentin becomes gradually aware of the universe that lies behind the stamp of human consciousness. Experience becomes a changing, sickening blur admitting no labels of either perception or name. It is this *nada* that stands behind many twentieth-century novels.

In madness, Anna Wulf experiences a chaotic state in an episode reminiscent of *Nausea*. All form dissolves for her: curtain material changes to a slimy texture; the floors and walls heave and buckle; time and space dissolve. The shape of Anna's ego-consciousness gives way to admit the shapeless total experience of which she is a part. It is a realm entirely inimical to human consciousness. In *Briefing for a Descent into Hell* there is a parody of a Greek myth in which the gods of Olympus discuss the earth and its solar system. They see that the observable universe is part of a larger experience that the human mind can in no way fully perceive. In *The Four-Gated City* Martha recognizes that she has occasionally experienced this realm in sex:

> Great forces as impersonal as thunder or lightning or sunlight or the movement of the oceans being contracted and heaped and rolled in their beds by the moon, swept through their bodies. (p. 470)

However, there is a great difference between Lessing's *nada* and that of twentieth-century existential thought. Sartre insists on the forlorn position of man in a meaningless universe. Lessing's universe is teleological, although man in his present state of evolution can not perceive its purpose. To glimpse this area of existence is healing because it affords a view of the interrelation of all things, allowing man a wholeness that is impossible to his ordinary, fragmented rationalism. Bearable for only short periods, it is a place of renewal. There the old mental constructs are destroyed, making room for the possibility of new ones that will be more comprehensive. Anna's plunge into the madness of this uncreated universe is healing. Afterwards, she is capable of a more unified view of existence. Saul Green, the American with whom she has an affair, half purposefully and half because of illness stays in this chaotic sphere as much as he can bear in order to prevent being limited by familiar forms of being. A mentally ill person is therefore in an ambiguous position in Lessing's work. His illness plunges him into an area that can either destroy or heal him. In part, *Briefing for a Descent into Hell* describes Charles Watkins's experience of it.

The next level of experience is the physical universe as it is perceived by man: the galaxies, the solar system with the earth whirling in it, and nature as it exists on this planet. This is the solar system described by Mercury and Minerva in *Briefing for a*

Descent into Hell, the cosmos Watkins sees from the Crystal. Here earth wobbles around the sun, torn between the forces of sun and moon. Part of a more remote set of influences, it also is subject to forces within the solar system itself. In *The Golden Notebook* and *Children of Violence* the natural world is Africa, of great importance in Lessing's work.

The third level of experience is the collective mind, conscious and unconscious. Similar to Yeats's *anima mundi,* it is composed of all past and present images created by the human imagination. For example, during a period of self-imposed madness, Martha enters psychic realms that resemble paintings by Salvador Dali and Hieronymus Bosch—regions she believes to be accessible to anyone, potentially. Here also is the "sound barrier" of living minds with its cacophony, predominantly unhappy. The narrator of *Landlocked* describes this collective mind as, "The soul of the human race, that part of the mind which has no name, is not called Thomas and Martha, which holds the human race as frogspawn is held in jelly—" (p. 463). In madness Anna Wulf perceives it when she enters the bodies of many different people, such as an Algerian soldier, a man being tortured, and a Chinese peasant. In this century, the collective mind is warped by violence.

Finally there is the individual, with his complex of thoughts, responsibilities, and roles. In *The Four-Gated City* it becomes apparent that most of what one takes for personality is scarcely individual; political ideas, philosophies, teen-age and middle-age points of view—all are simply like uniforms one adopts. To a large extent, people are interchangeable.[10] What is most oneself is consciousness: whatever it is that observes. After Martha's final exploration into the depths of consciousness, she writes in her notes, "I've seen the underneath of myself. Which isn't me—any more than the surface is me. I am the watcher, the listener . . ." (p. 524).

Everyone exists on four levels. As a child of nature he or she is part of the physical universe and the violent forces at work within and behind it—both destructive and constructive (seen from the human point of view). As a human being he or she is both an individual and part of the collective mind. Every attempt at significant action will have to take into account the way that a person is formed and influenced at all these levels. Whatever is completely veiled in the unconscious wields a destructive power.

Many of Lessing's symbols are models of wholeness. Most important is the ideal City, an image from traditional myth; but Lessing does not present it with the customary nostalgia for a lost paradise. Rather, it is a goal to work for and may even be attainable if human consciousness can only break out of its inhibiting grooves. But other forms of wholeness do exist and can provide inspiration to mankind's divided state—chiefly nature, and especially the veld of Central Africa.

Africa lends an extraordinary richness to Lessing's work, much as the moors do to Emily Brontë's. In *Wuthering Heights* they convey a sense of vast forces at work, uncontainable by ordinary, frail human beings. Heathcliff is of that other world and takes on his demonic quality as a result. For Lessing, in the same way, the veld suggests something wild and awesome that is foreign to human society and intelligence. However, her characters are not demonic; like Hareton and young Cathy who eventually tame moor flowers for their garden, Lessing's characters must use the materials of the veld for their own more orderly human purposes.

Lessing has expressed something of what Africa means to her in the preface to *African Stories*:

> I believe that the chief gift from Africa to writers, white and black, is the continent itself, its presence which for some people is like an old fever, latent always in their blood; or like an old wound throbbing in the bones when the air changes. That is not a place to visit unless one chooses to be an exile ever afterwards from an inexplicable majestic silence lying just over the border of memory or of thought. Africa gives you the knowledge that man is a small creature, among other creatures, in a large landscape. (p. viii)

In *Going Home* she describes her first experience of the bush after years in England:

> And now for the first time I was really home. The night was magnificent; the Southern Cross on a slant overhead; the moon a clear, small pewter; the stars all recognizable and close. The long grass stood all around, tall and giving off its dry, sweetish smell, and full of talking crickets. The flattened trees of the highveld were low above the grass, low and a dull silver-green . . . on that first night there was no barrier, nothing; and I was effortlessly and at once in immediate intimacy with the soil and its creatures . . . and if I had had to fly back to England the next day, I would have been given what I had gone home for.[11]

The African landscape nearly always conveys in Lessing's fiction a sense of awesome unity and lofty beauty. In *The Golden Notebook* and the first four volumes of *Children of Violence*, the passages dealing with the veld are particularly effective, acting as a counterpoint to the usual meticulous dramatization of the thoughts, actions, and interactions of her characters in society. The African landscape is described with no less careful detail, but the effect is quite different. These passages have an ecstatic quality similar, again, to those in *Wuthering Heights* dramatizing Catharine's passion for the moor. The following quotations from *Martha Quest* show the difference of effect between the two kinds of subject matter. The first illustrates Lessing's realistic style. Martha has recently left the farm for a job in the city and is undergoing an emotional reaction after the end of her first sexual affair:

> In the afternoon, she was standing by the door, with the thermometer in her mouth, when she saw herself from outside, and at the same time remembered her father, medicine bottles stacked in hundreds by his bed—her father, whose image persistently composed itself in her mind as a worried, inward-looking man, standing moodily at a window but seeing nothing out of it, holding one wrist between the fingers of his other hand, to measure his pulse. The thought frightened her; she slipped out the thermometer, and stood hesitating, thinking, I'll throw the thing away. She glanced at

the silver thread, for she might as well have a look at it first, and then it slipped from her hand and broke. Before it fell, she had seen that it stood at a hundred. Well, she had a temperature, she was justified. Soberly, she swept up the glass, and said consolingly that she would never buy another thermometer, she would not fuss over her health. But it was a relief, nevertheless, to be slightly ill, to be able to go to bed. (p. 207)

This passage is typical of most of Lessing's writing in its careful precision toward her character's thoughts and actions, and the dramatization of her battle with outside forces that threaten to control her—in this case, unconscious repetition of her father's hypochondria. Her thoughts then turn to the farm, and she considers how close one is there to the seasons. The next passage is worth quoting in entirety because not only does it illustrate the ecstatic quality of Lessing's descriptions of the veld, but it also reveals the unity from which they derive power and meaning.

On the farm, everything was vivid, a violent green, while the earth was a blaring red. The sky from Jacob's Burg to the Oxford Range, from the Dumfries Hills away back, over the unbounded north, was a deep, soft hall of blue; and the clouds wheeled and deployed and marched, day and night, flinging down hail, storming down rain, rolling and rocking to an orchestra of thunder, while the lightning danced about the thunder-heads and quivered over the mountains. On the farm, the bush on the hill where the house stood was so soaked and lush that walking through it meant red mud to the ankles, and saturated branches springing loads of sparkling water at every step. On the farm, the cattle were grazing with nervous haste on the short, thick grass, which they knew would be tough and wiry in so short a time. For this was the season when it was impossible to remember the burning droughts of the long dry season. The veld was like those blackened brittle sticks one picks off a rock on a kopje, apparently dead and ready to rot, which one places in water, only to find, an hour later, that this lifeless twig has burst into crisp, vivid little leaves. In January, the drought-ridden, fire-tortured veld was as teeming and steamy and febrile as a jungle. In the rotting trunks of trees the infant mosquitoes wriggled like miniature dragons; one might find the energetic creatures in the hollow of a big leaf, or in the imprint of a cow's foot or the tangled wetness of a low-growing clump of grass. (p. 208)

The main attribute and source of power here is unity of disparate elements: violent green opposed to blaring red, blue sky and raging storms, drought and junglelike wet, death and surging fertility. Above all, Africa stands for a unity of violent oppositions. Certainly this is not a comfortable scene. The cows are "grazing with nervous haste" because they will not have good grass for long. The walker is buried ankle deep in red mud and splashed with water. The veld is "fire-tortured," and mosquitoes crawl everywhere, grotesquely, like dragons. The power of this description comes not from the memory of a beautiful place but rather from a certain harsh majesty formed by a difficulty unity. The observer is part of it, but not comfortably. October, when the rains come, is the month most full of tensions and extremes (significantly, it is the month in which Martha was born):

> How terrible October is! Terrible because so beautiful, and the beauty springs from the loaded heat, the dust, the tension; for everyone watches the sky, and the heavy trees along the avenues, and the sullen clouds, while for weeks nothing happens; the wind lifts an eddy of dust at a street corner, and subsides, exhausted. One cannot remember the smell of the flowers without the smell of dust and petrol; one cannot remember that triumphant orchestra of colour without the angry, white-hot sky. (p. 31)

A vivid illustration of Africa's terrible beauty appears in "A Mild Attack of Locusts." Margaret, city bred, has been on an African farm for three years when a plague of locusts arrives and strips the farm bare. The next morning she goes to the window:

> And she gazed, astounded—and entranced, much against her will. For it looked as if every tree, every bush, all the earth, were lit with pale flames. The locusts were fanning their wings to free them of the night dews. There was a shimmer of red-tinged gold light everywhere. . . .
> Well, thought Margaret, we may be ruined, we may be bankrupt, but not everyone has seen an army of locusts fanning their wings at dawn.[12]

While the veld has an awesomeness that can inspire the human observer, it is absolutely remote from the social values that affect the health of society. Here only the main patterns count—the seasons and on-going life; the individual is of no importance. Consciousness and responsibility have no place on the veld; therefore Lessing frequently uses it as a foil to human values and achievements. Unity is desirable, but not on these terms. A good example is one of the episodes at the Mashopi Hotel in *The Golden Notebook*. Anna, Willi, Paul, Jimmy, and Maryrose pass a horde of mating grasshoppers, which appear obscene to them simply because there are so many. A few would be interesting, even beautiful in their bright, metallic colors; "But in thousands, crude green and crude red, with the black blank eyes staring—they were absurd, obscene, and above all, the very emblem of stupidity" (p. 357). Many are mismated, a small male and a giant female or the reverse. Like a deus ex machina Paul intervenes, separating two such couples and putting them together in matched pairs. Then, without warning, he casually smashes them with his boot. To Maryrose's shaken protest he makes a little speech about the prodigality of nature:

> Before many hours are out, these insects will have killed each other by fighting, biting, deliberate homicide, suicide, or by clumsy copulation. Or they will have been eaten by birds which even at this moment are waiting for us to remove ourselves so that they can begin their feast. When we return to this delightful pleasure resort next week . . . we shall take our well-regulated walks along this road and see perhaps one or two of these delightful red and green insects at their sport in the grass, and think, how pretty they are! And little will we reck of the million corpses that even then will be sinking into their last resting place all about us. (p. 360)

To Anna, the mating grasshoppers represent mindless fertility—and as Paul points out, death—on a mass scale that is foreign and repulsive. By contrast, human beings value order and, connected to it, the satisfaction of individual needs, as

Paul demonstrates when he steps in and sets right the mating of two pairs of insects. When he proceeds to smash them under-foot, Maryrose is shocked because she does not expect Paul suddenly to reverse himself and imitate nature, which is not concerned about individuals. The total design is formed with wide swathes of life and death; but one expects different values from men and women.

Nature's mindless force is beautifully illustrated in "The Sun Between Their Feet," in which the narrator spends a day watching the futile antics of two dung beetles trying to roll up a slope a bit of cow dung in which the female has laid her eggs. Instinct demands that the fertilized ball be firmed and shaped by rolling it down a hill. The story ironically contrasts reality with the science writer's flight of emotion over nature's plan:

> "The slope is chosen," says the book, "by a beautiful instinct, so that the ball of dung comes to rest in a spot suitable for the hatch-ing of a new generation of sacred insect."[13]

These particular beetles, however, play out a comedy of errors. They pick an impossible route and the dung ball falls again and again. Still the insects persist at the same hill, even when the watcher moves them to a more suitable spot. Finally the ragged ball is completely demolished by a summer shower. The nar-rator says ironically:

> Sacred beetles, these, the sacred beetles of the Egyptians, holding the symbol of the sun between their busy stupid feet. (p. 627)

A general pattern does exist; the reader knows that some bee-tles succeed in their endeavor. But it is by chance, because the force of instinct is blind, obeyed by creatures without reason or logic. It is the survival of the species that is important, not individuals within it.

"A Letter From Home" illustrates the remoteness of com-passion for the individual in the raw necessities of the veld.

The narrator is visiting an old friend, Hans, a talented poet who is trapped in an intolerable little town in the remote veld. On a walk they pass a thorn tree with a variety of creatures impaled on it, including a beetle, still alive and trying to wriggle off. It succeeds and falls to the ground, whereupon Hans picks the beetle up and puts it back on the thorn, carefully, trying to use the original hole.

> I said, "Hans, man, for God's sake!" And then he looked at me, and he said, reproachfully: "The ants would have killed it, just look!" Well, the ground was swarming with ants of one kind or another, so there was logic in it, but I said: "Hans, let's drink, man, let's drink."[14]

The point of this detail is to parallel Hans's own predicament, but at the same time it dramatizes the irrelevance of human compassion to natural forces.

This difference between the unconscious unity of nature and conscious human values is an important problem throughout Lessing's work. "The Story of Two Dogs" takes place on this borderline between human civilization and the wild natural world. Jock, "the gentleman," is cooperative and trainable until Bill comes into the household, a puppy fathered by a dog that has gone wild. Bill, unlike the civilized Jock, is always in a frenzy of vitality and is completely untrainable. As the narrator and her brother are away at school being taught civilized virtues, "learning, discipline, order, and sound characters," the dogs, to the contrary, get wilder and wilder. They are gone for days at a time, living off the land like wild dogs. One day, home for the holidays, the children see them after a kill: "We walked over to greet them but with restraint, for these two growling snarling creatures seemed not to know us, they raised eyes glazed with savagery, as they tore at the dead buck."[15] Jock and Bill live out their lives poised between the wild and the civilized, and it is this interplay that gives form and interest to the story.

To some degree the farmers on the veld all have to tread a line between the wild and the civilized, accepting nature for what it is and working around or with it as required. This is the human condition, dramatically visible in Africa. In "A Mild Attack of Locusts," for example, the men have the only attitude possible, recognizing the inevitability of the plague and going on with their work. They take it in stride and see its peculiar beauty. Margaret, the newcomer, is most shaken by the calamity, but she learns from the others that to survive one can not expect human justice from nature.

One of the best examples of this necessary attitude—and the difficulty of it—is in *Particularly Cats*. Recalling her childhood, Lessing tells how the population of farm cats had to be controlled by judicious drownings and that, by some "law of the household," her mother took on that unpleasant job:

> She was above all, and in every detail, practical. But more than that: she was one of that part of humankind *which understands how things work:* and work with them. A grim enough role.[16]

One dramatic episode shows the penalty for failing to work with nature. For a time the mother abdicates from this role for some unknown reason, with the result that the "senseless proliferations of nature" take over; the house and surrounding bush are infested with cats. Lessing and her father eventually have to get rid of them, a gruesome event leaving them feeling like murderers. Again it is evident that human values can exist only with difficulty in the natural scene. Nature kills impersonally. It is in the nature of things, and necessary. For mankind, killing is another matter altogether.

But if one expects humanity to be concerned with the pain and satisfaction of individual lives, "The Second Hut" dramatically shows that such values can exist only when basic needs are met. The poverty-stricken, struggling just to survive, may lose the luxury of ethics. In this story the new farm assistant,

Van Heerden, and his family have been forced into a poverty not much different from a state of raw nature. They live in a tent, off the land, and although there is scarcely enough food to go around, the babies keep coming. The children do not go to school but simply roam the veld; the assistant's wife, huge and maternal, is an earth mother. Van Heerden's reaction to the death of one of his children dramatizes his degeneration; though saddened, he takes comfort from the new baby, which arrives at the same time: "well, one comes and another goes." It is this glimpse of nature without the stamp of ethics and culture, the place where poverty is steadily dragging him, that horrifies Carruthers into finally leaving Africa:

> He felt weak. He felt as if Van Heerden had struck him, smiling. This was an absurd and unjust feeling, but for a moment he hated Van Heerden for standing there and saying: "this grey country of poverty that you fear so much, will take on a different look when you actually enter it. You will cease to exist; there is no energy left, when one is wrestling naked, with life, for your kind of fine feelings and scruples and regrets."[17]

The story that gives the most extreme illustration of the distance between the city and the veld is "Plants and Girls." Here the protagonist is mentally retarded and therefore closely attuned to nature, aware of the underground rivers and breathing soil beneath the pavement. He holds out fingers "like roots toward the earth" and holds a veld tree in a crushing embrace, as one might a lover.[18] While his mother lives, responsibility for her and her affection for him provide a thin fabric separating the boy from the preconscious mythic state of the veld. When she dies, the fabric is broken and he plunges in. All distinctions are lost. He embraces the neighbor girl as he once did the tree, in a crushing hold as if trying to merge with all reality. He crushes her to death, his teeth at her throat, murmuring, "Your hair, your leaves, your branches, your rivers" (p. 622). From the standpoint of society it is an act of madness, since society depends upon distinctions. Mythic perception is inimical to it.

Lessing's Africa—the veld and the country of "Zambesia"—is typically her own in the way that Joyce has made use of Dublin or Faulkner has created Yoknapatawpha County. The African veld is the natural arena where life and death continue mindlessly but with a certain awesome balance, a unity to which mankind may turn for beauty and inspiration but never as a model to be copied, because it is a violent, preconscious state. This is not the beatific nature of Wordsworth and Coleridge, though it does take on a similar unity, described in "The Story of Two Dogs":

> Watchdogs, in my experience, were never alseep; but they were not so much a guard against thieves . . . as a kind of instrument designed to measure or record the rustlings and movements of the African night that seemed to have an enormous life of its own, but a collective life, so that the falling of a stone, or a star shooting through the Milky Way, the grunt of a wild pig, and the wind rustling in the mealie field were all evidences and aspects of the same truth. (pp. 656–57)

"The one life within us and abroad" that Lessing dramatizes in the veld must make room for the devouring mother, those dark forces that human nature shares but consciousness often refuses. Somehow man must make room in his imagination for everything that is, so that he will no longer be an unconscious victim. Further, unity must lead to effective action.

Besides those of the African veld, Lessing uses other groups of images to convey wholeness: nature imagery in general and the material of traditional myths, mysticism, dreams, and madness, those products of imagination that have been suppressed in the age of science. These images do not have the same unique stamp upon them of Lessing's African materials. Rather, they are important because they are archetypal, shared by nearly everyone in every age, even though modern society as a whole has not given them serious attention. For while Lessing is calling for something new in the imagination of man, it is to be sought through recalling ancient knowledge that logic and reason have tended to ignore.

Lessing is similar to Coleridge in her attitude toward the unity and vitality of organic life. As Meyer Abrams has pointed out, organicism is the major influence on Coleridge's aesthetic. A plant grows, has the germ of wholeness within it, and "evolves spontaneously from an internal source of energy."[19] Lessing's sense of the wholeness and vitality of plants is a recurring motif throughout her work and stands in opposition to the sterility of human experience when it is uninspired by the inner life of intuition. For example, in *The Four-Gated City* Martha must hold the Coldfield household together even when she herself is ill. Her strength comes from the sight of the tree outside her window, when everything else is in a state of chaos.

However, for Lessing organicism is not by itself the main principle of life, the ideal always to be followed. Just as Africa is a composite of wet and dry and life and death, the principle of organic life is only half of experience. "Dialogue" gives one of the clearest illustrations of its significance and limitations. In this story it is a vital energy diffused among all living things. While looking at a fruit stall, the protagonist experiences "a pulse of vitality, like the beating colours of oranges, lemons, cabbages, gold and green, a dazzle, a vibration in the eyes. . . ."[20] Deadened by a visit to her ill friend, she is brought back to herself by a leaf, which she crushes and smells:

> She understood it was the smell of the leaf which, as she lifted it to her nostrils, seemed to explode with a vivid odour into the sense of her brain so that she understood the essence of the leaf and through it the scene she stood in. (p. 246)

After seeing Bill and being sucked dry by the sterility of his machinelike intelligence, the world around her seems made of cardboard, drained of vitality. The feel of the leaf with its life-force revives her. After she smells it, "The pulses were beating again. . . . She was saved from deadness, she was herself again" (p. 246).

Bill is her opposite. His world is seclusion and sterility, a point of view that sees only the sordidness of the street— which the protagonist allows herself only to glimpse. Above all, he stands for reason: "My dear, I don't understand the emotions, except through my intelligence" (p. 239). However, Bill is the more admirable character because he is forcing himself to face his "shadow" and break through to a new unity. The narrator is more appealing to the reader because she is in touch with emotional and organic life and senses their relationship. But she herself recognizes that this is only half of experience. The last lines of the story are the most telling:

> With one hand . . . she secretly touched the base of the tower whose shadow would always follow her now, challenging her until she dared to climb it. With the other hand she held fast to the leaf. (p. 247)

"The one life" of vitality, growth, and emotion is not to be denied; without it only sterility remains. But alone it is insufficient. Finally it must be encompassed by consciousness.

In *Landlocked* Martha is attracted to Thomas because of his vitality and energy. His body radiates warmth, and love to him is as essential as oxygen. During the height of their affair, Thomas is characterized with organic imagery. By his own definition he is a peasant, a man of the soil. As a nurseryman he lives in an aura of leaves and flowers, and Martha's affair with him takes place in a shed above the nursery, filled with the smell of fresh soil and growing things. After Thomas is possessed by the thought of Sergeant Tressel, he is no longer connected to organic images. He gives up the farm and the nursery. His sister-in-law takes away the shed and the affair must take place in Thomas's truck.

However, this early Thomas of warmth and vitality is only half the picture. Martha sees this later: "There had been a failure of imagination. A failure of sympathy. Her way of seeing Thomas, his life—it was that which had been wrong, at fault" (p. 454). He is also the thin, tight-lipped man who comes back from the bush filled with visions of death. One half may seem preferable, but both are true.

As has been seen, the leaf and the tower make up an important opposition in Lessing's work, standing for organic nature and human intellect. Similar are sand and water. Suggesting sterility and fertility, the two together make up a unity. Separate, they become the wasteland and the threatening sea. The traditional meanings of these images are particularly important in *The Grass Is Singing*. Its title originates from T. S. Eliot's "The Wasteland." In Lessing's novel, as in Eliot's poem, a dry, sterile period precedes the freshening rain, when the thunderstorm comes at last. The sterility of Mary and Dick's life is mirrored in the dry heat of an African summer, made palpable by the sun's beating on the tin roof. Mary's fervent wish for water, for rain, is only partly a need for physical comfort; it is also the need to end her intolerable psychic tensions. It comes at last, but only after those tensions are released by her death. At the end of *Landlocked*, Martha leaves the depressing meeting of young communists who are in the process of repeating the same mistakes of her own earlier group. She walks out the door into the freshness of sweet-smelling rain, like the promise of her own renewal.

Yet like organic life, the promise of fertility offered by water is only half of the truth. Martha's birthday is in October, the month of tension between drought and rain; the balance between the two must be maintained. When Martha is waiting to go to England, her life becomes unbearably sterile. As a direct result, she has dreams of the sea that seem more real than her waking life, a result of her unconscious mind trying to create a balance but becoming dangerously powerful as a result. In "To Room

Nineteen" Susan is not able to achieve a balance but is dragged ever deeper into illness. The death into which she drifts is a "sullen river," an image that suggests the unconscious elements of her psyche that have claimed her.

A passage in *Landlocked* illustrates the necessity for creating a truce between sand and water and the conditions of sterility and fertility they suggest. Martha contrasts the town where she currently lives and the house in which she grew up, a hundred miles away in "the red earth district." Once the family has left, water will be its conqueror; it had already "sunk to its knees under the blows of the first wet season after the Quests had left it. . . . Already it had been absorbed into a welter of damp growth. . . . The wet heat spawned, and the undersides of rafters sprouted fungus, and mosquitos bred in old shoes" (p. 457). On the other hand, "This city, if emptied, would be conquered at last by dust, not by wet; its enemy would be dryness, the spirit of the highveld where tall dry grasses have grown since—well, long before man first stood upright here. . . . Yes, this city could be like the minute brittle transparent cases that have held insects and now lie blowing about on the sand" (p. 457).

In nature, the wet and the dry can exist separately—for example, in the harsh dichotomy of the African seasons—and life adjusts to the various patterns. Should rain predominate, a jungle results; when dryness prevails, deserts form. It remains for the human imagination and will to mediate the two, keeping a house standing in the wet heat of the bush, a town full of life in the arid plateau. "Two Potters" illustrates the need for the human imagination to combine both wet and dry in a new, imaginative way. In this unusual story the narrator has a sequential dream of an old potter at work in a desert village, who appears to be emblematic of the human imagination throughout time. In each segment, the culture has become slightly more complex, but remains primitive; even in the last sequence the houses are cavelike, the river scummy, and the faces of the inhabitants shaped by poverty. The old man is always making the same kind of clay pot, splashing water onto the clay as he shapes it at his wheel, and the settlement is littered with shards. He desperately wants to make something that lives, and creates a clay rabbit; but nothing happens.

Meanwhile, the protagonist keeps a potter friend, Mary Tawnish, informed of the progress of her dream. Mary is a clear-headed woman who despite her matter-of-fact nature is tolerant of others' fantasies and even enters into them. For instance, inspired by the protagonist's dream story, she makes a pottery rabbit and gives it to her son, who does not often get to see rabbits because most of them have been killed by disease. He sets it out in the neighbor's garden, and the neighbor— remembering how previously rabbits would decimate his plants—shoots at and shatters it. The boy tells his mother that he has set the neighbor's house on fire in revenge, and even though he has not in fact done so, Mary sees that imaginatively to carry out an action, in one sense, at least, amounts to the same thing.

Finally Mary makes for the protagonist a pottery animal that resembles a rabbit but is actually shaped quite differently; it is made not for realism or beauty but for concealment. The protagonist incorporates it into her dream. The old potter flicks it with water, and it comes to life, running quickly off into the desert, unnoticed by the circling birds because of its peculiar shape.

This story provides an interesting play between traditional forms and new ones. The familiar forms will not do; the old potter has been making the same pots for thousands of years and society has scarcely changed. A few amenities have been added, and more people, but the quality of existence has not significantly improved. Or in other words: an English rabbit does not represent anything new and because of its past connotations as lettuce-eater and food for hawks, it is vulnerable.

However, the human imagination can create new forms; but doing so means to cross the customary boundaries and blend all levels of existence. In this story logic and intuition, dream and waking consciousness, clay and water blend together and create something new, something with vitality that is able to survive because it is different. The inference is: the creation of a healthy society will require this sort of effort.

As in "Two Potters," dreams are important throughout Lessing's work and represent the shadow-side of human experience that must be reintegrated. Jack Orkney is a typical example. He is characterized as a man who does not dream; that is, he lives only in the superficial, rational world. During his ordeal his dreams terrify him, making him aware of the other levels of existence and the futility—the danger, even—of confining oneself to the obvious, material world. Afterward, the one real change in Orkney's personality is that he has become a person with dreams and knows that they hint at an area that he is compelled to explore.

Lessing's theory of dreams appears to be similar to Jung's, that they are regulators, alerting people to imbalances in their conscious mind or bringing to full consciousness things that they had perceived only dimly. Martha and Anna dream profusely, and nearly always their dreams are descriptions of the state of their psyches or compelling messages of a course of action that demands to be followed. Their dreams add an imaginative richness to the long, realistic passages that describe the events of their daily lives.

Similar to dreams are the images of madness. As shall be seen in chapter three, for Lessing much mental breakdown is potentially creative, an automatic response by the body to achieve wholeness, to perceive the levels of existence shielded from the rational mind. All of Lessing's protagonists and many secondary characters have such experiences with their potential of healing unity.

Finally, Lessing makes extensive use of the symbols of traditional myth. At random one can cite many uses of it throughout her work. In *Briefing for a Descent into Hell,* Charles Watkins's voyage is compared to Odysseus', with all the connotations of homecoming expressed by that story. Also, in this novel Lessing uses Mercury and Minerva as characters in a modernized Greek myth, and Mercury plays his traditional role of messenger of the gods. In *Children of Violence* Martha's last name—Quest—is mythic and describes her life, a search for self-knowledge.

Traditional mythic patterns such as the Fall and rebirth are strong in Lessing's work. The idea of the Golden Age provides the most pervasive pattern, and she does not hesitate to use the term frequently. Most contemporary writers would hesitate to do so, fearing the paralysis of cliché. This image is appropriate to Lessing, however, since her theme is that to move ahead humankind must also move back. She warns that modern society has dangerously ignored many levels of experience; today people need to turn to the older forms of wisdom that take them into account. For example, in a contemporary society of individuals alienated by their private egos, humankind needs the lesson of traditional myth, which is social rather than personal; it affirms the solidarity of mankind and the patterns that are common to everyone. And myth is more emotional than conceptual, as is most literature: the image replaces argument. As dreams alert one to psychic imbalance, Lessing uses myth as antidote and warning, a signal that modern society has taken the wrong path in turning away from older wisdom.

However, the use of myth in no way implies a complete return to the past. Originally, myths projected unconscious "knowledge," and it has been an arduous intellectual journey to be able to understand them. If Lessing wishes to remind of the truth of mythic patterns and the communal consciousness they represent, she also wishes to show that the old patterns must be used in new ways: the English rabbit is out of date; something new is needed. Anna insists on the difference to Mother Sugar:

> And I don't want to be told when I suddenly have a vision (though God knows it's hard enough to come by) of a life that isn't full of hatred and fear and envy and competition every minute of the night and the day that this is simply the old dream of the golden age brought up to date . . . because the dream of the golden age is a million times more powerful because it's possible, just as total destruction is possible. Probably *because* both are possible. (*The Golden Notebook*, p. 404)

Reason combined with imagination can move either toward destruction, as typified in the hydrogen bomb, or toward a higher form of life than the world has known. Lessing's work is directed two ways. On the one hand, she analyzes the forces that are pushing the world toward Armageddon; on the other, she tries to envision an imaginative alternative.

There are two principal concerns that pervade Lessing's work: the fragmentation of both individual and society that leads to violent and sterile repetition, and the unified existence of nature and also myth. Correspondingly, Lessing moves freely between a logical and a symbolic narrative method. In her short stories she may use one method or the other; in the novels she usually alternates between the two, or combines them.

It goes without saying that poetry and fiction are expressions of a unified rather than logically divided experience. As Susanne Langer has said, art acts on people in a special way.

> What it does to us is to formulate our conceptions of feeling and our conceptions of visual, factual, and audible reality together. It gives us *forms of imagination and forms of feeling*, inseparably. . . . It is only when nature is organized in imagination along lines congruent with forms of feeling that we can understand it, that is, find it rational. . . . Then intellect and emotion are unopposed, life is

symbolized by its setting, the world seems important and beautiful and is intuitively 'grasped.'[21]

And Cassirer has suggested that in art the word "recovers the fullness of life" that it once had in myth—"but it is no longer a life mythically bound and fettered, but an aesthetically liberated life."[22]

By definition, then, Lessing's fiction conveys unified experience, as do all successful literary images. But at the same time, her style is frequently discursive. She seldom risks the ambiguity of the unexplained—or unexplainable—symbol; a story like "Two Potters" is rare in her work in the way its meaning is constructed through image pattern alone. Her constant aim is to show how lack of unity and harmony cripples the individual and his relationship with others. To dramatize this problem she most frequently uses realistic description. Nor does she often let the recorded actions speak for themselves; frequently the narrator or protagonist explains their significance. The result is that the reader is drawn into a logical as well as an emotional response.

In *The Golden Notebook*, a subsidiary theme is the problem of the twentieth-century woman who has been brought up in the traditional way, to be man's helpmate, yet who has found that such a life is impossible in the modern era. Anna verbalizes this problem throughout the novel as does Ella, Anna's fictional counterpart. As a result the reader not only is plunged into vicarious experience with these characters but he/she is also engaged in a discussion with them. To give just one instance, Ella goes to Paris at the end of a five-year affair with Paul, Anna's fictional version of her lover, Michael. Ella finds that she can not even sit alone at a sidewalk cafe and states the reason quite specifically: "she was unable, so weakened was she as an independent being, to enjoy sitting at a table publicly without a man's protection . . ." (p. 265). The reader shares Ella's painful experience but at the same time is given an analysis of it, which most modern authors would leave to the readers to make for themselves. The response is on two levels. The technique is successful because Lessing is extraordinarily perceptive to the nuances of feelings and relationships and gives them a uniquely searching exploration. Some have not been used in literature before; for example, Anna's reactions to the onset of her menstrual period in *The Golden Notebook* is a pioneer in its exploration of uniquely female experiences. As a result this novel is popular among many women who are not so much interested in its literary merit as its psychological accuracy.

Both Anna and Martha are dryly analytical, and readers share their observations in this manner throughout these six novels: on the Communist Party, the problems of women, the nature of repetitive behavior, the source and effect of violence, their own and others' personalities. Frequently the narrator summarizes what the character is thinking. For example, in *A Proper Marriage* Martha and Alice go to the town square to watch their husbands drill:

> It was a heavy rainy season that year. Many afternoons the square was a squelching mass of water and red mud. Once Martha and Alice drove up to watch, which they did in derisive silence. The drill was impossible, so the soldiers were scrambling and fighting across the mud, throwing great handfuls of it into each other's faces, yelling and whooping, knocking each other over. It was painful to the women, seeing their men turned into willing savages. . . . There was some sort of disloyalty to their husbands, and to their marriages, in remembering how the men had fought among the mud puddles with each other, their eyes gleaming with savage joy out of mud-streaked faces, because they were not allowed to go off and fight some enemy. (p. 393)

One shares the women's view of this vivid scene, but at the same time, the narrator interprets their reactions, making the reader consider the way marriage forces one to ignore a partner's faults. And spelled out is Martha's view of the reason some men are willing to go into war: it is an outlet for latent primitive savagery.

But Lessing also makes use of a symbolic narrative method in which the images have greater resonance than in such passages. Characteristically, the veld imagery has a symbolic power absent in the passages dealing with the problems of man in society, and Lessing frequently lets it speak for itself in the manner to which readers have become accustomed since Flaubert. For example, in "The De Wets Come to Kloof Grange" two contrasting philosophies of life are dramatized in the actions of Mrs. Gale and Mrs. De Wet but are given symbolic resonance in the story's images of nature. The loneliness of Mrs. Gale's life has led to an aloofness suggested by her favorite pastime, sitting and watching the mountains: "They were her mountains; they were what she was; they had made her, had crystallized her loneliness into a strength, had sustained her and fed her."[23] Her fear is that Mrs. De Wet's arrival as the wife of the new manager will prevent her from spending time in this way, and the remoteness the mountains suggest becomes concrete when Mrs. Gale is unable to give the young woman sympathy and comfort when she needs it.

Mrs. De Wet's refuge is the river, which is beautiful but dangerous from crocodiles and disease. Despite the risks, the young woman walks there daily to swim and enjoy the beauty. Her attitude toward the river mirrors her relationships with people: whatever the cost, she will risk involvement instead of giving in to the emotional sterility of her husband and Mrs. Gale. Mrs. Gale's strength is based on fragmentation; she has become divorced from feeling. Mrs. De Wet remains whole. This story is about the problems of emotional involvement, and their complexity is suggested by the natural images.

An episode in *A Proper Marriage* further illustrates the contrast between mimetic and symbolic modes in Lessing's work. Martha and Alice are both pregnant. Lessing has charted carefully the state of mind that led to Martha's pregnancy and failure to terminate it, the tedium of Martha's days, and the shallowness of her marriage. After a long stretch of analytical, realistic writing, Lessing paints a purely symbolic scene— especially powerful because by now the reader is hungering for this sort of thing. Martha and Alice are suddenly inspired to leave the shelter of their car and run through the bush, naked, in a pouring rainstorm. Martha immerses herself in a pothole, breast-deep in filthy water that stains her red. She is surrounded by frogs and frog spawn, snails, and snakes, while the rain beats down. The incident conveys a strong sense of exhilaration even though it is not comfortable: the water is dirty; the grass stings; and the snake flicks its tongue threateningly. Neither the narrator nor Martha attempts to explain; the reader is told merely that the women are refreshed by the experience. Certainly there is a contrast implicit between the unified and unifying life of the veld as opposed to the sterile, fragmented life the women have been living, but it is presented with imagery alone, without the analyses and judgments that are found in much of Lessing's work.

At times, images of sterility and fertility become reduced to a form of imagistic shorthand, possible because of their familiar meanings. In "To Room Nineteen" Susan must come up with a name for the man with whom she is supposedly having an affair. Pressed, she blurts out "Michael Plant." It is a small detail but one that suggests all the life force and health that would have characterized an affair, in contrast to the weary, emotionless sterility of her actual state of mind.

Similarly, the final lines of *The Four-Gated City* are a curt official memorandum to Francis concerning Joseph Batts, whom Martha has described as one of the new children with heightened consciousness. "It will be in order for him to inspect parks and gardens within the limits of seven miles from the city. No aliens are allowed outside that limit. It will be in order for him to attend courses on gardening. I take it that your statement that he is ten years old is a misprint?" The fragile figure of Joseph Batts becomes the bridge between two kinds of men: the type who has written the memorandum—those who run the known world—and the type that will be capable of achieving the City. One knows only that Batts has an odd maturity and that he will be a gardener, but that is enough. It is appropriate that Lessing should end her apocalyptic vision with such a small detail. She scarcely ever allows herself the artistic exaltation that can result from the resolution of a short story or novel; "The Antheap" and "Hunger" are rare exceptions for her. Like the blade of grass that Anna Wulf envisioned thrusting up after the holocaust, Joseph Batts as gardener is a sturdy but very small beginning.

Lessing occasionally uses imagery in a near-allegorical sense. In *A Proper Marriage* Martha is haunted by the ferris wheel visible from her bedroom window, symbol for the repetition of behavior that she fears for herself and her child. Martha's clothing is another example; it frequently expresses her personality at that particular stage. Her first dance dress, white and romantic, is out of place at Marnie's party. Ruined with mud, it signifies the disenchantment she suffers during the evening. When Donovan dresses Martha for another dance, his creation is bizarre, not Martha, a sign of the influence he has had over her.

Significantly, this type of conscious, obvious imagery is typical of another writer with a message, D. H. Lawrence. In *Women and Love* Gudrun's appearance at the ball in her silver beetle's costume signifies that she has been reduced to the level of Loerke, the insectlike artist. Ursula and Birkin crossing the Channel, huddled together for warmth, are described as nuts in one shell—like Lessing's organic imagery, a detail that suggests vitality and optimism.

Unlike Lessing, Lawrence frequently uses techniques that

seem out of keeping with his themes. Both share the philosophy that the flaw in Western culture is inflation of the intellect at the expense of intuitive "knowledge." However, Lawrence's allegories and frequently discursive style are themselves intellectual and force such a response from the reader, conflicting with the theme that one must do away with all that. Lawrence is at his best when idea is submerged in image, as depicted in the characterization of Mr. Morel.

Lessing, on the other hand, never undervalues the intellect. One of her main themes is the importance of consciousness, since in order to change, humanity must first understand. As a result, her discursiveness and use of allegory do not go against the current of her work. Typically, even in the chaos of madness, Anna and Martha are as rational as scientists in a laboratory. Even while enduring this psychic realm where all the rational distinctions of ordinary life are gone, they carefully chart their discoveries and analyze their significance: reason and unreason joined. It is this combination of the two extremes, in both subject matter and narrative method, that is one of Lessing's most distinctive characteristics.

3
Madness and the Unity of Personality

Mental breakdown is a recurring pattern in Lessing's fiction. *The Grass Is Singing, The Golden Notebook, Briefing for a Descent into Hell,* "The Temptation of Jack Orkney," *The Summer before the Dark:* in every one of these works, psychological crisis or degeneration is the main action; and in *Children of Violence* Martha's flirtation with madness climaxes the long series of explorations into roles and experiences that has given continuity to the series. Not only Lessing's protagonists but also a host of secondary and minor characters suffer breakdowns: Dick Turner, Thomas, Saul Green, Lynda, Dorothy, Charlie Themba, and Phoebe Coldridge, to give only a partial list. Madness is also a frequent theme in Lessing's short stories. "To Room Nineteen" records Susan's poignant drift toward death with the harsh immediacy of a Plath poem. In "The Eye of God in Paradise" Dr. Kroll, who spends six months of every year as a patient in his own mental hospital, exemplifies the schizoid split of Germany itself. In "Dialogue" Bill concentrates all his effort toward facing and overcoming madness.

Some of Lessing's finest passages take the reader into the distorted world of insanity, especially the golden notebook section of that novel, Martha's daring probes into inner consciousness in *The Four-Gated City,* and parts of Charles Watkins's mental journey in *Briefing for a Descent into Hell. The Grass Is Singing,* in some ways a crude first novel, is convincing and compelling in its dramatization of Mary's gradual degeneration. Not surprisingly, mental breakdown is not entirely a matter of fiction for Lessing. In *Going Home* she tells how she began to dream continually of world destruction and in a fight for her sanity had to restore to conscious memory every detail of her childhood home (much as Martha in *The Four-Gated City* fights a nervous breakdown by forcing herself to recall the painful experiences of her childhood). And Lessing has told how in writing *The Golden Notebook* she deliberately evoked the different levels of experience of that novel, especially where Anna is "a bit mad."[1]

Lessing has said that she was very young when she first began to see the eccentricity of the human race. Her father would sit in a deck chair near the farm house and look out over the veld.

> After a silence which might well have lasted several hours, he would start to his feet, majestically splenetic in shabby khaki, a prophet in his country, and shaking his fist at the sky, shout out: "Mad! Mad! Everyone! Everywhere! Mad!"[2]

This appears to be Lessing's own view of the world. Here and there appear a few apparently sane and stable characters such as Johnny Lindsay of *Children of Violence* and Jan Brod of *Retreat From Innocence*—both patient and unselfish fighters against injustice. But most of Lessing's characters are in some sense neurotic, and all the protagonists of the major novels experience neurosis or madness, or both.

However, within these terms there are important distinctions. For example, one phenomenon Lessing calls madness is irrationality in human relationships. The quotation cited above aptly introduces *In Pursuit of the English,* a series of portraits of the "mad" inhabitants of Lessing's London boarding house:

Rose, who can not part from the lover who makes her miserable; Flo and Dan, spending money on improbable schemes while they neglect their beloved daughter, Aurora; the Skeffingtons, with their sadomasochism. The irrationality or madness of these people is to destroy themselves or those they love with greed, masochism, or self-interest.

In the novels, most relationships are as flawed as these, but in her fiction Lessing's emphasis is the social forces that cause neurosis. Mr. Quest is a hypochondriac, but only because of his very real war injuries. Mrs. Quest, cheated of a full life by circumstance, must try to live vicariously through her children, and she ends by hating as much as loving them. Thomas, Sally-Sarah, and Michael (Anna's lover) retain psychic injury from Hitler's pogroms. Paul Coldfield, warped by his traumatic childhood, never quite matures into an independent, responsible adult. Phoebe Coldfield's rigidity, like her nervous breakdown, has its source in thwarted idealism and the failure of her marriage.

Other characters are not so much neurotic as stunted. Mr. Maynard has built his personality around a dry cynicism. The sports-club crowd of Zambesia lives only for pleasure, and most members of the leftist organizations settle for triviality and self-gratification.

For Lessing all fragmentation, neurosis, and madness imply some failure in psychic unity from lack of vision or openness to experience. Partly this lack of unity is an inability to integrate the conscious and rational with the unconscious and alogical. Partly it implies failure to recognize one's relationship with humanity as a whole. Yet neurosis and madness may be constructive if recognized and dealt with correctly, as Anna and Martha are able to do. Unheeded, they may be purely destructive, as occurred in *The Grass is Singing*. Memories of breakdown may be a goad to future growth, as shown in "The Temptation of Jack Orkney," or be overcome and ignored, as happened in *Briefing for a Descent into Hell*.

The Grass Is Singing, Lessing's first novel, like all the others is about the fragmented personality. This novel is usually seen to be chiefly about the color bar and miscegenation, and to some degree it is. However, the main subject is Mary's mental degeneration and absorption by unconscious elements in her psyche, her Jungian "shadow."

Lessing is very precise about the nature and cause of Mary's division. Her problem is repressed sexuality, and the more insistently she represses it the more control it gains over her. The facts are given about Mary's childhood and all illustrate the origin of her contempt for men and distaste for sex: her father's drinking problem, the poverty and degradation of her mother and herself, her hatred for her parents' sexuality. These emotions and memories remain harmlessly in Mary's unconscious during her pleasant single life. However, she remains static; as a woman of thirty she is still living as she did ten years earlier, with the clothes, social life, and living arrangements of a young girl. Inevitably she is eventually confronted by her difference from other women. Once she becomes aware of society's expectations, trouble stirs. Another girl's comment about her— "She is not like that" (that is, interested in sex)—forces Mary to question herself and her way of life.

Once Mary overhears these words, her repressions begin to exert a power of fatality that she is helpless against, since she is unable to analyze and deal with them. After making the mistake of marrying Dick and finding herself in surroundings as dreary as those of her childhood, she half senses that she is no longer in control of her life. She is "possessed with the thought that her father, from his grave, had sent out his will and forced her back into the kind of life he had made her mother lead."[3]

Indeed, because Mary never confronts her neuroses directly, she becomes increasingly their victim. Exacerbated by the grimness of her life, the psychic split deepens, and she gradually loses control over herself. Hysterically unreasonable demands on a succession of kitchen boys are a transference of her inability to order her own emotions; and when Dick is ill, she takes a perverse pleasure in whipping the farm workers into line, first with her tongue and then in fact, when she slashes Moses across the face.

When Moses becomes Mary's kitchen boy, her final destruction begins; she regards this virile man with a growing attraction and fear. There is no question that he represents Mary's repressed sexuality, a neurosis originating in her childhood. His increasing power over her symbolizes the fatal power of her psychic shadow:

> He approached slowly, obscene and powerful, and it was not only him, but her father who was threatening her. They advanced together, one person, and she could smell, not the native smell, but the unwashed smell of her father. It filled the room, musty, like animals. (p. 176)

The more violently Mary tries to impose her will on Moses the more insistently she is possessed by him until her will simply dissolves and she completely succumbs to the "dark attraction" he holds for her. The decor of her house, African materials left over from the store and usually held in contempt by the whites, is an outward sign of the way she has been taken over by Moses physically and psychologically. It is also a sign of the fatality that has pursued her from childhood, where the store with its cheap goods stood for everything she hated in that way of life. Mary's final grotesque parody of coquetry shows the complete reversal of her personality; she has been consumed by her shadow, a psychological state witnessed in " 'Leopard' George" and it will recur in *The Four-Gated City*.[4]

The racial theme complements the theme of mental breakdown in this novel, since Mary's attitude to the black workers on the farm expresses not merely her own neurosis but also a fairly typical example of white supremacy. To the degree that

Lessing allows the racial theme to be subsidiary to the psychological theme, it is very successful. However, the chief weakness of this novel is that Lessing's passion against racial prejudice causes her to disrupt her main concern. She wished to show that prejudice destroys everyone, white and black, and to do so she framed Mary's story with an unconvincing murder and the subsequent reactions of Charlie Slatter and Marston. Finally, since Moses is a powerful character mainly because he symbolizes Mary's own shadow, it is disastrous to enter his point of view after he has killed her. *The Grass is Singing* would have been a stronger novel if the frame had been eliminated and it had ended with the final vision of Mary's bizarre coquetry and the twisted relationship that Dick, Mary, and Moses have finally evolved.

The Grass Is Singing has several motifs and minor themes that appear again in Lessing's later work. While Mary's destruction is caused by her particular psychological problems, her plight is also representative of the European farm wife in Africa, isolated from family, friends, and the amenities of society—a common theme in Lessing's African stories. Also, Dick and Mary both illustrate the danger of illusions. Mary's false expectations of farm life, which allow her to marry Dick, and Dick's unrealistic dreams about family life and making money show the danger of such an approach to life. Martha's illusions are a major theme of the first three volumes of *Children of Violence*.

In *The Grass is Singing* the motif of the African seasons is as important as it is to *Children of Violence*. Unlike Martha, Mary detests the summer heat. The intolerable sun on the tin roof of the farm house—there is never enough money for ceilings—effectively symbolizes all that makes life intolerable. Heat is unavoidable, always following her, a concrete image for the inner and outer pressures that ultimately destroy her. Mary fails to find any sort of unity—either within herself or with nature, husband, or society. All these failures combine to cause her destruction, which Lessing describes with surprising skill for a first novel, and these chapters are as fine as anything she has written.

Lessing wrote *The Golden Notebook* with the experience behind her of five novels and a host of short stories. It is here for the first time that her major themes appear in their full complexity. In *The Grass Is Singing* neurosis and madness are completely destructive. However, in *The Golden Notebook* it appears that they may be the source of creative vision.

It is an ancient idea that the mad are touched by the divine and have greater vision than the sane. The outstanding contemporary spokesman for this belief is R. D. Laing, whose work with schizophrenics convinced him that many of the so-called mentally ill have actually embarked on meaningful explorations of the inner world. The real problem is that they are hindered in their return to sanity and often completely destroyed by the psychiatric treatment they receive.

Like Jung, Laing believes that the central evil of modern time is the split between the inner and outer worlds of human perception, that "society, without knowing it, is *starving* for the inner":

> If the human race survives, future men will, I suspect, look back on our enlightened epoch as a veritable Age of Darkness. . . . They will see that what we call "schizophrenia" was one of the forms which, often through quite ordinary people, the light began to break through the cracks in our all-too-closed minds.[5]

Although it would appear to be chaotic, the schizophrenic experience seems to Laing "to be part of a potentially orderly, natural sequence of experiences." If such a person were guided through it with understanding and genuine assistance — perhaps by someone who has been through it himself — he would perhaps experience an existential rebirth. "This process could have a central function in a truly sane society." Instead, many lose their way and are completely lost in the maze of the inner world.[6]

> This journey is experienced as going further "in," as going back through one's personal life, in and back and through and beyond into the experience of all mankind, of the primal man, of Adam and perhaps even further into the beings of animals, vegetables and minerals. . . . We are far more out of touch with even the nearest approaches of the infinite reaches of inner space than we now are with the reaches of outer space. We respect the voyager, the explorer, the climber, the space man. It makes far more sense to me as a valid project—indeed, as a desperately and urgently required project for our time—to explore the inner space of consciousness. Perhaps this is one of the few things that still make sense in our historical context. (pp. 126–27)

Such an exploration is dangerous, risking "chaos, madness and death," but the rewards can be the release of the "wretched mind" of the unenlightened ego into a finer state:

> True sanity entails one way or another the dissolution of the normal ego, that false self competently adjusted to our alienated social reality; the emergence of the "inner" archetypal mediators of divine power, and through this death a rebirth, and the eventual re-establishment of a new kind of ego-functioning, the ego now being the servant of the divine, no longer its betrayer. (pp. 144–45)

In the later novels—*The Golden Notebook, Landlocked, The Four-Gated City,* and *Briefing for a Descent into Hell*—Lessing's views of madness are like Laing's. In each of them certain characters spontaneously or deliberately journey deep into consciousness, shed their confining egos, and gain a more inclusive vision than they had before. *The Golden Notebook* is the first of these novels to dramatize such an exploration.[7]

In *The Golden Notebook* the focus is on Anna Wulf. Like Mary Turner, she is neurotic because of a fragmented personality. However, the point of the novel is the complexity of Anna's fragmentation and eventual integration. Anna is Lessing's most fully developed character in the sense that she comes to life vividly and completely for the reader. Mary Turner is vividly realized but her character is oversimplified. Martha Quest is more a consciousness than a three-dimensional heroine; as the series progresses she gradually sheds the personality traits by which readers have come to know her. One views Charles Watkins from the oblique angles of his schizoid consciousness and others' views of him. His rational mind, or ego, is left out in order to emphasize the symbol-making underside of his psyche. However, Anna deserves to take her place among the great, fully realized protagonists of the novel.

Lessing does not present a traditional portrait. There is that and more, and the Anna who emerges is a hall-of-mirrors composite of imagination and "fact," past and present, ego and alter ego. Lessing is here engaged in the same search delineated by Virginia Woolf in "Mr. Bennett and Mrs. Brown"—how to convey the complexity of personality within the traditional forms of fiction. Anna, the writer, faces the same problem within *The Golden Notebook* itself. One of her difficulties is to know that truth can not be captured in words and that the known forms of the novel are particularly unable to express it.

For Lessing all reality is dual, two sides of a coin, and the narrow beam of consciousness can not light up both sides at once. Since in *The Golden Notebook* Lessing's chief aim is to show the essential duality of personality and the need to find a way to balance the opposites within oneself, she uses a complex blend of Anna's conscious thought, dream, madness, and fictional creation to complete her characterization. The great artistic achievement of this novel is its merging of form and content despite the complexity of its material.

Doris Lessing has described the structure of *The Golden Notebook*:

> The shape of this novel is as follows: There is a skeleton, or frame, called *Free Women*, which is a conventional short novel, about

60,000 words long, and which could stand by itself. But it is divided into five sections and separated by stages of the four Notebooks—Black, Red, Yellow, and Blue. The Notebooks are kept by Anna Wulf, a central character of *Free Women*. She keeps four, and not one because, as she recognizes, she has to separate things off from each other, out of fear of chaos, of formlessness—of breakdown. Pressures, inner and outer, end the Notebooks; a heavy line is drawn across the page of one after another. But now that they are finished, from their fragments can come something new, *The Golden Notebook*.[8]

The black notebook begins by describing Anna's wartime years in Africa, especially a series of weekends spent with a group of communist friends at the Mashopi Hotel. The climax is a disastrous episode in which this idealistic group inadvertently causes the hotel's black cook to be fired, forcing him to leave his family and find work elsewhere. During this period Anna shares a loveless marriage with Max Wulf (called Willi Rodde in the notebook) and becomes pregnant with Janet. Anna is attracted to Paul Blackenhurst, a member of the group, with whom she has a brief affair. Shortly afterward, the group breaks up, and Paul dies in an accident. Further sections of the black notebook describe Anna's encounters with agents who wish to buy the television or film rights to her novel, *Frontiers of War*, and parodies of her own book, writer's notebooks, film scripts, and communist book reviews. One further African segment recalls a pigeon hunt at the Mashopi Hotel.

The red notebook describes Anna's joining the British Communist Party and also her cynicism at the disparity between it and its ideals. The second segment records a dream of a unified world that suddenly unravels like a ball of yarn: a concise view of Anna's failing idealism. The third segment records how Tommy, son of Anna's friend Molly, becomes a socialist of the same idealistic bent as the young Anna and Molly—a painful reminder to Anna that each generation fails to move beyond the mistakes of its elders. The final entry describes the disillusion of a man who has devoted his life to the study of Russian history and communism, but who is never called upon to use his education in service to the Communist Party.

The blue notebook, meant to be a journal of daily events, begins by describing the complicated and unhappy relationships among Molly, her ex-husband Richard, and their son Tommy, who is torn between his two parents. In this notebook Anna describes her first encounter with Mrs. Marks, her analyst. Mrs. Marks insists that Anna's real problem is a writer's block, while Anna admits only to an inability to experience emotion. The notebook is then dropped for three years, until the end of Anna's analysis. She can then feel, although she complains that the result is merely pain. The segment ends with a dream about a jeweled crocodile.

The second entry describes one entire day in detail. Anna has spent the night with Michael, who says he will be back that night. She plans her day accordingly, shopping for fresh groceries and making sure she is attractively dressed. After dealing with her unexpected menstrual period, she tackles her work at the Communist Party headquarters, answering letters and reading manuscripts. In a moment of complete despair about the inadequacies of the Party, she quits her job and comes home to prepare dinner for her daughter Janet and then for Michael and herself. Hours later, Michael calls to say he is not coming, and Anna knows that it is a permanent break between them.

The third entry describes a meeting with Mrs. Marks that actually took place several years earlier. Here Anna states many important ideas that I shall refer to later in the chapter. This segment also records two disastrous affairs—with a neurotic American writer, Nelson, and the cruel De Silva. In the final segment, Janet leaves for boarding school, and the reader learns that Tommy is to marry. Saul Green, an American writer, rents a room in Anna's apartment for a short while, and Anna plunges into a disordered mental state similar to his. They have a complicated relationship, in which they share each other's personalities and those of many others. As Lessing says, "They 'break down' into each other, into other people, break through the false patterns they have made of their pasts; the patterns and formulas they have made to shore up themselves and each other, dissolve."[9] For the first time Anna admits that she has had a writer's block. Healed, she buys a golden notebook and decides that she can write in just one instead of four. Saul asks for it, and Anna refuses to give it to him.

The inner golden notebook is written by both Saul and Anna. In it Anna describes the events of her relationship with Saul and he (one is told) writes a short novel after Anna does finally give the notebook to him. In this complicated section of the novel, a combination of dreams, hallucinations, and "facts" bring together all the themes of the novel. Finally, Anna and Saul give each other the first lines of their novels. Anna's is the first line of *Free Women* and also *The Golden Notebook*, "The two women were alone in the London flat," establishing Anna of the notebooks as the author of *Free Women* and also *The Golden Notebook* itself. Lessing has said that it is an ironic sentence,[10] presumably because one of the main themes of the novel is that mankind is a unity and therefore no one is ever alone.

The yellow notebook is an unfinished novel, *The Shadow of the Third*. It concerns the love affair of Ella and Paul Tanner, surrogates for Anna and Michael. Divorced, Ella lives with her son Michael in the home of her friend Molly. She meets Paul, a psychiatrist, at the home of her employer, who is a psychiatric consultant for a woman's magazine. Paul is married and has children, but gives his family only cursory attention. The first episode deals with Paul and Ella's first encounter: Ella immediately falls in love, but Paul sets careful limits to the affair. Several incidents during their five-year affair show Paul's cynicism and critical attitude toward Ella; for example, he can not take seriously her novel about a suicide. The segment ends with a description of the end of the relationship. Paul leaves for Africa, and Ella hopes to join him; however, she is told by her employer that Paul has written complaining about a "flighty piece" he had wanted to get away from, a "not-so-young woman" who was pestering him to marry her.

The next episode shows Ella's difficulty in trying to adjust to the break with Paul, to whom she is still emotionally tied. She can not enjoy a business trip alone to Paris, and a brief, unsatisfying affair with an American neurosurgeon depresses her further. The third segment takes place a year later and describes Ella's various unsuccessful affairs, which are followed by a complete lack of interest in men. Ella visits her father, a retired army officer who has retreated from warm relationships into a life of solitude. Ella fears she is headed for a nervous breakdown and tries to envision the novel she would like to write from her experiences, but her creativity seems to be dried up. At this point Anna drops the novel and simply lists story ideas that are related to events in the other notebooks.

The five segments of *Free Women* begin and end *The Golden Notebook*. This short novel opens with Anna and Molly talking in Anna's kitchen. Richard, Molly's ex-husband, comes in, followed by Tommy, and the clash of attitudes among the four is witnessed. In the second segment Tommy's resentment of his mother heightens. He comes to Anna, apparently for soothing words to calm his cynicism and despair, but she is unable to give him what he needs. He attempts suicide with a pistol and does not die, but blinds himself. In the third segment, Anna goes to Richard's office at his request. He hopes to get her aid in dealing with his second wife, Marion, an alcoholic, to facilitate a divorce. Marion, seeing that her marriage is collapsing, turns for solace to politics. She and Tommy begin a bizarre friendship based on a naive socialism. Anna rents a room in her apartment to two homosexuals, Ronnie and Ivor. In the fourth segment Marion leaves Richard and her children and moves in with Tommy. After Marion and Tommy are arrested at a political demonstration, Anna tries to give Marion a sense of what political activity really is, telling her about Charlie Themba, imprisoned for his beliefs, becoming mad. Faced with emotional problems on all sides, Anna evicts Ronnie and Ivor because of their satirical attitude toward her and Janet. In the final segment Janet goes off to boarding school. An American, Milt, rents a room in Anna's apartment for five days. In a calm episode that nevertheless suggests the chaotic, timeless events of the final blue notebook and the golden notebook, Milt takes down clippings about the world's violence that Anna has neurotically pinned to her walls. He himself is suffering a mental breakdown, and Anna gives him five days of care. This brief affair over, Anna decides to give up writing and take a job as a teacher and marriage counselor. Molly announces that she is getting married.

It is important to note that Anna steps in for Doris Lessing and writes not just *Free Women* (Saul gives her the first line in the golden notebook) but *The Golden Notebook* itself. There is evidence for her authorship in the text. At the end of the first *Free Women* section, Anna is sitting on her music stool looking down at her four notebooks "as if she were a general on top of a mountain, watching her armies deploy in the valley below" (p. 52). Also, Anna's notebooks play an important part in this little novel; it is after reading them that Tommy tries to commit suicide.

However, evidence for Anna's authorship is indicated in more far-reaching ways. One reason that Anna has not written a second novel is that "The thinning of language against the density of our experience" convinces her that fiction will always be a distortion for her (p. 259). Life is "crude, raw, tentative" and is valuable for those very qualities, whereas art is finished and therefore unreal, with a "terrible lying nostalgia" (p. 61). It is this quality of nostalgia that disturbs her in *Frontiers of War*. Also, art distorts because it is shaped in terms of the end. Her chief criticism of the novel fragment in the yellow notebook, *The Shadow of the Third*, is that every word is written with the knowledge that Paul leaves Ella (as Michael left Anna). The result is a distortion of the experience it attempts to dramatize: "As soon as one has lived through something it falls into a pattern. . . . That is why all this is untrue. Because while living through something one doesn't think like that at all" (p. 196). Yet without the pattern of form and analysis, "it would be chaos" (p. 196). Also, Anna states unequivocally that the only sort of novel that interests her is the kind that makes a philosophic statement. She herself would not be interested in writing another unless it produces a "new way of looking at life."

There is no reason to suppose that an Anna who holds these ideas about literature would be interested in writing *Free Women* by itself, even as a therapeutic exercise.[11] However, *The Golden Notebook* meets her demanding criteria: it makes a philosophic statement and provides a new (or at least nontraditional) way of looking at life. It combines the raw, tentative crudeness of experience with the finish of artistic form. It even evades the problem of being molded by its ending, for Anna of *Free Women* and *The Golden Notebook* embark on different careers, the former to teaching and social work, the latter to writing. In the light of Anna's authorship, a comment by Mrs. Marks, Anna's psychiatrist, affords a pleasant bit of dramatic irony. Speaking of Anna's sessions with her she says, "And you will write of this experience. . . . You will see. In a few months' time, perhaps a few years' time" (p. 215). It is three years later that Anna does so, incorporating their conversations into *The Golden Notebook*.

The result of Anna's authorship is an unusual distancing of

the writer from the work. Lessing can stand aside to the degree normally possible only in a first-person narrative, yet be free of its restrictions. As a result, the entire novel is part of Anna's self-revelation even as the reader seems to move out of her mind and look at her (or a surrogate) through the vision of an omniscient narrator. This method of narration is perfectly designed to accomplish Lessing's purpose, dramatizing Anna's growing knowledge of her own nature and illustrating the complexity of the psyche.

The reader experiencing *The Golden Notebook* for the first time is left with a mental collage of each character made up of the various views given in the different sections. (*See* appendix for chart listing parallel characters.) Lessing undoubtedly intends such a reaction, since one of her themes is that truth has this sort of complexity. At the same time, she wishes to convey how much complex experience lies behind any fictional representation. She insists on having it both ways. As a result, it is important to distinguish as much as possible between "fact" and fiction even while being sensitive to the way Lessing blends the distinction between them.

When I differentiate between fact and fiction, it will of course be obvious that all the characters are fictional, originating in Doris Lessing's imagination. However, since Lessing wishes in this novel to deal with the relationship of fiction and experience—to show how fiction inevitably simplifies and distorts—she carefully sets up two levels of fiction. What I shall call the "real" Anna is just once removed from life; she is the author of the notebooks, *Free Women,* and *The Golden Notebook* itself (standing in for Lessing as a first-person narrator would do). Similarly, other "real" characters appear in the blue, black, and red notebooks, which purport to be the facts of this Anna's life. What I shall call fictional characters are twice removed from reality, the "real" Anna's creations in *Free Women* and *The Shadow of the Third* (novels within the novel), and to some degree the final notebooks: the last blue notebook and the golden notebook.

However, the division between what is real and fictional is not always clearly defined, since there are discrepancies, undoubtedly intentional. For example, the first segment of the black notebook is supposed to show the source material for Anna's novel, *Frontiers of War*, but she uses a fictional name, Wilhelm Rodde, for her husband Max Wulf. Also, the final, significantly undated, segment of the blue notebook (which has supposedly been Anna's factual diary) gives contradictory information on an important point, her selling the film rights to *Frontiers of War*. At one point she says she has sold it "for the third time," knowing the film will never be made. As a result, she need not get a job. Shortly after, she says she has refused to sell, despite the high offers. "They do want to make the film, I think, so what is the use of standing out all these years simply to give in now, just because for the first time I am running short of money" (pp. 464, 471). The other blue notebook entries, which are dated, do not have discrepancies, nor does the red notebook, in which Anna writes about her experiences with the Communist Party.

In the following study I am making the assumption that the first three blue notebooks and the red and black notebooks are essentially true except for possible name changes, while the final blue notebook and golden notebook are an indeterminable mixture of fact and fiction. However, since Lessing always wishes to blur the distinction, the reader needs to hold in mind that Lessing's whole point is that "truth" is virtually impossible either to discern or communicate, that the written word inevitably distorts. Still, to see clearly where art and life merge, it is necessary to distinguish between them where possible. *The Shadow of the Third* and *Free Women* present no problem, since they are obviously fiction based on Anna's life: the heroine of *Free Women* bears Anna's own name, and the Anna of the notebooks sees that her creation, Ella, is at least partly based upon herself. She writes, "I, Anna, see Ella. Who is of course, Anna. But that is the point, for she is not. The moment I, Anna, write: Ella rings up Julia to announce, etc., then Ella floats away from me and becomes someone else" (p. 393).

Like Anna, Ella is a writer, although she is not suffering from a writer's block. In *The Shadow of the Third* Ella writes and publishes a novel that itself deals with the split personality: the protagonist unconsciously heads toward suicide, a motive not apparent until the end. Ella works for a magazine, *Women at Home*, answering letters from lonely, defeated women who write for help. Similarly, Anna does what she calls "welfare work" at the Communist Party headquarters, answering letters from party members and trying to help them with their problems. Both Anna and Ella become disillusioned with the party and leave it. Ella has a young son, Michael, who is the counterpart of Anna's daughter Janet and is named after Anna's lover. Like Anna, Ella has a five-year affair with a doctor, who leaves her.

The Anna of *Free Women* bears a close resemblance to the real Anna. Like her, she is having difficulty overcoming her desertion by Michael. She has a daughter Janet. Like the real Anna she has once lived in a small apartment in her friend Molly's house but has left it when the novel begins. She has written a best-selling novel but is not interested in writing another. She has undergone analysis with Mrs. Marks, or "Mother Sugar" as Anna and Molly call her. And again like the real Anna she has a brief affair with an American, Milt. (This is the only name in *Free Women* that differs from those in the diaries. The American of the blue and golden notebooks is Saul Green.) Anna of *Free Women* differs from her counterpart in deciding to become a teacher and marriage counselor; she does not intend to write again.

Marion and Richard are almost entirely fictional. All that one knows of them in the blue notebook is that they live in an expensive country house from where Richard commutes to London. The real Richard once bullied Molly financially to try to get her to return to him and threatened to jeopardize her job with blackmail about her membership in the Communist Party. But the Richard of the expensive office, the financial power who has a weakness for "nut brown maids," is pure fiction. In the blue notebook there is not even a name for Richard's second wife: Marion the alcoholic is fictional.

Tommy, the son of Richard and Molly, is both real and fictional, but the facts differ greatly from the version of him in *Free Women*. It is known that he is torn between his father's and his mother's values. He becomes a conscientious objector, which pleases Molly, but in most instances he simply tries to antagonize her. He spends his two years working in a coal mine and then begins a tour of lectures about the life of a coal miner. He marries a girl whom Molly dislikes. Like Molly, Tommy and his wife are socialists, but Molly is appalled to see that they use the same jargon she and Anna once used and have the same out-worn ideas; they have learned nothing from their elders' mistakes.

Tommy of *Free Women* has a character similar to the Tommy of the notebooks, but the facts of his life are exaggerated for the sake of fiction. Torn between his parents' views, unable to come up with any workable view of life, he attempts suicide. Reading Anna's notebooks appears to have brought on this crisis. The real Tommy's way of bullying Molly and Anna is imaged in the strange power the blind Tommy seems to wield over them. His relationship with Marion is of course fiction.

Molly is mostly fictional. From time to time, however, she does appear in the notebooks. For a time, Anna has lived in her house. Molly has been a communist, and she is Jewish. These are the only facts. Molly the actress, open and warm, always ready with advice, delighting in her various roles both on and off the stage, is a product of *Free Women* and *The Shadow of the Third*, where her name is Julia. The main difference between the two characters is Julia's anger and hurt feelings when Ella leaves her apartment to live on her own.

Michael, Anna's real-life lover, is not as fully developed as his counterpart, Paul Tanner, in the yellow notebook, but there are some important facts about him. Unlike Paul, Michael is not English but European and Jewish; most of his family died in the gas chambers. He was a communist but left the party, although he gets pleasure from Anna's activity in it. Most of his friends are dead, "communists murdered by communists." Michael suffers the same fate of many characters in *Children of Violence*—a distortion of personality because of the fabric of violence that has spread worldwide since World War I. As he says at one point, "My dear Anna, if you insist on sleeping with a man who is the history of Europe over the last twenty years, you mustn't complain if he has uneasy dreams" (p. 284). Like Paul he has a wife and children (of whom nothing is said), but never spends any time at home. He is a doctor.

It is in *The Shadow of the Third* that the full impact of this affair and Michael's departure is evident; indeed, this is where Anna herself discovers it. Reading her notebooks for the first time she says, "I had not realized before how the experience of being rejected by Michael had affected me; how it had changed, or apparently had changed, my whole personality" (p. 407). Paul Tanner is different from Michael in many of the outward details of his life. He is from the English working class and has had a difficult time arriving at his present status—and hints that the adjustment has taken its toll on him. He is a psychiatrist and helps Ella with her letters. He works extremely hard, dividing his time between patients and executive work, trying to improve methods of dealing with the mentally ill. He speaks frequently about his wife, and Ella builds up a mental picture of her.

Paul's attitude toward Ella is dramatized in more detail than is Michael's toward Anna. He is rather domineering: he makes fun of Ella's writing, tries to change her manner of dress, and tends to be jealous. In deference to Paul's jealousy, Ella has scarcely any social life during the five years she is with him. In this fictional version of the affair, it is an emotional crisis that finally makes him leave: Ella insists that she *is* his wife. Finally, Paul leaves for Africa, which has no weight of tradition to hinder his work.

It is in *The Shadow of the Third* that the pain that Ella/Anna endures from the loss can be seen: Ella can not exist as an independent person; after five years, she requires the company and protection of a man. She vacillates between sexual hunger and sexlessness and can not go out with another man without being haunted by the memory of Paul. Such emotions are merely hinted at in the blue notebook and *Free Women.*

Saul Green appears only in the final blue notebook and the golden notebook, which are combined fact and fiction. Therefore, it is impossible to know how much basis for fact is in these episodes. One can probably assume that Anna has a brief affair with an American who is fighting mental illness and that the experiences she shares with him are instrumental in her final vision and integration.

These are the main characters of *The Golden Notebook,* and except for Anna and to some degree Saul the image of them is almost entirely from Anna's fiction and in the traditional mode. Both Anna and Saul are a blend of fact and fiction, but it is only Anna's psyche that is explored deeply. The contrast in methods speaks eloquently of the ability of traditional fiction to bring scenes and characters to life by simplification and exaggeration, but it also shows its failure to convey the true complexities of character and experience as Lessing sees them.

Dramatically, the reason for the different views of Anna is that she is suffering from a neurotic fragmentation of personality. The outward sign of her condition is her inability to put all of herself in one book; since her ideas and experiences conflict, she feels compelled to put them in separate compartments. The notebooks cover a seven year period, from 1950 to 1957. The following chart will show their relationship in time to one another and to some of the main events in Anna's life:

BLACK NOTEBOOK	RED NOTEBOOK	BLUE NOTEBOOK
	1/3/50– first entry.	1/7/50– first entry. Anna is living with Molly.
	2/5/50– short entry, showing criticism of C. P.	1/10/50– first visit to Mother Sugar. Has known Michael three weeks.
	8/19/50– short entry, critical of C. P.	3/27/50– last entry for four years. One is told that clippings describing world violence supplant entries.
Begins in 1951, no exact date.	9/15/51– re: Jack Briggs, victimized journalist.	
1952– refuses film rights to *Frontiers of War*.	1/3/52– begins series of undated entries: death of Rosenbergs and Stalin; criticism of English C. P.	
1953– satire on fantasized film version of *Frontiers of War*.		
1954– long story of African years: source of novel.	8/28/54– Quemoy incident in news. Dream of a beautiful world that dissolves.	4/54– End of analysis with Mother Sugar. Blue notebook begins again.
Undated entries under "money."	1952 incident pasted in, re: communist naiveté.	9/17/54– One day recorded in detail: quits C. P.; Michael leaves her.

		10/15/54 to circa 3/55	Short fac- tual entries (examples included). – Moves to own apart- ment.
11/11/55– pigeon episode in London recalls hunt at Mashopi.	11/13/55– C. P. meeting. (Political materials attached. Theme: new coopera- tive C. P.)		
Undated: satires on popularization of literature.			
Newspaper clippings on African violence.	Newspaper clippings describing acts of violence.		
9/56– Dream of complete sterility.	9/20/56– Complete disillusion with politics.		
	More clippings.		
	Undated entry: Harry Mathews, disap- pointed expert on Russia.		
Clippings to 1957	Clippings of world violence to 1957		
			1957 Final espisode including key conver- sations with Mother Sugar and episode with Saul Green.

1957–Novel *Free Women'* takes place summer of 1957 and is integrated
with the notebooks, which are edited for this purpose: certain comments
and summaries are added in brackets. Most clippings and factual entries
of blue notebook for 10/17/54 through 3/55 are eliminated.

In Anna's relationship with Mother Sugar is learned that Anna makes some important distinctions in her views of neurosis. Anna went for help originally not because of an inability to write in one book, but because she was no longer touched by emotion, and when she has regained feeling, she no longer goes. Anna believes that neurosis may be a sign of superiority, "of being highly conscious and developed." In a world of conflicts, the only "whole" people are those who have "chosen to block off at this stage or that. People stay sane by blocking off, by limiting themselves" (p. 402). Anna does not wish to live without conflicts, and she finally parts company with Mother Sugar on this central difference: Jungian psychology would have Anna neutralize her painful memories and dreams by relating them to myth—that is, to general human experience—and be cured by placing her problems outside herself in this manner. (This comforting view is no doubt the basis for Anna and Molly's nickname "Mother Sugar.") However, Anna insists that it is more important to be "morally better" than "clinically healthy." She would prefer to live with the pain and the unresolvable conflicts. Anything that is whole and finished has a dead quality, whether it is a work of art or a human being. Those who refuse a sterile, artificial unity may be tomorrow's saviors. As Anna says to Mother Sugar in a passage reminiscent of Laing:

> sometimes I meet people, and it seems to me the fact they are cracked across, they're split, means they are keeping themselves open for something. . . . *Yes*, there's a hint of something—there's a crack in that man's personality like a gap in a dam, and through that gap the future might pour through in a different shape— terrible perhaps, or marvellous, but something new—(p. 405)

Anna finally achieves the sort of unity that is not sterile and dead, but to do so takes an enormous effort. In *Free Women* Richard, Marion, and Tommy are examples of the cost of failing to do so. All have substituted artificial unity for an attempt to deal with unreconcilable conflicts. Richard has given up his youthful ideals in favor of the power politics of big business. His personal life reflects the same diminution. Unable to relate to any woman as a complex individual, he finds one "nut brown maid" after another in his secretaries. His wife Marion and his children are the victims of this pattern. Marion's alcoholism is a result of her sensitivity and suffering. Her real fragmentation occurs when she trades alcohol for an unrealistic political liberalism, which to Anna is worse: "All the same, Anna thought, better for Marion to be a lush and a whole person; better a drunkard, and bitter and truthful; than sober, if the price of being sober is that she must be an awful dripping coy little girl—" (p. 340). Perhaps the most dramatic image of fragmentation is Tommy's blindness. When the Tommy of *Free Women* causes his own loss of sight, he is willing his limitation much as the real Tommy has done in his easy acceptance of out-worn ideas.

Unlike these others, Anna refuses to cut herself off from difficult experience. But before she can once again function creatively, there are a number of basic dualities that she must learn to balance. This is the classic problem of the Lessing protagonist, but *The Golden Notebook* is Lessing's most intricate study of the difficulty of achieving this unity.

Anna's integration and the attempts toward it of all Lessing protagonists bear a strong resemblance to Jung's process of individuation and also the alchemical art that described the transmutation of base metals into gold. The alchemical "work" is actually a metaphor, usually unconscious, for the integration and refinement of man himself. Jung studied alchemy deeply and discovered in it a parallel to his theory of individuation, which he has described as the "developmental process" by which "the psychic human being becomes whole." It is "experienced only by those who have gone through the wearisome but, if the unconscious is to be integrated, indispensable business of coming to terms with the unconscious components of the personality."[12] When this reconciliation is accomplished, "the centre of gravity of the total personality shifts its position. It ceases to be in the ego, which is merely the centre of consciousness, and instead is located in a hypothetical point between the conscious and the unconscious, which might be called the self."[13] The result is the birth of a "superior personality" without *participation mystique* (projection of one's own personality to the outside world) and on a high level of being somewhat detached from the joys and sorrows of ordinary life. Individuation has a freeing effect:

> It is as if a river that had run to waste in sluggish sidestreams and marshes suddenly found its way back to its proper bed, or as if a stone lying on a germinating seed were lifted away so that the shoot could begin its natural growth.[14]

Anna's integration follows this Jungian pattern. She explores her unconscious and discovers there the essential opposites to her outward personality.[15] The result of this integration is that she takes an entirely new stance toward life: she is somehow able to rise above the emotional and intellectual dilemmas that had entangled her, and her creativity is freed.

For Lessing, unification of the city and the veld involves something more than personal integration of the conscious with the unconscious, the rational with the intuitive and emotional. It also implies responsibility for one's actions and for the welfare of others. Anna suffers from neurosis because she is already "more conscious and developed" than the average person. Since she has a strong sense of responsibility, she is deeply ashamed of her novel *Frontiers of War*, which seems to her written out of a destructive "nostalgia," her term for a longing for death and dissolution—an emotion she believes is fed in everyone who reads her book. At the same time, Anna has strong empathy for the world's misery and is overcome by her helplessness in the face of modern enormities. The result is a backing away from emotion, although she does not see the cause of her neurosis until later: "In a world as terrible as this, limit emotion. How odd I didn't see it before" (p. 466).

Besides her disgust for *Frontiers of War*, Anna is fragmented because she deliberately holds to her complexity, even before she realizes the significance of doing so. She could put all of herself in one book if she were willing to suppress part of her nature. Instead, she consigns the conflicting areas to different notebooks. Since she can not concentrate her power on one creative work, she suffers from a writer's block. Mother Sugar sees from the beginning that this is Anna's main problem, although Anna does not admit it herself until seven years after her first session.

It is quite clear, then, that Anna's writer's block is the focus of all the motifs in the novel. It is a result of Anna's superior responsibility and openness to experience on the one hand and of her paralyzing fragmentation on the other. When she is finally able to return to writing, it is because she has found the vision necessary to reconcile the dualities in her own nature and in reality as a whole.

There are seven main dualities that Anna must resolve. First is the need for emotion set beside the difficulty of enduring it in a world that offers so much pain. Second is the problem of the traditional versus the modern woman. Anna of the 1950s must lead an independent life, free of what she considers out-dated conventions; yet her emotions are from another era in which she might have hoped for a permanent and loving marriage. The third duality is between "creative naivety" and cynicism. Closely related is the fourth, between idealism and a hopeless sense of fatality. Fifth is the dichotomy between the individual and, as Lessing says elsewhere, "the collective": humanity as a whole, the sum of individual lives. Sixth is the duality between form and chaos. Finally, there is the dichotomy between generosity or helpfulness and "joy-in-spite" or "joy-in-destruction." The nature of these opposites as Lessing defines them will become clear as I trace Anna's reconciliation of each of them through psychiatric help, self-revelation in the notebooks, and a pilgrimage into her psyche during a period of madness. In the final installment of the blue notebook and in the golden notebook all of these motifs are orchestrated and resolved in a complex mixture of fact, fiction, dream, and hallucination. After this unifying experience Anna is once again able to write.

Unlike its treatment of the other dualities, *The Golden Notebook* does not dramatize either Anna's lack of emotion or her regaining of it. It merely provides Anna's statement that this symptom led her to an analyst and that after three years she has learned to live with what she calls her *private-pain* material. She then refuses to neutralize the pain by relating it to myth, saying that it is simply a manifestation of ever-recurring human patterns, since she believes that pain and conflict may be the harbingers of new forms of experience: "I'm tired of the wolves and the castles and the forests and the priests. I can cope with them in any form they choose to present themselves. But I've told you, I want to walk off, by myself, Anna Freeman" (p. 403). Learning to face experience squarely is the first step toward her complete integration, the other elements of which are fully dramatized.

The problem of Anna the modern woman forced to deal with traditionally female emotions is explored predominantly in the yellow notebook in *The Shadow of the Third*. It is only here, after the fact, that Anna realizes the extent of this split in her nature. Rereading the notebooks for the first time she says, "I had not realized before how the experience of being rejected by Michael had affected me, how it had changed, or apparently had changed, my whole personality" (p. 407). Ella sums up the problem as Anna would, concluding that women's emotions are all still fitted for a kind of society that no longer exists. My deep emotions, my real ones, are to do with my relationship with a man. One man. But I don't like that kind of life, and I know few women who do. So what I feel is irrelevant and silly . . . I am always coming to the conclusion that my real emotions are foolish, I am always having, as it were, to cancel myself out. (p. 269)

Anna considers herself free of traditional conventions about women. She supports herself financially and is sexually liberated. Michael tells her at one point that she is the least jealous woman he has ever known. Nevertheless, part of her longs for marriage and is happiest when cooking for and looking after a man, a fact poignantly dramatized in the blue notebook for 17 September 1954, the day Michael leaves her, in Anna's careful preparations for Michael's supposed return that evening. Later she tells Saul that her strongest need is "being with one man, love, all that. I've a real talent for it" (p. 535). So while Anna appears to be independent, she has actually become deeply dependent on Michael during their five years together. Part of her integration must be to recognize this deep split in her nature; only then will she be able to resolve it.

Anna's dependence on Michael is understated in *Free Women* and the notebooks; it is only in *The Shadow of the Third* that the reader and Anna herself become aware of it. Anna feels that the point of her novel, reflected in the title, is the way Ella and Paul's affair brings both their "shadows" into existence. Paul's is the careless rake. Ella's is the "serene, calm, unjealous, unenvious, undemanding woman, full of resources of happiness inside herself, self-sufficient, yet always ready to give happiness when it is asked for" (p. 174). Ella sees that as she becomes more dependent, jealous, and demanding (until Paul finally leaves her), her view of this unselfish figure gets stronger, centered on an imaginary vision of Paul's wife, whom she has never seen. Just as Ella is projecting her own shadow onto Paul's wife, Anna is projecting hers onto Ella. Anna is the serene, unjealous woman; through her fictional creation she learns to recognize the jealous and demanding female who lies on the underside of her personality.

In the yellow notebook Anna breaks into her narrative, informing the reader that as Ella's alter ego gets stronger, her personality disintegrates. One symptom is a new dry cynicism and disillusion with men. At this point Anna and Ella are clearly alike. Reading back over the notebooks, Anna is disturbed by the growing sterility, "The deepening note of criticism, of defensiveness, of dislike" (p. 407). Anna would like Ella to overcome her negative outlook and describes what would have happened had she written more of the novel:

> Then she [Ella] finds herself thinking: I've got to accept the patterns of self-knowledge which mean unhappiness or at least a dryness. But I can twist it into victory. A man and a woman—yes. Both at the end of their tether. Both cracking up because of a deliberate attempt to transcend their own limits. And out of the chaos, a new kind of strength. (pp. 399–400)

Ella waits in vain for a story to form on this theme, for the images "to take on life." At this point Anna drops her interest in the novel, apparently because she then sees her own split more clearly and chooses to solve it in life rather than fiction, or at least in some combination of the two. In the final installment of the blue notebook and the golden notebook Anna and Saul do succeed in creating mutual strength from the chaos of their madness.

While Anna's dependence is dramatized obliquely through the story of Ella, it is in the final notebooks that Anna overcomes this problem in her relationship with Saul. In madness she encounters the shadow side of her female nature. In the blue notebook she becomes insanely jealous, accusing Saul of seeing other women and even reading his diary to find out if he has been doing so. Jealousy is unlike Anna's outer personality, but it is only a step from the emotional dependence she has learned to recognize in herself. By recognizing her shadow, Anna lessens its power over her.

With Saul Anna experiences for the first time a truly creative experience with a man that does not sap her independence, and one watches her intense struggle to be capable of such a breakthrough. In one final crisis she cradles Saul in her arms out of pity for his illness and her own need to be needed: "I was thinking how extraordinary, that an act of kindness, of pity, could be such a betrayal." He echoes her thoughts: "We can't either of us ever go lower than that" (pp. 547–48).

It is a great victory for Anna to be able to tell Saul to leave when she sees that they are becoming bad for each other, in danger of mutual dependence. When he goes, she is able to face his departure with equanimity and her affection is on a new, high plane:

> I felt towards him as if he were my brother, as if, like a brother, it wouldn't matter how we strayed from each other, how far apart we were, we would always be flesh of one flesh, and think each other's thoughts. (p. 548)

Anna's dependence on men has not been her only failure in emotional independence. The yellow notebook and *Free Women* dramatize the undercurrent of complexity in Anna's relationship with Molly. In fact, Molly is less important in the novel for herself than for what she shows about Anna. In both *Free Women* and *The Shadow of the Third* one of the strong bonds between the two women is their mutual criticism of men. For example, in *Free Women* Anna sees that after a year's separation, they have grown apart, but as soon as she is willing to start complaining about men, the two recapture their former intimacy. Ella describes a similar relationship with Julia as psychological lesbianism. And when Anna leaves Julia's apartment she thinks wryly that it is "like the break-up of a marriage" (p. 385). Cynicism toward men may be seen as the mirror image of dependence on them. In her relationship with Saul, Anna rids herself of both.

The other important undercurrent of Molly and Anna's friendship is their mother-daughter relationship. In *Free Women* Molly constantly remonstrates with Anna about not writing. Both Molly and Julia advise Anna/Ella about social life and clothes. In *The Shadow of the Third* Ella sees that Julia has dominated her and that she "had been prepared to be dominated. . . . Leaving Julia's house was like a daughter leaving a mother" (p. 385). It is a necessary step before she can walk off alone, Anna Freeman.

Anna's dependence on others is closely related to the duality of cynicism and "creative naivety," a spontaneous idealism that is necessary to prevent cynicism from destroying the personality. As has been seen, Anna learns from the yellow notebook that her rejection by Michael has made her cynical. The opposite emotion is the naiveté of a woman in love, "which is another word for a spontaneous, creative faith" (p. 183). Anna sees that her cynicism (based on shrewd, rational logic) would no longer allow her to feel such an emotion, yet she feels that this loss is destructive to her personality.

In the final blue notebook and golden notebook several important events signify Anna's defeat of cynicism. In the blue notebook Paul Blackenhurst of her African years appears in a dream. Paul, the model for Anna's hero in *Frontiers of War* and probably the source of the name for Ella's lover, is charming and likable, but his outstanding characteristic is a mocking cynicism, which he often directs against others cruelly. It is a trait characteristic of Anna in *Free Women* until Tommy's disaster. Her first recognition of this pernicious trait in herself is dramatized in a dream vision. Various acquaintances from her African years try to fit themselves into her body as she lies on the bed. When Paul tries, Anna is suddenly aware of danger:

Then he dissolved into her, and I, screaming with fear, fought my way through a crowd of indifferent ghosts to the bed, to Anna, to myself. I fought to re-enter her. I was fighting against cold, a terrible cold. My hands and legs were stiff with cold, and Anna was cold because she was filled with the dead Paul. I could see his cool, grave smile on Anna's face. After a struggle, which was for my life, I slipped back into myself. (p. 512)

Anna's displacement of the dead Paul is an image for ridding herself of the cold cynicism she has slipped into since Michael has left her. She sees later that as a result she has been "delivered from disintegration."

In *The Golden Notebook* a still more positive experience occurs: in a dream Anna sees Paul Tanner, Ella's lover, whose "quality of dry critical irony" has "slowly defeated the idealism in him," as it has in Anna. In *The Shadow of the Third* Paul had voiced a rather cynical idealism, that instead of being the researcher he had hoped to be, his job was to be a "boulder-pusher," pushing the boulder of truth that great men instinctively know, up the mountain of human stupidity. He hates his job, "treating illness that is caused by a society so stupid that— . . . I wish I had died, Ella. I wish I had died" (p. 182). In Anna's hallucination, Paul and Michael merge, forming a new man of heroic size and strength. He voices Paul's idealism, but this time without cynicism:

All our lives, you and I, we will use all our energies, all our talents, into pushing that boulder another inch up the mountain. And they rely on us and they are right; and that is why we are not useless after all. (p. 528)

The creation of this imaginary hero marks Anna's ability to defeat her destructive cynicism with "naivety," or creative faith. At the end of *Free Women* there is a significant exchange between Molly and Anna. Molly comments on Anna's plans to be a teacher and marriage counselor:

"So we're both going to be integrated with British life at its roots."

"I was carefully avoiding that tone."

"You're right—it's just the idea of you doing matrimonial welfare work."

"I'm very good at other people's marriages."

Anna's fictional surrogate has willingly accepted the role of boulder-pusher, without the mocking cynicism that would once have been natural to her, as the real Anna is now able to do as a writer.

The duality of idealism and a sense of hopeless fatality, closely related to naiveté and cynicism, is the subject of the red notebook.[16] Anna joins the Communist Party because of her idealism; she hopes that it can provide a viable alternative to money and power as the motive forces of government. Ostensibly merely an account of Anna's experiences with the Communist Party, the red notebook charts her gradual and complete disillusion with it. The final blow is the news of Stalin's enormities that finally comes out of Russia with his death. To remain a communist is to be fragmented like Jack, her co-worker at communist headquarters, who must close his eyes to much of what is going on within the party.

The importance of idealism is a major theme of *The Golden Notebook,* and Anna's regaining of it, even as she paradoxically holds to her belief in a pessimistic fatality, is an important part of her integration. As has been seen, Anna above all is socially conscious. She wishes to work for the good of humanity, but all effort seems doomed to negation. One of her central nightmares is reported in the blue notebook. The commander of a firing squad, about to have an enemy shot, hears loud cries announcing the defeat of his side and victory of the captive's. With ironic looks, the two men change places, and the former commander is himself shot by the other's command: "no right, no wrong, simply a process, a wheel turning." Such knowledge "cancels all creative emotion" (p. 295).

Because people have nothing to believe in, they suffer from a lack of feeling, a condition of the times:

> People know they are in a society dead or dying. They are refusing emotion because at the end of every emotion are property, money, power. They work and despise their work, and so freeze themselves. They love but know that it's a half-love or a twisted love, and so they freeze themselves. (p. 467)

Without idealism, a person can not act responsibly. It is in *Free Women* that Anna makes this point most clearly, dramatized in the relationship between Anna and Tommy. When the hysterical Tommy comes to her, she knows he wants something from her, but she does not know what it is. Their conversation centers on her notebooks, which have upset him. Later Anna is haunted by guilt that she has somehow failed Tommy and unwittingly contributed to his attempted suicide.

It seems clear that Tommy is looking for something to believe in. He sees that Anna's separate notebooks are a sign of her own uncertainties and divisions. When she tells him her philosophy, that mankind does occasionally lurch forward, she can not help an ironic attitude and a "self-accusatory smile" (p. 235). The implication is clear: cynicism begets despair, whereas idealism may inspire. Anna of the separate notebooks, cynical and divided, can not act responsibly. Only after her integration will she be rid of her "paralysis of will"; then, as a counselor and teacher, Anna of *Free Women* will be able to help others, and the Anna who writes *The Golden Notebook* will be able to share her creative vision.

Anna has a model for the balance of idealism with a sense of fatality. One of her heroes is Tom Mathlong, the "courteous, ironical" African who knew he would probably spend most of his life in prison and perhaps accomplish very little, but who nevertheless continued his fight for human rights. In the final blue notebook Anna says of him:

He was the man who performed actions, played roles, that he believed to be necessary for the good of others, even while he preserved an ironic doubt about the results of his actions. It seemed to me that this particular kind of detachment was something we needed very badly at this time, but that very few people had it, and it was certainly a long way from me. (p. 510)

Mathlong's attitude represents a point of balance that Anna tries to reach in the final blue notebook, during her descent into madness. At first she is unsuccessful: she tries but fails to enter Mathlong's consciousness as she has—only too easily— entered the mad Charlie Themba's.

Later, however, Anna seems able to reach a detached idealism similar to the one she has described in Tom Mathlong. It is first exhibited in her tolerant attitude toward the distance between her own personality and the ideal woman she would like to be. She catches herself thinking about Ella, building an impossibly perfect image of her much as Ella did of Paul's wife. But Anna is no longer depressed by her distance from the ideal:

I was thinking that quite possibly these marvelous, generous things we walk side by side with in our imaginations could come into existence, simply because we need them, because we imagine them. Then I began to laugh because of the distance between what I was imagining and what in fact I was, let alone what Ella was. (p. 545)

In this passage Anna expresses the importance of idealism: to imagine something is to help create it. As Anna says to Tommy at one point, "If people can imagine something, there'll come a time when they'll achieve it" (p. 235). Once cynicism and bitterness have been overcome, Anna can live tolerantly with the disparity between the ideal and reality. She can then calmly agree with Saul that "we've got to believe in our beautiful, impossible blueprints," accepting this paradox with equanimity much as Tom Mathlong would do.

Another difficulty standing in the way of personal unification is the need to balance the dichotomy between the individual and collective humanity. Part of the attraction of communism for Anna has been its camaraderie, its ability to unite people working for a cause. But full knowledge of participation in humanity goes even deeper. It is during the madness of the final episodes that Anna experiences dissolution of her own personality and gains a vision of an underlying fraternity in which the individual merges with the collective. At one point in the blue notebook she becomes a variety of people with whom she has a common bond through political concern: a victim of torture, a revolutionary, a dead soldier, a Chinese peasant. And in a dream she finds herself playing out all possible female roles:

> It was like living a hundred lives. I was astonished at how many of the female roles I have not played in life, have refused to play, or were not offered to me. Even in my sleep I knew I was being condemned to play them now because I had refused them in life. (p. 516)

Both Saul and Anna are invaded by alien personalities to such a degree that Anna says a tape recording of the hours of their talking "would be a record of a hundred different people living now, in various parts of the world, talking and crying out and questioning" (p. 533).

Pointed out earlier, Jung's individuation process involves centering the personality in the self, the hypothetical point between the conscious and unconscious, rather than the ego. According to Jung's theories, the unconscious is only partly personal; in addition to the materials of one's individual repressions (the personal unconscious) lies the vast uncharted collective mind. In this context Anna and Saul's experience of collective humanity may be seen as an example of Jungian psychic integration at one of the deepest levels.

After Anna has experienced being part of mankind as a whole, she is left with a strong feeling of solidarity with others.

The event no doubt helps her to the new fraternal closeness with Saul, which eases the pain of his leaving. More, Anna comes to value the steady courage that she shares with others: "It's a small painful sort of courage which is at the root of every life, because injustice and cruelty is at the root of life" (p. 543). The camera of her dream sequence focuses on one person after another: the ignored wife, the woman fighting not to commit suicide, the soldier on a hillside, painful moments in the lives of people she has known or created in her fiction. She comes to see that all share "the small endurance which is bigger than anything" and she has been mistaken in giving her attention only "to the heroic or the beautiful or the intelligent" (p. 544).

Perhaps the most important part of Anna's integration is to learn to face this injustice and cruelty "at the root of life." The central duality of the novel concerns what Anna calls joy-in-spite or joy-in-destruction. It is balanced against generosity and every human or nonhuman creative impulse. Anna must recognize and accept the destructive impulse not just in the universe as a whole but also in herself. To do so is to disarm its potential to destroy her personality.

Joy-in-destruction is pervasive and unavoidable. Ella has had a vision of it since her six-month stay in a tuberculosis sanatorium: "some dark, impersonal destructive force that worked at the roots of life and that expressed itself in war and cruelty and violence" (p. 164). It is dramatized in Anna's memory of the pigeon hunt at the Mashopi Hotel (pp. 355, ff.): Paul Blackenhurst, Anna, young Jimmy (a homosexual), Willi, and Maryrose go for pigeons for a pigeon pie. After passing hordes of mating grasshoppers, the group reaches a large kopje (a mound of boulders) with a clump of trees at the foot, where pigeons are cooing. The kopje has been a scene of battle between the Mashona and Matabele and is still decorated with bushman paintings, now defaced by hotel guests. Paul kills a pigeon and in an unpleasant scene orders Jimmy to fetch it.

Jimmy does so because he is in love with Paul, although he knows he is being treated like a hunting dog. More pigeons are killed, and the stench of blood becomes sickening. Various conflicts among members of the group appear, and Jimmy causes another: he pits a tiny ant-eater against a beetle, and both insects die in the evenly matched battle. A group of black workers who had been laughing and talking are silent and avert their eyes as they pass the group. Paul says to Willi, the most ardent communist among them, "Comrade Willi, would you not say that there is some principle at work not yet admitted to your philosophy? Some principle of destruction?" (p. 367).

In this vivid episode, such a force is at work in all living creatures: ant-eaters eat ants; people shoot pigeons for food, but also sacrifice a beetle and an ant-eater in a battle to the death, just out of curiosity. Joy-in-destruction appears in the personal conflict between Jimmy and Paul and also the general conflict implicit between the passing gang of black workers and the white group from the hotel. The hunt itself takes place on an ancient battle ground where black fought against black. Joy-in-destruction is all pervasive and ancient as creation.

It takes many forms. In Anna's dreams joy-in-destruction is a grinning, malicious demon. "And the creature was always powerful, with an inner vitality which I knew was caused by a purposeless, undirected, causeless spite. It mocked and jibed and hurt, wished murder, wished death. And yet it was always vibrant with joy" (p. 408). In life it is embodied in Nelson, who in some moods lashes out cruelly at the women he cares for. More purely it is in Da Silva, who tells his friend's wife about her husband's affair with the cleaning woman just to see what will happen. And it is in Anna when she uses a tone of mocking irony. It is the emotion "nostalgia" from which she wrote *Frontiers of War*.

The black notebook is ostensibly about Anna's novel, its sources in her African experience and her business dealings in connection with it. However, the real theme of this notebook is joy-in-destruction, as the opening words suggest:

> black
>   dark, it is so dark
>   it is dark
>   there is a kind of darkness here

[And then, in a changed, startled writing:]

> Every time I sit down to write, and let my mind go easy, the words, It is so dark, or something to do with darkness. Terror. The terror of this city. Fear of being alone. Only one thing stops me from jumping up and screaming and running to the telephone to ring somebody, it is to deliberately think myself back into that hot light. (p. 55)

Anna is not interested in writing another novel because of her horror at the emotion from which her first book originated:

> And yet it is so powerful, that nostalgia, that I can only write this, a few sentences at a time. Nothing is more powerful than this nihilism, an angry readiness to throw everything overboard, a willingness, a longing to become part of dissolution. This emotion is one of the strongest reasons why wars continue. And the people who read *Frontiers of War* will have had fed in them this emotion, even though they were not conscious of it. That is why I am ashamed, and why I feel continually as if I had committed a crime. (p. 62)

Anna's main revelation is the paradox that joy-in-destruction has an inherent creative power. Mother Sugar hints as much. Recognizing the malicious elf of Anna's dreams she says, "It is dangerous to you as long as you fear it" (p. 409). However, Anna must experience its creativity for herself. Only when her ego disintegrates in madness and she emerges with a new and finer vision does she see the creative potential of destruction and dissolution. The central paradox of *The Golden Notebook* is that the same force that gives rise to malicious cruelty, war, hopeless madness like Charlie Themba's, and novels that feed mankind's death wish—this same force may also be the seedbed of new creation. It may be the crack through which "the future may pour through in a different shape"—from someone like Saul Green, perhaps, who refuses to be molded into one of society's shapes and courageously endures his bouts of madness until he can come through them in a form acceptable to him.

The paradox of creation and destruction is embodied in the central image of *The Golden Notebook* in one of Lessing's finest passages. Anna dreams she is back at the Mashopi:

> The hotel building seemed to have exploded in a dancing whirling cloud of white petals or wings, millions of white butterflies had chosen the building to alight on. It looked like a white flower opening slowly, under the deep steamy blue sky. Then a feeling of menace came into us, and we knew we had suffered a trick of sight, had been deluded. We were looking at the explosion of a hydrogen bomb, and a white flower unfolded under the blue sky in such a perfection of puffs, folds and eddying shapes that we could not move, although we knew we were menaced by it. It was unbelievably beautiful, the shape of death. (p. 528)

This image with its union of life and death carries the reader ahead to *The Four-Gated City* in which it is the explosion of nuclear weapons that causes not just grotesque physical mutations but also the mental ones that may lead to perfection of the human race.

It is while in the deepest throes of mental dissolution that Anna is able to perceive the merging of creativity with destruction. She enters this state of madness willingly because she senses its creative potential. In a perception similar to R. D. Laing's view of schizophrenia, she believes that, "Something has to be played out, some pattern has to be worked through . . ." (p. 498). This pattern involves going beneath all mental formulations. She goes beyond thoughts and words, seeing through newspaper headlines to the naked reality of the destructive forces they inadequately describe. Even the constructs of time and space dissolve: time has no meaning, and the solidity of the room simply gives way. During this visionary state of dissolution and chaos, Anna sees the creative potential of destruction, that "war was working in us all, towards fruition" (p. 506). Only at that point does she have a dream in which she herself embodies joy-in-destruction; but instead of being left with a sense of fright, she awakes suffused with peace: in some way still unclear to her she has "dreamed the dream 'positively.'" Having come to terms with this basic destructive force and experienced total dissolution, she is ready to write *The Golden Notebook*, which describes her final integration.

It is in this section also that the final dichotomy is resolved: chaos versus form. Chaos has been illustrated throughout the book in several ways: fragmentation of personality, the formlessness of the psyche when it merges with the collective at the deepest level, and most profound, the area of existence that lies beneath the ordering power of sense perceptions, words, and ideas. Joy-in-destruction thrusts toward chaos and formlessness, one of the reasons Anna has feared it. However, at the end of her plunge into madness, Anna is able finally to come to terms with it:

> The fact is, the real experience can't be described. . . . The people who have been there, in the place in themselves where words, patterns, order, dissolve, will know what I mean and the others won't . . . and it's not a question of fighting it, or disowning it, or of right or wrong, but simply knowing it is there, always. It's a question of bowing to it, so to speak, with a kind of courtesy, as to an ancient enemy: All right, I know you are there, but we have to preserve the forms, don't we? And perhaps the condition of your existing at all is precisely that we preserve the forms, create the patterns—(p. 542)

Finally Anna is once again able to create form, even with—or rather because of—her full knowledge of the chaos that lies beneath. Form, like most things, is paradoxical. A finished idea or human being may be dead and sterile, but at the same time form is necessary to survival and also potentially useful. For example, Anna can control the painful experiences of her life by "naming them"; in this way, as Anna puts it, she "buttons up" the various periods of her life and aspects of her relationship with Saul by describing them in a phrase. Also, the "beautiful, impossible blueprints" that may lead to the creation of something new are a way of using form powerfully and with imagination. Finally, Anna can give form to the bewildering complexity of experience by writing. The human mind can not tolerate formlessness: this is apparently what Saul means when he tells Anna that she must start writing again, that if she does not she will crack up: "I was thinking that if you could simplify it in your mind, boil it all down to something, then you could take a long look at it and beat it" (p. 546). The result is *Free Women* and later its integration with the notebooks to form the completed novel. The whole point of adding this typical, realistic novel is to contrast traditional fiction (form), with complex, hodge-podge experience. One incident after another echoes the rush of events in Anna's life, culminating in the calmly told affair with Milt, which grossly oversimplifies the bedlam shared in the notebooks.

All the final resolutions of duality occur in the golden notebook section: Anna learns to balance her independence from tradition with her emotional dependence; she imagines Michael and Paul Tanner merging in a heroic new voice that balances hopeless fatality with idealism; she is able to defeat cynicism with creative faith; she can merge her individual personality with the collective, gaining a new faith in the courageous endurance of ordinary lives; she learns to balance creativity with joy-in-destruction and form with chaos. In every case she has had to retrieve from her unconscious the opposite to every emotion, trait, or idea that she displayed at the beginning of the novel.

Gradually the narrative pace slows to a peaceful rhythm as Anna and Saul exchange the first lines of their novels—a concrete image for the way each has nourished the other's growth and creativity. Their new spiritual union is dramatized by their both writing in Anna's new golden notebook. They have then brought to life Ella's once sterile idea:

> A man and a woman—yes. Both at the end of their tether. Both cracking up because of a deliberate attempt to transcend their own limits. And out of chaos, a new kind of strength. (p. 400)

The basic movement of *The Golden Notebook* is Anna's psychic dissolution first into paired opposites (her condition at the start of the novel) and then into complete chaos and, finally, integration into a new unity characteristic of a finer consciousness. This pattern of dissolution and integration is characteristic of alchemy and both *The Golden Notebook* and *Briefing for a Descent into Hell* show striking parallels to this ancient art in philosophy and symbolism.

Jung considered his long and detailed study of alchemy to be one of his most significant achievements.[17] He believed that the true alchemists (as opposed to the charlatans and those who misunderstood the art) were involved in a dimly perceived spiritual quest, that their search for the philosopher's stone was actually a projection of an instinctive desire for psychic wholeness. Jung saw strong resemblances in alchemical patterns and symbols to his own theory of individuation. Laboratory work was essentially a metaphor, a theoretical guide for carrying out chemical procedures that actually was directed toward transformation of the spirit much as Jung describes it. Alchemical texts speak of their general aim as bringing about the dissolution of what has been "falsely joined" in order to form "the true conjunction." In its imperfect state, matter lies as if chained in a sleeplike state; but when treated with the "divine tincture" from the philosopher's stone, it will be reborn to a "new and more beautiful life."[18] Similarly, according to Jung (and Lessing) there is a psychic process by which men and women can develop a finer and more integrated consciousness than most people possess. It involves dissolution of the "falsely joined" personality followed by a new "conjunction" or unity. The result is a superior, unified consciousness.

Put another way: the search for psychic wholeness may be seen symbolically as a search for the golden flower or "diamond body" of Lao Tzu in Chinese alchemy, or for the philosopher's stone. These or comparable symbols frequently appeared in the dreams of certain of Jung's patients; for example, Jung consistently states that a stone or crystal symbolizes the "self," the balanced, whole psyche.

Jung apparently did not know about the connection between alchemy and Sufism, a transcendental philosophy with roots in the Middle East; however, Idries Shah (whose books are the most important modern source for Sufic thought and literature) has shown it to be far-reaching. Lessing is a student of Sufism under Shah, and the effect on her work from *Landlocked* to the present is profound. However, the present concern is the light shed by Sufism on the connection between alchemy and human development. Sufism maintains that humanity has an inherent ability to evolve consciously toward a new and perfect state. The first step in such a development appears to be destructive, since old patterns must disintegrate. As the Sufis put it, people must throw off the "old Villain," the constricting bonds of conditioning with its faulty perception. In an analogy of Jalaludin Rumi (thirteenth century), an important Sufi philosopher and poet, a person must pull down his house to find the priceless treasure within. Having finally achieved the highest state, the Sufi is completed—in tune with creation, able to perceive connections in the universe and his role there.

Idries Shah gives convincing linguistic evidence[19] that alchemy is, indeed, a metaphor for such psychic development and that the father of alchemy as it is known in the West was an eighth-century Sufi, Jabir Ibn el-Hayyan. Unlike Jung, who takes the position that medieval Western alchemists were unconsciously projecting psychic materials onto the apparatus of the laboratory, Shah gives evidence that many knew precisely what they were doing and veiled their work with abstruse symbols because of the analogical method of Sufi thinking and to avoid persecution by the established church.

The alchemical work may be seen, then, as an essentially spiritual exercise, a metaphor for the integration and transformation of consciousness. Shah summarizes the process within the context of Jabir Ibn el-Hayyan's terms:

> The regeneration of an essential part of humanity, according to the Sufis, is the goal of mankind. The separation of man from his essence is the cause of his disharmony and unfulfillment. His quest is the purification of the dross and the activation of the gold. The means of achieving this is found within man—it is the Philosopher's Stone. . . . The stone, according to the Sufis, is the *dhat*, the essence, which is so powerful that it can transform whatever comes into contact with it. It is the essence of man, which partakes of what people call the divine. It is "sunshine," capable of uplifting humanity to a next stage. (p. 263)

Considering the importance of the metaphor of alchemy to Jungian and Sufic ideas, it is not surprising that one should find specific alchemical symbols in Lessing's work, especially as her main concern—the development of a more advanced consciousness—is similar to theirs.

The importance of the paired opposites in Anna's psyche has been discussed; she had to become aware of them and accept them before she could become whole. Throughout his writings on alchemy Jung points out the importance to alchemy of this principle of opposites. Every symbol is paradoxical; for example, the sun may stand for the soul, divinity, but also for a destructive element. Also pairs of symbols frequently stand for two opposites, such as king and queen (male and female), eagle and toad (air and earth), or winged and wingless dragons (soul and spirit). Mercury, one of the three elements to be joined in the alchemical process, is a particularly important symbol of duality; "He is metal and yet fluid, matter and yet spirit, cold but fiery, poison but also the healing draught—a symbol that unites the opposites."[20]

> The pairs of opposites constitute the phenomenology of the paradoxical *self*, man's totality. . . . The intensity of the conflict is expressed in symbols like fire and water, height and depth, life and death.[21]

As the alchemist, both in the laboratory and as a spiritual allegory, sought to join the opposites into a final integration, Anna succeeds in a similar quest.

The Golden Notebook, in which Anna's final resolution occurs, has a number of alchemical parallels. As seen along with the final blue notebook, its general pattern is analogous to alchemical dissolution and integration. In addition, the climactic dream of the tiger cage uses symbols characteristic of the alchemical "work."

To summarize the dream briefly, Anna finds that she is trapped in a cage with a tiger, and she is ill from fear and from the smell of dead flesh from strips of food the tiger has left. Anna is lying in water, and deep beneath her are monsters and crocodiles, some scarcely imaginable because they are so "old and tyrannous." She is pulled down, attracted by the danger. Then a voice warns her that she is sinking into her own subjectivity and urges her to fight. She then sees that the water is actually shallow, although putrid. Nearly fainting from the close, fetid breath of the tiger, Anna manages to fly out of the cage. At once the tiger ceases to appear dangerous and she recognizes that "the tiger is Saul." She does not wish him to be caught but to run free through the world. At her urging, he runs away from the people who are chasing him and, as he does so, accidentally wounds Anna with his claws. However, the wound heals immediately. At this point Anna begins to experience the series of integrating dream images that have already been observed.

On one level this scene may be viewed as merely an allegory for the important actions of the book. Anna is threatened with disintegration because of the lure of joy-in-destruction (the monsters) and also by her own subjectivity (the water, as the voice suggests). When she is able to "fly" out of her own needs, Saul, the tiger, no longer has the power to hurt her, and both of them are free of the cage of their own egos and of society's forms. However, this scene becomes more meaningful when its images are compared with some of the symbols of alchemy.

The literature of alchemy is vast and ambiguous. Nevertheless, it is possible to isolate some persistent motifs. Throughout all alchemy since Jabir Ibn el-Hayyan, the basic alchemical process has been to unite sulphur, mercury, and salt. These three substances have multiple meanings. Sulphur stands for the sun (Sol), king (the male principle), soul, air, fire, and consciousness. Mercury stands for the moon (Luna), queen (female principle), water, spirit, duality, and the unconscious.[22] Salt stands for the principle of fixity, body, earth, "in a mystical sense . . . the body of man."[23] Paracelsus, the Swiss alchemist, says, "Know they therefore that . . . the soul, which is indeed sulphur . . . unites those two contraries, the body and spirit, and changes them into one essence."[24] On the phsycial level, the purpose of the alchemical work was to find the philosopher's stone, which would be able to change everything it touched into gold. If impure sulphur and mercury were used, the result would be base metals. Pure sulphur and mercury produced gold; "quintessentialized" they produced the philosopher's stone.[25]

Clearly, the events of *The Golden Notebook* are analogous to the alchemical process. Anna, the dual being, suffers disintegration but comes together on a new, high level, where she joins Saul in a unity that transcends the usual emotional and physical dependency that Lessing has portrayed as the usual substitute for love. Saul's name is surely not chosen at random; he is Sol the king, sulphur of the alchemical work. His last name, Green, naturally suggests growth and fertility, but it also has specific meaning in alchemy as a creative principle.[26] Anna is Luna, the female principle. When they are joined like brother and sister, they recall the unifying image of the hermaphrodite. Their creative union is described in the "gold" of the notebook. There is given the recital of Anna's new integration of personality, and evidence of the heightened creativity of both: Saul (it is told) writes his novel in Anna's pretty book, and there also is recorded the first line of *Free Women*, "The two women were alone in the London flat," which becomes the first line of *The Golden Notebook.*

Anna's tiger dream, which climaxes her integration, is carried out in images much like those of the alchemical work: there are striking similarities between it and a typical progression described in the *Rosarium*, a sixteenth-century alchemical treatise. Here it is not Luna but Sol who is the main actor. He "passes through various stages of transformation from the dragon, lion, and eagle to the hermaphrodite. Each of these stages stands for a new degree of insight, wisdom, and initiation."[27] In the beginning of the dream, Anna is threatened by her own attraction to the crocodiles and sea monsters (dragons) deep in the water. Her next danger (or so she believes) is not a lion but a tiger, an image that gains extra force from its traditional association with energy. Like the tiger of Blake's poem, which suggests the vitality at the heart of the universe, it has its frightening but also its opposite, gentle side. Blake's illustration belies the poem, showing not an awesome beast but a smiling, lamblike tiger. Similarly, when Anna passes into a higher state of awareness, she is able to see the tiger's gentle side. It is no longer a threat to her; the wound it gives her heals immediately. Finally Anna flies—like an eagle—out of the cage altogether. This episode results in her being able to join with Saul in the hermaphroditic stage of brother and sister.

The Golden Notebook is the one Lessing novel in which a tight structure mirrors the main theme. The notebooks represent the city, the forms of half-knowledge that have bound Anna. Even traditional literature *(Frontiers of War, The Shadow of the Third, Free Women)* turns out to be a structure of the city, form made possible only when the chaotic mass of experience, and life's tentativeness, are set aside. However, gradually Anna overcomes all divisions, when she sees deeply and broadly enough; the result is the final golden notebook and then *The Golden Notebook* itself, which encompasses not just Anna's new psychic unity but also a truce between art and the formlessness of experience.

The final symbol of integration is the shape of the completed novel, which reflects two symbols adopted by the alchemists—the mandala and the uroboros, the serpent biting its own tail. Aniela Jaffé has explained the importance of such unifying symbols, especially the mandala:

> The alchemists exalted the mysteries of matter and set them alongside those of the "heavenly" spirit of Christianity. What they sought was a wholeness of man encompassing mind and body, and they invented a thousand names and symbols for it. One of their central symbols was the *quadratura circuli* (the squaring of the circle), which is no more than the true mandala.[28]

The structure of *The Golden Notebook* includes the circle and square of the mandala. The four notebooks—black, red, blue, and yellow—represent the foursquare structure of Anna's divided psyche, finally united in *The Golden Notebook*. When *Free Women* is added, beginning with a line given to Anna by Saul in the golden notebook, they are joined in a circle—the uroboros, the serpent biting its tail. Thus, psychic experience is united in the completed novel by means of the artistic imagination; once completed, *The Golden Notebook* forms a mandala, symbol of Anna's unified consciousness. To her reason has been added emotion, knowledge of the personal and collective unconscious, perception of the area of existence where all human values cease to exist, and, finally, the creative and responsible member of society.

However, the uroboros suggests more than just unity. As Erich Neumann has pointed out in *The Origins and History of Consciousness*, it is the symbol of the Great Mother, "the state of being contained in the whole, without responsibility or effort, with no doubts and no division of the world into two."[29] This is the paradise of childhood and of the human psyche before the ego developed, and man was separated from creation. In Lessing it is dramatized in the African veld. However, the essence of this paradise is repetition; as long as unconsciousness continues (in a race or an individual), then the uroborus takes on its more sinister meaning as the devouring mother: in this state "the uroborus reigns on as the great whirling wheel of life, where everything not yet individual is submerged in the union of opposites, passing away and willing to pass away" (p. 16). Throughout *A Proper Marriage* Martha is disturbed by the sight of the ferris wheel whirling outside her window; like the biological and social pressures that Martha obeys in this novel, it represents the cyclical repetition of nature and of society, too, when like nature it remains unconscious.

However, the uroboros means more; it "also symbolizes the creative impulse of the new beginning; it is the 'wheel that rolls of itself,' the initial, rotatory movement in the upward spiral of evolution" (p. 18).[30] It is this completion at a higher level that is suggested by the circular structure of *The Golden Notebook*. Similarly, the mandala may have a dual purpose as M.-L. von Franz in "The Process of Individuation" points out:

> The mandala serves a conservative purpose—namely, to restore a previously existing order. But it also serves the creative purpose of giving expression and form to something that does not yet exist,

something new and unique. . . . For, in most cases, what restores
the old order simultaneously involves some element of new creation. In the new order the older pattern returns on a higher level.
The process is that of the ascending spiral, which grows upward
while simultaneously returning again and again to the same point.[31]

Lessing echoes this idea. In *Briefing for a Descent into Hell* Jupiter, "the sun's deputy," describes creation: "it's a harmony, it's
a pattern, bad and good, everything in turn, everything spiralling up."[32] Throughout her work Lessing uses mythic patterns
in this way. They are never a return; they always represent
ascension to a higher level.

The development of Martha's unified consciousness is the
central action in *Children of Violence*, as Anna's is in *The Golden
Notebook*. And like Anna, Martha must first experience mental
breakdown before she can reunite with her conscious mind the
deeper levels of experience. An important difference between
the two novels, however, is the relative degree of success the
characters enjoy. Anna is part of a fragmented and violent world
and as a result can never hope for a truly harmonious life;
nevertheless, *The Golden Notebook* ends with a sense of completion. Anna accomplishes something definite; she frees her
creativity and writes a novel that suggests the complexity of her
experience, *The Golden Notebook*. Her disintegration and reintegration follow alchemical principles, and, as it does in alchemy,
her *opus* is a work of art. It is so on two levels; she makes a
whole of the materials of her life and then turns them into art.

Nevertheless, there is an ambivalence in the final result.
Without question, Anna is better off in a worldly sense at the
end of the novel than before: she has pulled herself together;
she has accomplished a superior perception; she can then write
a novel that breaks through many of the limitations of traditional narrative. However, there is no reason to suppose that
Anna has changed her passionate belief that it is the nature
with a crack that will let the future pour through, or her scorn

with Mother Sugar's near worship of art. That is, tight form of any kind repels change, and this view must include Anna's final psychic state and her creation, *The Golden Notebook*. As Dagmar Barnouw has said, "The structure of *The Golden Notebook*, then, hinders the process of self-knowledge." And one must remember that the golden notebook, where Anna resolves her dualities, has been cursed by Saul Green.[33] Anna admires Saul for his ability to stay in a state of formlessness without giving in, as she is forced to do. However, the effect of Lessing's careful structure in the novel does war against this important theme: it gives the reader a sense of rest and completion. The alchemical art dramatized in Anna's psychic transformation remains essentially that—art. It remains for the late work to develop the theme of developing consciousness in a way more consonant with Lessing's deeply held beliefs concerning the dichotomy between form and change. She will return again and again to the motif of the mandala. Significantly, in later novels its shape becomes less important; rather, it becomes a symbol for a new, more inclusive psychic unity not constricted by boundaries that become barriers.

An important boundary-barrier in Lessing's work is the individual ego, which raises an important problem that *The Golden Notebook* does not satisfactorily answer. Before Anna can become whole enough to write, she must recognize that at some deep level she is one with humanity, that in a very Eastern sense her individuality is a chimera. But if no man is an island, if deep within mankind is a collective mind where all become one, how can any person be unified in a splintered world? How can anyone be sane when everyone else is going crazy? Here one needs to refer to R. D. Laing, for whom the schizophrenic may be more sane than the man perfectly adjusted to a sick society. Lessing poses this problem in *The Golden Notebook* but does not answer it. Anna finds strength from "the small courage which is bigger than anything" and manages to pull herself together and write about her experience. End of story. It is in *Children of Violence* that Lessing confronts this question, taking it relentlessly as far as she can. Here she never settles for aesthetic solutions; the strength of *Children of Violence* lies elsewhere.

Martha's experience is quite different from Anna's. The disintegration of both is tied to a failing society; but when Martha pulls herself together, there is no sense that she has become a more creative person. She has produced no gold except knowledge, and it is grim enough, the perception that the contemporary consciousness—including hers—is beyond redemption. Then she can only hold on (as indeed she has been doing all her life) and help nurture the children of Pharos, who are the New Men of the future. Destruction and reintegration are central to both *The Golden Notebook* and *Children of Violence*. *The Golden Notebook* describes one woman's refinement in the hermetic vessel. *Children of Violence* dramatizes the dissolution of society as everyone knows it. From these radioactive ashes appears the "gold" of a new race, the mutated children of Pharos with their finer consciousness that transcends original sin—the perverted consciousness that leads always to sterile repetition and violence.

Many readers are more comfortable with such novels as *The Summer before the Dark* and even the complex *The Golden Notebook* than with *The Four-Gated City*, because in these novels Lessing's protagonists are at least somewhat traditional literary characters, dealt with by means of customary narrative techniques. (*The Golden Notebook*, in challenging the traditional novel, makes the whole subject of traditional narrative techniques one of its themes.) On the other hand, Lessing's main purpose in *Children of Violence* was to achieve clarity. It poses these questions and attempts to answer them without equivocation: What is the shape of the human psyche? How much of it simply is a reflection of society? Where does the instinct for wholeness reside? What is the nature of the collective mind? Further, given that at some deep level humanity is one, what are the ramifications of such a bond? Is personal unity really possible in the world of today? (The answer is a pessimistic no.)

Martha's life is a quest for self-delineation, instinctive and fumbling at first, finally becoming a daring, conscious exploration. Modern theorists as different as Laing and Heisenberg have stated emphatically that the universe that today demands exploration is the inner one of consciousness. Lessing has consistently made such an attempt in her fiction; and in Martha she gives the entire life of a character devoted to this effort.

Martha's compulsion toward growth is inspired by the veld, quite literally: from childhood she has experienced there illuminations that she calls her *lodestone moments*. They leave her with some instinct that eventually forces her out of each of the successive roles that she temporarily slips into. It is as if having known unity in some difficult way, she is never satisfied for long with the fragmentation that the city imposes on her as socialite, working woman, wife, mother, or communist. However, leaving these roles sometimes means to shed responsibility—of her child, for instance. In *The Four-Gated City* Martha finally sees that her goal in life is self-knowledge. At the same time she takes on responsibility for others—not in an idealistic, often impractical way as she did in her communist days, but very concretely, holding the Coldridge family together during difficult times. Goaded by a mental breakdown, which forces her to reclaim her past, Martha eventually goes on to experience all the levels of consciousness necessary for integration. Like Anna, Martha discovers the opposites in her nature and also the collective mind; but this defeats her. Unlike Anna, who is nourished by her recognition of unity with others and the courage everyone shares, Martha just barely escapes being wrecked on the reef of this collective mind.

Martha's psychic explorations give Lessing's most detailed

map of the psyche as she perceives it. The motive force is the guide, or guardian, as Martha sometimes calls it, that keeps her moving through outgrown stages and guides her in dreams—an inner voice comparable to the Jungian self, the mediating point between the conscious and the unconscious. Jung has said that to achieve individuation, "one must surrender consciously to the power of the unconscious, instead of thinking in terms of what one should do, or of what is generally thought right, or of what usually happens. One must simply listen, in order to learn what the inner totality—the self—wants one to do here and now in a particular situation."[34] Similarly, Martha says at one point in *The Four-Gated City* that everyone makes decisions "in obedience to something we don't know anything about" (p. 70). Certainly this has been true for her. Only in middle age does she see that her own growing point, the forward direction of her life, is her own developing consciousness; however, she has always acted intuitively, if haltingly, toward such knowledge.

At the beginning of *The Four-Gated City* Martha begins to realize the difference between what is essentially herself and what is simply a reflection of others. For weeks she deliberately tries on different personalities with different people: with Olive and Jimmy she is the clownish, self-deprecating "Matty"; with Stella she becomes the "hip-swinging sexually gallant girl." On trains and busses she makes up different names and life stories at random. The result of this conscious role-playing, combined with having no job or any other commitment, is an ability to sense the "real" Martha: "a taste or flavour of existence without a name. Who remembered. Who noted. And not much more" (p. 16). These pages are essentially a summary of what Martha struggled through laboriously in five years of successive errors before leaving Africa for London.

It is many more years before she understands her psyche deeply. In these first months in London she gets a glimpse or two, walking the streets at night with little food or sleep, until her mind becomes a sensitive instrument: a jumble of sound that occasionally throws up a distinct phrase or song and also a menacing figure that raves like an idiot. These are her brief introductions to the collective mind and shadow. She also has tantalizing moments of heightened vision in sex with Jack. Through timing and control, he carries them both to the same "high stretch" of being she knows on her night walks, and from where she has an uncanny perception of good and evil: she has a glimpse of a golden age and also the hell that is before her— being chief support for a group of half-grown, terrified children during a difficult time.

However, Martha leaves her mental explorations at this point, apparently knowing instinctively that she has unfinished business to take care of. Although she has up to this point resisted every claim on her that might limit her freedom, she finds herself staying with Mark Coldridge because she is needed, even though she knows she is in for a bad time.

The interplay between freedom and responsibility is always an undercurrent in Lessing's work. Martha can not move forward without freedom; marriage, motherhood, and service to a rigid political movement all placed her in stultifying positions. Service to the Coldridge family prevents her from exploring further the discoveries she has made in her first free weeks in London. Nevertheless, Lessing takes the position that freedom from responsibility can be dangerous. Jack is the clearest example. He refuses all commitments; for example, he would like all his girl friends to have his children but is adamant that he would never take responsibility for them. Martha sees that Jack is for some reason not to be taken seriously, and she intuitively prophesies his downfall in a perceptive moment, hearing the line "Jack fell down and broke his crown" among the jumble of sounds she calls the *wavelength*. At the time she has only a sense of foreboding, later fulfilled. Jack is completely one-sided. Totally physical in his approach to life, he lacks intellect and reason. The result is complete dissolution of his personality; he is possessed by a spirit of cruelty and bestiality. A statement from Jung illuminates Lessing's position toward responsibility and is particularly appropriate to Jack. Jung is discussing the importance of knowing what is ego and what belongs to the collective psyche:

> It is essential, in differentiating the ego from the non-ego, that a man should be firmly rooted in his ego-function; that is, he must fulfill his duty to life, so as to be in every respect a viable member of the community. All that he neglects in this respect falls into the unconscious and reinforces its position, so that he is in danger of being swallowed up by it.[35]

In *The Golden Notebook* the title of the novel *Free Women* is seen eventually to be ironic. People are not free—of their own natures, their responsibilities, their society, the forces behind all creation. Or they may be said to be free only in the paradoxical Miltonic sense—free to do what they must do. In Lessing this means to follow not the laws of a God separate from oneself, but those of an inner law of growth combined with outer social responsibilities. Martha eventually finds that the right course to follow, the least dangerous and most fruitful, is to give up the freedom she sought by leaving her marriages, her child, and her political commitments. "You start growing on your own account when you've worked through what you're landed with. Until then, you're paying off debts" (p. 432), says Martha when she has been with Mark for over ten years. At that time she is still not finished paying off her own debts. Before she can continue growing on her own account she must make up for her abandonment of her own child by taking on the children of the Coldridge clan. She has left two husbands, but then she must stand by Mark. Also, there is the debt of her childhood: she must work through the conflicts implanted then before she can move ahead. Finally, years later, Martha is ready to return to the business of self-exploration.

But if responsibilities are a difficult prerequisite to personal integration, they also provide stability against the dangers inherent in it. Anna knows that she will return to normal because she must, to be Janet's mother when the child returns from school. And Martha is afraid that the "self-hater"—summoned from her unconscious during her explorations—will be beside her permanently. However, she finds that he fades away when she returns to normal life, helping Mark and welcoming Rita, her friend Maisie's daughter, from Africa. Lynda is closest to normal in the years she fulfills her responsibility as a mother, grandmother, and—as much as possible—wife. A chief symptom of her illness is that she does not like to be touched; she cannot enter into a normal, loving, responsible relationship with Mark or her son Francis.

Only when the Coldridge family is fairly peaceful does Martha have time to be concerned about herself. Her responsibilities over, neurosis overtakes her—always in Lessing a sign that forward growth is blocked. The present hurdle is Martha's personal unconscious, which she must face. Anna went through such a task herself; she went to Mother Sugar because she could not feel emotion, and the cure was the recovery of the "private-pain material" of her past, as she put it. This process is not dramatized; it is simply recorded that it happened. In *The Four-Gated City* Martha's experience is shown.

Here again, the similarity of Jung's theories is striking. Jung has said that recovery of one's past is necessary for individuation, that Freud has shown that one must be freed from the fragments of childhood experience that remain in the personal unconscious:

> Only when they are rejoined again to the adult consciousness can they lose their infantile aspect and be corrected. This "personal unconscious" must always first be disposed of—that is to say, made conscious; otherwise, the entrance to the collective unconscious cannot be opened.[36]

Martha's past centers on her mother. Hearing that she plans to come from Africa, perhaps to live with her, Martha takes to her bed, paralyzed with inertia. She visits Dr. Lamb, a psychiatrist, but soon decides she can do better on her own. She works to recall her past, "As one puts a hand into hot water, withdraws it, puts it back, gingerly holds it there, withdraws it—" (p. 220). Finally she sees that she has blocked off half her life in order to protect herself from the pain that accompanies it: "Martha heard herself crying. She wept, while a small girl wept with her, Mama, Mama, why are you so cold, so unkind, why did you never love me?" (p. 221).

When Martha has finished wrestling with her personal unconscious, she has achieved normalcy; a psychiatrist would announce her cured. It is at this point that Lessing begins to dramatize Martha's supranormal development and to ask the question: how far can one go toward integration and expansion of consciousness? Sign of this new growth is Martha's sense that during the difficult period of regaining her past, she has created a new, fragile being that must be guarded, as it "might easily again be lost into the dark":

And [she] had made discoveries. She had found doors she had not known existed. She had wrestled herself out of the dark because she had had to, and had entered places in herself she had not known were there.

She was like a woman with a secret, or one who is pregnant. (p. 286)

Again, family responsibilities engross Martha as the "children" occupy Mark and herself with their emotional problems. Paul, accused of theft, returns to the house and goes to day school, and Mark's increasing work load requires her secretarial help. Nevertheless, the new doors remain open. Martha finds that she has found an ability to listen in to the thoughts of others. Suddenly she is able to understand something of Lynda's mental state:

> And Martha was already feeling extremely foolish. For what else had Lynda been saying all this time, in so many different ways. But Martha had not heard. She had not been *able* to hear. She had not had anything to hear with—there being no substitute for experience. (p. 354)

Martha and Lynda begin "working" together, trying in various ways to go beyond their present experience. "They did not really know what they were doing, or how, really, they did it. Yet out of all this material gathered, they began to get glimpses of a new sort of understanding" (p. 357).

Two episodes give Lessing's clearest picture of her view of the psyche. In the first, Martha allows herself to slip into Lynda's mad state much as Anna did into Saul's. Here she is able to view what lies beyond the barriers of human thinking, where words are inadequate, unable to express anything of the truth behind them, or conversely, a word repeated over and over may mystically suggest all truth. In this state Martha receives waves of turbulent energy from Lynda. Jung cites a similar phenomenon that may occur when one leaves the safety of the conscious ego for deeper areas of the psyche. Strong forces may "burst out of the collective psyche" with "confusing and blinding effect." The conscious mind loses control and is pushed about.[37] Similarly, Martha is racked by forces that she is only by great effort able to control and use:

> Martha sat still in her chair, feeling herself shake, almost shake apart with the force of whatever power it was that was being generated in that room, and made herself remember what she had learned through leaving Jack. Essentially, it was keeping still, holding, waiting . . . —you must let it build up. (p. 472)

In this state of heightened awareness Martha encounters the "sound barrier." Fifteen years ago she knew it as a faint jumble of sounds throwing up banal songs and phrases to her attention. This time it is like a "million radio sets" running simultaneously. "It is the human mind, or part of it, and Lynda, Martha can choose to plug in or not" (p. 472). She rides like a small boat on a river of "words, shrieks, gunfire, explosions, sentences" (p. 474), then realizes that fear makes her vulnerable, capable of being taken over by this chaos. Calming herself, she moves through the sound barrier to a still more heightened state in which she can move freely in time and space and see beautiful gardens—once again a vision of Eden, reminiscent of the glimpse of paradise she had with Jack. But when Martha goes outside to a London street, her new consciousness tortures her with a Swiftian view of mankind, half-evolved and sluglike. For the first time Martha understands Lynda's circular movement around the basement room, leaving her rusty trail of blood stains from chewed fingers. It is a protest against the imprisonment of the spirit in this vile, lethargic, deadened creature. At this point Martha experiences it:

> Why can't I get out? What is this thing that holds me in? Why is it so strong *when I can imagine, and indeed half-remember, what is outside?* Why is it that inside this room I am half asleep, doped, poisoned, and like a person in a nightmare screaming for help but no sounds come out of a straining throat? (p. 468)

Finally Martha meets what she later terms "the self-hater" or the devil—a mocking, jeering figure who sets her writhing with misery. At this point Lynda begs Martha to stop; in her own precariously balanced condition she can not bear Martha's outcries. Later, when Martha goes to a room alone for several months for further explorations, it is the self-hater who stops her. She is never able to get beyond that point.

The phenomenon of the self-hater is clearly discussed in Jung (although not in those words) as a necessary and dangerous part of the integration of personality. He sees Goethe's

Faust as the archetypal statement of this problem for the modern age:

> It is on the one hand an endeavour to understand the archetypal world of the psyche, on the other hand a struggle against the sanity-threatening danger of fascination by the measureless heights and depths and paradoxes of psychic truth.[38]

In *The Integration of the Personality* Jung states that "The character of the inner voice is 'luciferian' in the most proper and unequivocal sense of the word":

> The inner voice brings to consciousness whatever the whole—whether the nation to which we belong or the humanity of which we are a part—suffers from. But it presents this evil in individual form, so that at first we would suppose all this evil to be only a trait of individual character.[39]

Jung emphasized the danger in meeting this inner voice or shadow:

> If the shadow succeeds in assimilating the ego, a reversal of the whole personality comes about. Outwardly, this becomes perceptible through a change for the worse in character. When this is the case, there also unfailingly arises a kind of possession.[40]

The situation is therefore precarious: one must succumb in part to the shadow or no integration or renewal can take place. But if the *I* succumbs completely, the contents of the psyche "act as if they were so many devils, and a catastrophe follows."[41]

In Martha's second experiment with madness she sees that Thomas and Jack have both been taken over by the self-hater—literally possessed by the devil. And she believes that Lynda possibly met the self-hater when she was too young and without help and has never been able to banish him completely. All three have had extraordinary powers of perception, but like Renaissance explorers wrecked on unknown reefs, they were destroyed on psychological reefs, the modern counterpart.

Like Anna, Martha discovers the opposites in her personality: "Every attitude, emotion, thought, has its opposite held in balance out of sight but there all the time. Push any one of them to an extreme, and . . . over you go into its opposite" (p. 520). The uniting of opposites was Anna's major discovery. Here it is secondary. Martha's most important realization is the degree to which she is not unique. Every quirk of personality is general, as are thoughts, emotions, and creative images: Martha encounters psychic areas that look like paintings by Salvador Dali and Hieronymus Bosch and sees that anyone can plug into them. This psychic realm seems to be like the Jungian collective unconscious. Although Jung insisted that this phenomenon could never be completely explained, he compared it to an ocean of images and figures that drift into consciousness in dreams or abnormal states of mind and containing characteristics of both sexes, all ages, and all human experience—frequently expressing itself in myth.[42] So Martha's ultimate discovery is that every discernible trait is simply part of this general human experience: "I am what the human race is" (p. 511). Unique to her is only "the watcher, the listener" (p. 524).

Jung felt that integration of the personality would lead to a superior consciousness and a freeing effect, like a river finding its proper course. Anna achieves such a result. However, in *The Four-Gated City* Lessing takes a different point of view. Throughout *Children of Violence* she has dramatized the extent to which the individual is embedded in the collective "like frogspawn in jelly," and in this epoch that collective mind is unhappy and violent. As a result, Martha, Jack, Thomas, and Lynda are unable to push through the self-hater, the universal shadow who embodies the scourges of the modern age. Thomas and Jack were wrecked because they were not aware of the nature or dangers of the mass psyche. Lynda was ruined by misguided psychiatric treatment (although it is revealed toward the end of the novel that with the help of an enlightened doctor she eventually becomes a first-class seer). Martha believes that she escaped disaster only because she has had Lynda for a guide and did not put herself into the hands of psychiatrists. The prescription for the future is clear. First, society needs wiser psychiatric care. But more, it needs a human race with a more evenly balanced psyche. Then the self-hater would no longer be all powerful and mankind would once again be able to perceive good as well as evil.

In "The Temptation of Jack Orkney" Orkney goes through in a period of weeks many of the experiences that take Martha a lifetime. The subject of this novella is the need for a different sort of awareness than even the most responsible members of society generally cultivate.

"The Temptation of Jack Orkney" is very simple in design. For many years Orkney has been an important figure in English liberal politics. Never doubting himself or his aims, he has devoted his life to socialism. He is a very rational man who prides himself on not dreaming and being "delivered from" interest in the nonrational. However, at the time of his father's death, Orkney begins to have disturbing dreams, giving him a new angle of vision toward things. He and his fellow liberals at this time appear to be wearing masks of vanity, and the younger generation is blindly following a similar pattern. Meanwhile his dreams continue to draw him to some frightening knowledge beneath rationality. Finally, the experience becomes too much for him, and he takes sleeping pills and tranquilizers to quell it. Still, he knows that he will continue to explore the world of dreams that he has newly discovered.

Like Charles Watkins in *Briefing for a Descent into Hell*, Orkney's breakdown occurs spontaneously. Unlike Anna or Martha he can not bring himself out of this state by willpower; however, he does have the choice of doing so by drugs. At first he does not choose to take them because he is aware that something important is happening. The imagery clearly suggests that it is a spontaneous attempt by his psyche to correct an imbalance in his nature caused by lack of development of his nonrational self. Under the mask of vanity that he newly perceives in his everyday face he feels "something small, formless, blind—something pitiful and unborn."[43] And when Orkney finally does take medication, he does so "with the same miserable determination that he would have had to use to kill something that had to be killed" (pp. 302–303).

Whatever new consciousness is developing sees—as Martha came to see—that all beliefs and attitudes are roles selected like clothes off a rack. Orkney selected atheism, for example, because it was fashionable. If he had been young today he sees that he might well have been a "Jesus freak." When his daughters Carrie and Elizabeth and his niece Ann argue over their Christian and Eastern religions and women's liberation, Orkney sees that they are all expressing ideas that are simply momentary possessions and that they can (and do) trade in a day for a new set. But unfortunately, as the girls' arguments illustrate, all opinions are divisive:

> Again he felt like a threatened building, the demolition teams at work on its base. He was seeing, like a nightmare, the world like a little ball covered over with minuscule creatures all vociferously and viciously arguing and killing each other over beliefs which they had come to hold by accident of environment, of geography. (p. 285)

Beliefs can never give rise to social change because they always splinter and divide. New generations accomplish nothing because they can never go on to something new; Orkney's son is the image of himself at that age. And opinions give rise to vanity and the love of power that he perceives like masks on the faces around him.

Orkney's dreams instill in him a fear of death, for the first time (even though he was close to death in the war). There is a suggestion that the warning is not so much against physical death as a certain meaninglessness, a negation of his life. And when Orkney has refused the challenge of his "temptation," he feels his face take on a look similar to his father's at one point in the older man's life: "the face of a Roman, heavy-lidded, sceptical, obdurate, facing into the dark: the man whose pride and strength has to come from a conscious ability to suffer, in silence, the journey into negation" (p. 308).

The dreams appear to hold a second warning. Frequently a female figure, who he is certain stands for his wife and daughters, beckons Orkney threateningly into a black tunnel, and he ends gasping for air. Waking, he has a nauseating sweetness in his mouth. Orkney has always relied on women. Throughout his marriage he has had affairs; that period over, he has turned to his wife and daughters for comfort. But the dreams cause him to see them as "great dolls who supplied warmth, charm, sympathy, when the buttons of duty or habit were pressed" (p. 303). There is an implication that depending on women as he has done has somehow impeded his development and speeded him toward negation.

However, there is evidence that life might have been different, and that the breakdown is an alert to whatever it is he failed to do or perceive:

> His life had been set in one current long ago; a fresh current, or at least, a different one, had run into it from another source; but, unlike the springs and rivers of myth and fairy tale, it had been muddied and unclear. (p. 308)

This new stream has left Orkney with "a question as urgent as a wound that needed dressing," but he has "no idea what the language was in which he might find an answer" (p. 303). And he sees that the situation is desperate: "the future of humanity depended on humanity being able to achieve new forms of intelligence, of being able to learn from experience" (p. 273).

Nevertheless, Orkney shuts out the urgent question with drugs. His own "temptation" to new intelligence appears to be only partly successful. Nevertheless, it is a beginning. He has been unalterably jogged out of fatuous patterns of thought: "Behind the face of the sceptical world was another, which no conscious decision of his could stop him exploring" (p. 308).

In *Briefing for a Descent into Hell* Charles Watkins's plunge into new awareness is much more extreme than Orkney's; he leaves the rational world behind him completely. However, Watkins has shock treatment, which seems to destroy completely the knowledge he gained from his madness. He then immerses himself completely in his old life.

Watkins's breakdown takes him on an extended voyage into the recesses of his psyche. The epigraph for this novel is, "Category: inner space fiction. *For there is never anywhere to go but in.*" In over half the novel the reader observes Watkins from the underside of his ego, experiencing with him the images he meets there. The persona of Professor Charles Watkins, specialist in classical studies, husband of Felicity and father of two boys, is presented only through letters written by his wife, friends, and ex-mistress.

In *Briefing for a Descent into Hell* true sanity is to be found in so-called madness; Watkins's ordinary world of normality is like sleep and is without any saving vision. This view is once again similar to R. D. Laing's theories of schizophrenia. In fact, Charles Watkins's story bears strong resemblance to a case history presented in chapter three of *Politics of Experience*. [44] It is interesting that Laing's friend is also named Watkins—Jesse Watkins, a sculptor. Jesse Watkins experienced his three-month schizophrenic episode as an enormous journey back into time. He felt as if he were an animal like a rhinoceros and then, further back, as if he were "just struggling like something that had no brain at all," fighting for existence. At one point, like Martha in *The Four-Gated City*, he was conducted through the stations of the cross. Watkins knew that he had made such a journey but also that it would continue for a horrendously long time in the future. He saw three levels of existence. The first was like a waiting room—the ordinary state of humanity, firmly placed in time. The second area, where Watkins appeared to be at this point, was where people were "sort of awakening." Finally there was a higher level of existence where gods or superior beings somehow took charge of running the universe. The most agonizing knowledge was to see that "everybody had to take on the job at the top" after having arrived at "awareness of everything."

When leaving the hospital, Jesse Watkins felt that some of the heightened awareness of his experience remained with him along with the memory of his vision. Everything was more vivid and "more real" than before. "I could see the bad things and the good things and all that. I was much more aware" (p. 166). He agreed with Laing that specific treatment—such as electroshock—might have caused him to lose his grip on himself completely, simply adding to the stress he was already experiencing. Likewise, he felt sedatives were dangerous. When Watkins began to feel that he could not take any more stress, he made a conscious decision to "come back" and was able to do so.

Some of the parallels to Lessing's fiction are striking. In *Briefing for a Descent into Hell* (written in 1971, four years after *The Politics of Experience*) there are superior beings who are in charge of running the universe, as in Jesse Watkins's highest level of existence. Both men experience a journey that transcends space and time. Like Jesse Watkins, Charles finds that the sedatives given to him leave him with a sensation of drowning, of going under. After his "journey" but before shock treatment, Charles is highly perceptive. He is able to perceive character at a glance and read thoughts. His conversation and written stories make a good deal of sense within terms of his new knowledge, but because they are not verifiable in the rational world they appear mad by ordinary standards.

Unlike Jesse Watkins (or Jack Orkney), Charles is not left with a permanent sense of vision. Through the device of amnesia, Lessing makes his a case of one extreme or the other. Without treatment he will stay in his new, aware state and perhaps find a way to capture the elusive knowledge that tantalizes him—but he will also fail to remember his previous life. The knowledge that eludes him is what Mercury was sent to earth to divulge: that man must obey the cosmic laws of harmony; otherwise, he will destroy himself. However, shock treatment simply "cures" Charles Watkins, ironically causing amnesia toward the inner life he has so recently discovered. This device allows Lessing to make a strong statement about the blindness and damaging effects of prevalent views of psychic disturbance.

Watkins's amnesia gives an ironic twist to Lessing's ever-present theme of responsibility. Watkins can scarcely be responsible to a wife and children whom he does not remember. However, during his period in the hospital he takes on a new responsibility, Violet Stokes. The two would like to live together, although such an arrangement would be beyond the pale of society's laws; and the implication is that both would benefit. By contrast, Watkins's wife Felicity is self-centered and demanding; to return to her is like going back to the arms of the Circe he feared as a young man (and unwittingly found in Felicity). Lessing implies that Watkins's responsibilities to Violet and for his own continued growth are higher than those to his family, recognized by society. Faulty psychiatric treatment results in a wrong choice. Rosemary Baines's comment about Watkins's amnesia is a clue to the attitude Lessing favors: "I am sorry he is so ill. I have it in me to envy him. There is a good deal in my life that I would be very happy to forget" (p. 243).

Briefing for a Descent into Hell is about the attempt and failure of integration of personality. Like Anna and Martha, Watkins explores his unconscious, and integration would have meant to balance its wisdom with the intensely logical and rational ego, imaged by Watkins's profession, professor of classical studies. In spite of his weaknesses, however, Watkins even before his breakdown is farther than most toward a sense of community. Jeremy Thorne in his letter to Doctor Y recounts with incredulity and anger certain traits that seen from another light are signs of Watkins's superiority. Superficial trappings have meant little to Watkins. When Thorne criticized his manner of dress as a professor at his own college, Watkins began to dress like Thorne himself, as if aping him, wearing cast-off clothes that Thorne's wife had planned to throw out until Watkins asked for them. What looks like an affront is actually a sign of Watkins's lack of concern for such things; he assumes that he is merely following Thorne's request—to look more like him. When Thorne and his wife have a serious quarrel, Watkins tells the wife not to be "so personal," that it scarcely matters whether one is married to one person or another.

Constance Mayne, Watkins's ex-mistress, reports that after the war "he couldn't believe that people found important the things they said they found important." He had to "learn to 'play little games.'" In other words, Watkins has been struck by the superficiality of society's rigid patterns of behavior and belief. On the surface one might think that Watkins has mistreated Constance, who changed her life for him, but in whom he eventually lost interest. But Watkins's behavior follows the pattern he first displayed in failing to show "proper" appreciation to Thorne for giving up a school yachting trip so that Watkins could take his place: if people see fit to make certain decisions, they should not expect set responses from others. In "The Temptation of Jack Orkney" Orkney perceives that his wife and daughters turn on certain emotions like pressing a button because of duty or habit. This is the sort of response that Watkins has always avoided, but to do so naturally looks strange by society's standards.

Before Watkins's breakdown an inner guide similar to Martha's "guardian" seems to be directing him. He begins to stammer during lectures, a physical reaction to a deep, unconscious sense that what he teaches is meaningless. Thorne reports that one evening Watkins was belligerent, saying that "everything taught under the heading of Classics is pigsfeed from beginning to end . . . and that we have never had any idea at all of what Plato or Socrates and Pythagoras were teaching" (pp. 228–229). The evening of his breakdown Watkins appears at the apartment of Rosemary Baines, a stranger who has written him a long letter about her sense that Watkins belongs to a special fraternity that shares a certain "wavelength"—a "quality of matching, of ringing together, of substances being in tune" (p. 183). That Watkins seeks her out is a sign that she has perceived some deeply buried knowledge that in his breakdown is striving to emerge. The first sign of this nonrational knowledge is Watkins's behavior at Rosemary Baines's apartment. She observes that his talk is disconnected but seems to make a poetic sense and have a certain "inner logic" (p. 242). At this time he talks about making a voyage. As it turns out, the voyage is into his psyche or "inner space," as earlier spasmodic attempts of the unconscious to penetrate Watkins's ego give way to his complete immersion in it.

Previously seen in connection with *The Golden Notebook*, alchemy historically has been a metaphor for the refinement of human consciousness and Lessing uses its imagery to illustrate that theme. The image of the crystal, which figures at the beginning and the end of Watkins's "journey," is the Chinese Taoist version of the philosopher's stone, found in *The Secret of the Golden Flower*. As Jung points out, "The creation and birth of a superior personality is what is meant by our text when it speaks of the 'holy fruit,' the 'diamond body,' or refers in other ways to an indestructible body" (p. 46). While mad, Watkins believes that the crystal has swept up his friends and left him behind. To be absorbed into it is his main preoccupation throughout his mental journey, and when it happens he does achieve a superior consciousness. Certainly one does not need the parallel to alchemy to perceive the sense of clarity, perfection, and order implied by the crystal.

Watkins's vision from within the crystal is similar to those observed in the other novels. Like Anna and Martha, Watkins senses his unity with the rest of humanity:

> In that dimension minds lay side by side, fishes in a school, cells in a honeycomb, flames in fire, and together we made a whole in such a way that it was not possible to say, here Charles begins, here John or Miles or Felicity or Constance ends. And so with us all. (p. 106)

However, in the midst of the fullness of this sense of unity, Watkins sees the destructive element that was Anna's chief foe and for which he uses an image similar to one of hers. He becomes aware of

> the cold weight, a compulsion, a necessity, as it were, a menace only just held at bay by humanity, and always waiting there, the crocodile's jaws always there, just under the water. It was a grief and a fear too ancient for me, it was a sorrow bred into the essence of the race. I saluted it and passed on. . . . It was too old a lodestone for any individual to fight away from, or even accurately to know and place. It was there. (p. 106–7)

It is the broad patterns that Watkins sees from the crystal. As Jupiter says at one point, "it's a harmony, it's a pattern, bad and good, everything in turn, everything spiralling up—" (p. 131). Everything is in a tightly knit harmony, forming patterns, one thing affecting another. Man's sin is to forget the laws of harmony for the *I-I-I* of self. The moon of subjectivity—or egocentricity—pulls man like a tide so that he ignores "God's singing centre," the sun (p. 117).

But before reaching this awareness of cosmic harmony, Watkins makes a journey through time, an allegory of man's existence on earth from the beginnings to the present age. Watkins begins on a ship. He compares himself to Odysseus, establishing the mythic nature of the allegory. When the crystal leaves him behind, he moves to a raft and continues to go "around and around," waving at his friends as he circles the world. Then he begins a progression analogous to man's development on earth, part mythic, part scientific. He finds that he is then deep in the sea, able to eat plankton (p. 33). Then he emerges from the water on the back of a porpoise, suggesting the time when man's ancestors made the same step, leaving the memory of the experience in the collective unconscious:

> And now leaving the sea where I have been around and around for so many centuries my mind is ringed with Time like the deposits on shells or the fall of years on tree trunks. I step up on the dry salty sand, with a shake of my whole body like a wet dog. (p. 40)

After a difficult climb up a seemingly insurmountable cliff—perhaps a metaphor for man's ascent to consciousness—Watkins arrives at the peaceable kingdom of the golden age of myth, where fruit grows on the trees, and lions and man can lie down side by side. He comes to a ruined city that in some way embodies all his friends: once again the City of human harmony with its mandala center—a square with an inner circle. But it is unfulfilled, a blueprint only. Watkins knows that he must clear this center before he can be accepted by the crystal. But before he can do so he becomes moonstruck; that is, the subjectivity of *I-I-I*—egocentricity—has taken over with its insistent greed: "the thoughts of the moon are very cold and hungry" (p. 65). A direct result is the Fall. A shadow separates itself from the edge of the city and kills a cow peacefully grazing; "and suddenly there was a strong sickly smell of blood on the air that I knew, though I had no proof of this, had not been made to smell of blood before."

> I knew that I had arrived purged and salt-scoured and guiltless, but that between then and now I had drawn evil into my surroundings, into me, and I knew, as if it had been my own hand that had drawn that bow and loosed that arrow, that I had caused the shining milk-white beast to fall dead. (p. 66–67)

That is, original sin, and with it death, originated in man's egocentricity.

Claimed by sin, Watkins is then divided by sun and moon, standing for harmony and subjectivity. By day he tries to escape the guilt-filled town, but by moonlight he is drawn back and joins in bloody feasts. The crystal comes, but Watkins is too heavy with physical decadence to become part of it, and his eyes are "not evolved enough" to see it (p. 76). He suffers, feeling as if his "whole being had suffered a wrenching away from its proper level" (p. 76).

The city becomes inhabited by vile rat-dogs and monkeys, apparently an allegory for the ruthlessness and violence of society, reminiscent of Martha's Swiftian view of London's half-evolved human creatures. In a version of destruction comparable to the realistic one in *The Four-Gated City*, Watkins sees from the back of a bird the polluted sea and a vicious war between the monkeys and rat-dogs that leaves them nearly destroyed. The final terrible scene shows a female rat-dog giving birth and defending herself from enemies; snapping at her attackers she sometimes kills or wounds her young. A male attempts to mate with her and "she died in a spasm that was as much a birth- as death-spasm" (p. 98). This powerful and grotesque image marks a turning point. As if things have spiraled to their lowest, life and death merging on the most vicious and carnal scale, Watkins again sees the bird, who has come to guide him back to the city square. Once again he is compelled to clean it, clearing away the dead bodies and freeing the waterways from rubbish. At this point the crystal comes and absorbs him. Properly attended to, the center of the city becomes his own center of consciousness from where he can perceive the world and the universe with godlike objectivity; the "diamond body" is completed.

In *The Four-Gated City* certain characters, such as Martha and Lynda, laboriously acquire a finer consciousness than they have had before. In his schizophrenic experience Watkins is accomplishing the same thing, integrating his rational mind with the Jungian collective unconscious, the complete history of the race. Martha's self-hater, the shadow side of humanity, is in *Briefing for a Descent into Hell* the guilt of the blood feasts, tied to man's egocentricity. And just as Martha discovers that she is one with all life, Watkins sees that he is a tiny microbe in one complete pattern. From the crystal he sees not just man's evil side but also his good; the dross seems to dissolve and a pattern of light remains, stronger in some creatures than in others. When Watkins is able to talk to the doctors this ability to see the good in people remains with him; for example it is the steady light of Dr. Y.

The crystal is not the only reference to alchemy in *Briefing for a Descent into Hell*. Many of the images of Watkin's voyage gain significance in reference to it—the sun, for example. In the Sufi view of alchemy, the philosopher's stone stands for the divinity in man, his light or essence, the "sunshine" capable of lifting humanity to a higher stage.[45] When Watkins is in the crystal he is lifted to a higher state in which he is able to see the light, or divinity, in certain people. He perceives that it is related to the sun, whose energy is "the controlling governor of them all." It is "the deep low organ note that underlies all being" (pp. 116–117). Earth and her creatures, distant from the sun and pulled out of shape by the moon, forget this knowledge of cosmic harmony.

Mercury is another important alchemical image in *Briefing*, creating the metaphor around which the novel is structured. In *The Golden Notebook* Mercury is the uniter of opposites, one of the three elements of the alchemical "work." In *Briefing* it figures as a messenger of the divine—a tradition Mercury-Hermes holds in Roman and Greek mythology, also. Idries Shah outlines the importance of Mercury, and his counterpart Hermes, in Sufic alchemy. Like the philosopher's stone, the name refers to mankind's hidden sunshine, or divinity, which has the potential to lead him to a state of harmony and fulfillment; as such, it is a messenger. Alchemy is traditionally called the *Hermetic art* after its founder, Hermes (probably several teachers); but this figure blends into Hermes the messenger-god who moves at great speeds, out of time and space—as does the mind. In his athletic prowess and connection to wisdom, music, letters, and medicine he stands for the perfected man of Sufism, and as such he has a place in many religions under different names. Lessing clearly had in mind this alchemical figure, making almost direct use of the following passage, in which Idries Shah cites the history of Thoth or Hermes as given by the eleventh-century Spanish-Arab historian Said of Toledo:

> 'Sages affirm that all antediluvian sciences originate with the first Hermes, who lived in Sa'id, in Upper Egypt. The jews call him Enoch and the Moslems Idris.'[46]

In *Briefing* Watkins refers to Mercury as "the sun's closest associate," the only one who can "maintain steadily and always the consciousness of the sun's underlying song, its need, its intention. Mercury whose name was, also, Thoth, and Enoch, Buddha, Idris, and Hermes, and many other styles or titles in the earth's histories, Mercury the Messenger, . . . the disseminator of laws from God's singing centre" (p. 117). Further, Hermes-Mercury is often represented as a bird, or a man with the head of an ibis, a fact that lends an extra dimension of meaning to the bird that instructs Watkins in the steps he must take to be finally absorbed into the crystal.

Most important, the whole idea behind *Briefing* is based on the figure of Mercury. The title of the novel derives from an Olympian drama in which Mercury and others are sent down to earth (hell) to become human and try to warn others of their impending disaster if they continue to disobey the harmony of the sun. The message is carried in the form of "brainprints," and the gods are warned that it will be extremely difficult to remember once they are members of a drugged and violent humanity. Next is witnessed the birth of Watkins; obviously *he* is this messenger. The reader is led to believe that Rosemary Baines and Frederick Larson are part of the group as well. Mrs. Baines has written to Watkins, speaking about an intuitive connection she feels toward him. Possibly this letter has contributed to Watkins's breakdown, forcing him to a crisis; on the evening of his collapse he goes to Mrs. Baines's apartment and takes it for granted that the three are friends, perhaps those he speaks about on his circular voyage. "I'll see you next time round," he says to Larson. Watkins's purpose in life is to break through his conditioning, which begins in infancy when he is encouraged to sleep (an ancient metaphor for dulled consciousness, frequently used in Sufism) and to remember his mission. His breakdown is a spontaneous and abortive attempt to do so.

This fable is a metaphor for the Sufic idea that man has a portion of divinity within himself—that is, an ability to perceive the cosmic pattern and his own place in it. He is born with it, but the knowledge tends to get lost under the stress of conditioning. Alchemy is a metaphor for this Sufic idea: Mercury, man's dual substance, when given proper attention, will regain its gold, its sunshine, its divinity.

Another important alchemical symbol is the moon, repeatedly cited throughout *Briefing* as a malign influence or necessity that causes mankind's egocentricity and all the world's troubles. Specifically, it causes Watkins to join the death rites of the old women, pulling him away from his spiritual quest.

Titus Burckhardt in his study *Alchemy: Science of the Cosmos, Science of the Soul,* is clear on the importance of the moon to alchemical theory. Gold and also the sun are symbols of the Divine Spirit in man, an active principle, traditionally male. Silver and also the moon symbolize another cosmic force— soul, a passive and receptive principle, traditionally female. In the unpurified state, these two parts are crude and one-sided; in order to lift the human spirit out of its paralyzed, leaden, impure condition, one must find the way to separate or divorce spirit and soul and then "marry" them again in the hermetic vessel, by fire, in order that they may be reformed as a perfect crystal.[47]

This particular version of alchemy provides a model for much of Charles Watkins's experience. His Fall is the separation of soul and spirit, and in this lopsided state, he is prey to the passive moon within him; unable to exert himself against it, he is always drawn back to its power. Then after Watkins has endured the ultimate in chaos and despair, the bird, symbol of Hermes the divine messenger, protects and guides him. Finally transcending the power of the moon, Watkins once again clears the center of the city (by moonlight and sunlight, a sign of balance), and shortly thereafter the crystal absorbs him.

The broad scope of alchemy makes it an appropriate metaphor for the central structure of *Briefing.* While it refers to the integration and purification of the individual consciousness, it does so in the broadest terms; its symbols extend from those of deepest consciousness out to the cosmos. Alchemy recognizes a unity among the souls of all living creatures and also of inert matter, in and out of living forms. Astrology stems from the same tradition and is intimately connected to it, interpreting the zodiac and planets as alchemy does the elements and metals. Yet, as in all esoteric knowledge, the macrocosm is reflected in the microcosm: thus within a single man are the zodiac, the traditional four elements, a universal soul, and universal matter. This pattern exists on a larger scale in the solar system, which then becomes a unit in a larger scale unknown by man.

Such is the scale of *Briefing for a Descent into Hell*. The novel moves from deep inside Watkins's consciousness, out to society as a whole, the solar system, and the cosmos. For example, the moon is the source of Watkins's imbalance, and the entire world's as well. Seen from another perspective, it is a cosmic accident that eventually will right itself. Also, Watkins becomes Hermes, who in turn is either fragment of sunlight or cosmic messenger. By such methods Lessing moves freely—as alchemy does—between realism and myth, inner consciousness and outer reality, the individual and the group, the solar system and creation as a whole, blurring the distinctions among them.

In *The Summer before the Dark*, the protagonist recovers psychic health as a result of a breakdown that is both mental and physical. *The Summer before the Dark* opens at a crisis in the life of Kate Brown, wife of a successful London neurologist and mother of four children, the youngest being nineteen. Since the family members are all going their separate ways for the summer, for the first time Kate is not needed. An intelligent and introspective woman, she is intellectually aware of her crisis and that it was to be expected eventually, but she nevertheless feels extremely depressed. By chance, a job is offered to her as a translator for Global Foods, an international service organization. With trepidation she accepts, beginning a four-month period during which she is stripped of all the illusions that have borne her up during her life. Also, the narrator informs, she grows old suddenly. However, it turns out that to grow old is also to achieve spiritual maturity.

Kate becomes invaluable to her employers because it turns out that besides being fluent in Portuguese she is good at looking after people; the traits once useful in caring for her family become able to keep conferences running smoothly. She is given an executive position for a conference in Turkey. Nevertheless, as Kate sees her "mothering" skill in new light, she begins to look on the years of household management as a form of dementia rather than a virtue and becomes increasingly aware of something in herself that has remained unfulfilled because of her constant "fussing."

A young man, Jeffrey Merton, offers her the opportunity of an affair, and she accepts, going to Spain with him when the conference is over. He becomes ill, and Kate is convinced that he has an identity crisis rather than a disease. In a small impoverished Spanish town the convent takes Jeffrey as a patient. Then Kate feels herself getting ill, a sign of her own mental crisis, which has been steadily approaching. She flies to London and checks into a hotel to endure her illness. For several weeks she is extremely ill with symptoms that are as much mental as physical. When she partially recovers and attempts to take a short walk, she notices people staring at her. Once a "pretty, serviceable" wife and mother, later an alluring executive, she has become a strange, old woman with frizzled hair, the undyed streak widening at the part. When she returns to her own neighborhood on a brief visit (the house is rented for the summer), her neighbors fail to recognize her, even Mary Finchley, her best friend. (Throughout the novel Mary figures prominently in Kate's thoughts as a woman without any sense of guilt. She openly has affairs and attaches no importance to them. Also, she dresses and acts as she likes, with no sense of propriety.)

The change in Kate's appearance teaches her an important lesson—that she is dependent on others' attentions, which she receives as a direct result of a polished appearance. Kate goes to

see Turgenev's *A Month in the Country* and gets a keen perception of the triviality of most human concerns: on stage, the
frustrations of the heroine in facing old age and the growing
indifference of men; in the audience, the triviality of concern
over clothes and hair. Things that once seemed of all-
consuming importance appear to be ridiculous.

Well enough to leave the hotel, Kate takes a room in the
apartment of a young woman, Maureen, who is in the midst of
her own crisis, wondering whether she should marry William,
the aristocrat, Philip, the social idealist bent on law and order,
or Jerry, a fellow dropout from established society. Eventually
Kate and Maureen confine themselves to the cavelike
(womblike) apartment, absorbed in their immediate problems.

At first Maureen seems to be a free spirit with no inhibitions.
However, it is an unearned, childish freedom, the innocence of
Blake's Beulah land. Maureen is continually characterized as a
little girl: she eats baby food; her stubbornness and outbursts of
temper are childlike; while she seems to be independent, in
fact, her father supports her. She drifts off to sleep against
Kate's shoulder and wakes up sucking her thumb. While Kate
gradually achieves real freedom, Maureen "falls" into the
bonds of ordinary adulthood, dramatized by her urgency to
choose one man, one role. "Tell me a story, Kate," she pleads
constantly, searching for clues from Kate's experience. With
anger and cynicism she finally decides that it does not matter
what she does—no choice seems good—and at the end she
goes to William, the father image, privileged member of a
traditional class structure.

Maureen's hair becomes a reflection of her state of mind: she
cuts it off short as she might wear it in prison or boarding
school, because she has indeed surrounded herself with invisi-
ble walls. As if to flaunt her new dissociated personality, Maureen gives a party, dressing seductively in a costume of the
thirties; but its devil-may-care mood is contradicted by the
severe hairstyle. Her spirit is as if withdrawn into a cocoon: the

puppet she has made of the cut-off hair, which Kate calls a harvest or corn doll. She scarcely greets her guests but dangles it in front of them. When William in disgust tries to snatch the doll, Maureen keeps it from him, crying out that he is not supposed to like it. As puppet it signifies the lifelessness of Maureen's new constraints. As harvest doll, it projects new life, the possibility that someday, like Kate, she will move out of ordinary adulthood to real maturity. The doll is her badge of resistance and represents that part of her that stands sulkily aside while she allows William to embrace her.

As Maureen just begins to face her battles, Kate nears the end, breaking out of the dissociation she has always lived with into a new psychic unity. In this novel the fragmenting city is all the automatic responses one gives to others in the name of love. On the surface Kate has had an impeccable life: an extremely successful marriage, by most standards; the successful raising of four children; friends; and finally the chance to have a glamorous career in a service organization, Global Foods. It is a life characterized by intelligence, humanity, and love, usually considered the highest attributes of mankind. A major theme of this novel is that, as usually displayed, they are superficial and ineffective.

Kate's experience is an indictment of the bonds that hold together even the most apparently satisfactory families. She herself has been the mainstay, but she has allowed herself to become inauthentic in the Sartrian sense, merely a reflection of others; her dress, morals, actions—and dyed hair—are all for pleasing. She is not subject but object, an image in a mirror. However, the problem is deeper than merely a failure to develop one's own personality in favor of devotion to others. Kate eventually realizes that there are no deep connections among any of them. "Intelligent" discussion and banter have replaced deep emotion. She and her husband Michael, in spite of carefully working on their marriage, live in different worlds.

Mary Finchley is important to the novel because she illustrates, by contrast, how much of Kate's life is based on habit, propriety, guilt, and the romantic ideal. When Kate goes to *A Month in the Country* while ill, she recognizes for the first time the triviality of most people's concerns, something Mary has always known. Mary has dressed and spoken as she pleased, without regard for rules. She knows deep affection but not morality and possessiveness. If she wishes to go to bed with a man, she does so; sex is sex—nothing more. Her affairs are not a criticism of her husband or a gesture for freedom but like having an ice cream soda when the mood strikes. Kate's husband Michael also has affairs but with a discretion based on guilt. In him infidelity is hypocrisy and self-indulgence; in Mary it is like a cardinal being red. The issue is not whether one should have extramarital affairs but the degree to which one acts according to one's nature, neither giving in to popular morality nor defying it. Kate has lived her entire life in response to propriety and the knowledge that she would feel guilty if she did certain things. She has always felt superior to Mary; at the end of the novel she respects her, seeing that Mary has always been her own woman.

An incident at the zoo shows in cameo form the muddles that ensue when people fail to perceive their own motives. Maureen and Kate observe a young couple in front of the animal cages. The boy is upset, having just realized that the parrot has been caged for half a century, never allowed to fly free. His adoring friend is sure she can comfort him with love. Then Maureen audaciously flirts with him, even kisses him, until the young man realizes he is being used. Feeling guilty, he turns to his friend, now tearful and miserable, and comforts her while half his attention is with the seductive Maureen, at that time walking away. There is an interplay of emotions: the young girl's need, Maureen's joy in conquest, the young man's mixture of guilt, responsibility, and desire. When misunderstood, such emotions trap people like parrots in cages of their own making. The three play out a little drama of distorted sexuality.

It is Mary Finchley's genius to cut through to the center and accept sex (and other basic emotions) on its own terms. She does not confuse it with conventional morality, proof of her own desirability, the need for security, or the affectionate loyalty of marriage.

Most of the emotions people show for one another prove to be distorted, on a social as well as personal level. The delegates to the Global Foods convention squabble like children, preserving their own interests, and the organization itself, despite its wish to help, is as slick and impersonal as any business. Meanwhile, the problem of hunger goes unsolved, and television coverage of the demonstration by London's poor becomes just another program on the evening news, followed by the weather report.

What then is important? What is a healthy substitute for the superficial level on which most people live out their lives? There is no suggestion in the novel that living like Mary Finchley is the answer. Rather, there is a suggestion that once stripped of illusion, like Mary, something else quite different becomes visible. The only clue to it is Kate's serial dream about a seal: she somehow has a responsibility to carry the dying animal to water: "Oh the seal, my poor seal, that is my responsibility, that is what I have to do. . . ."[48] She comes to see that the whole point of the summer has been to finish this dream, and that outward events have served merely to "feed" it. The seal has often been close to dying; she has poured water on it and revived it. A princely lover has invited her to stay, but she is forced to refuse. She heads north, into the dark and snow. It is during the weeks with Maureen that Kate finally finishes the dream. In the snow and dark she comes upon a flowering tree. Then she sees light ahead and comes to the sun and a group of seals playing in the water. It is spring. Kate deposits the seal in the ocean, and he swims off, not looking back, to join the others.

When Kate has finally come to the end of her dream, she

makes plans to return home to her family, who are then back in the house. She knows that her face is aged, and her hair half-gray; however, she determines never to dye it again in an attempt to fit into a certain mold: "The desire to please had gone out. And about time, too . . ." (p. 269).

The Summer before the Dark is unusual among Lessing's novels in that the themes are not spelled out. Kate's most important experience, the seal dream, is nonverbal, and the narrator never explains it except that in some way it represents Kate's true responsibility. It is not a simple metaphor, easily summed up in a phrase or two. In its weight and Kate's struggle to carry it, the seal stands partly for all the freight of her life that she has worked through during the summer. Like Charles Watkins laboriously clearing the city's mandala center, Kate has cleared away the assumptions that have choked her life. Releasing the seal is to release that burden. The seal also suggests Kate's essential self, whatever is most enduring in her. In the beginning it is half-dead, nearly overcome by dryness and cold, but taken to its true home, it revives and swims away in the sea among others of its kind. Thus it revives only as Kate sheds the baggage that she once saw as her life. But if the seal is Kate, it is also impersonal; it swims off, not looking back, showing that in some way she has shed her sense of self-importance. Finally, Kate's dream journey also represents the approach of old age and death, where worldly concerns are irrelevant and only the essential self counts. Unlike Jack Orkney's father and perhaps Orkney himself, who comes to see death as a journey into negation, Kate rediscovers the sun at the end of her dream—a sign of rebirth.

When Kate has finished her series of dreams, she is no closer to knowing analytically what is important—a fact that throws Maureen into despair, since she is looking for guidance. However, Kate is relaxed and at peace; she has learned to avoid self-deception and has glimpsed something within herself that is eternal. Like Maureen, she seems to have come to the conclusion that it really does not matter what roles one plays; however, for Kate this conclusion stems from knowledge, not cynicism. It hardly matters whether she returns to her family, works for Global Foods, or does something else altogether; Kate treats the matter lightly. Having recognized roles for what they are, she can no longer be injured by them. This is not a message that she can easily pass on to Maureen, though she makes a tentative effort by wondering aloud whether one's dreams can be for others, too.

For Kate as well as Maureen, hair becomes a statement. She will no longer dye it; the ever-widening strip of gray will remain. This decision is more than a refusal to live by pleasing others. Kate points out that hair is the one part of the body that does not respond to being stroked or injured. As such it represents the center of being that is free from the fears and needs that dictate most behavior. To leave it undisguised is a gesture of inner strength. Becoming gray is also an acceptance of old age and death—less frightening after all was done, perhaps, because of the suggestion of eternity Kate has experienced in her dream of the seal.

The Summer before the Dark marks a new direction in Lessing's work. Lessing's customary analysis is here applied only to Kate's social milieu and her relation to it, her discovery of the persona. The major theme is nonanalytical and even religious: an emerging spirituality through which the individual can apparently bypass the problem of the collective and discover a unity that exists within, if one can just dig deeply enough.

4

The Fragmented Society

In Lessing's novels, the characters are never separate from their society; their individual ills are always reflections of larger social ills. In *The Golden Notebook* Anna makes the greatest strides of any Lessing character toward integration, but because of the times she lives in, her success is not so much a triumphant victory as simply the ability to function, to tolerate the intolerable. As Lessing has pointed out, Anna's writer's block is linked to the fact that she, a "tiny individual," mirrors overwhelming problems of war, famine, and poverty.[1] Nevertheless, Lessing's individual novels focus predominantly on their protagonists, and the reader's interest centers on their failures or successes.

On the other hand, the novels in *Children of Violence* have a strong double focus. While they are concerned with the personal conflicts of Martha Quest-Knowell-Hesse, they are equally intent on the society that formed her and in which she must survive or fall. Martha shares the stage with myriad characters, some sketched in with a few lines, others nearly as well developed as Martha herself. This double focus of *Children of Violence* is what Lessing refers to when she insists that this series is "a study of the individual conscience in relations with the collective" and that a proper view of man should see him neither as an alienated individual nor "collective man with a collective conscience": "The point of rest should be the writer's recognition of man, the responsible individual, voluntarily submitting his will to the collective, but never finally; and insisting on making his own personal and private judgements before every act of submission."[2]

Because of Lessing's social habit of mind, she has been drawn to the idealism behind communism and socialism, which express concern for the equality and welfare of all. She has been strongly influenced by Jungian psychology in its attempt to define the individual in terms of humanity as a whole. More recently, Lessing has been attracted to Sufism, with its position that the individual can perfect his consciousness but that having done so, he then has a duty to serve society by helping humanity as a whole to evolve toward a higher consciousness.

Like Jung and the Sufis, Lessing holds the view that if society persists in its present patterns, global catastrophe will inevitably follow. She does not believe that *The Four-Gated City* is fanciful in its view of the destruction of large parts of the earth and of the society of today. As she has said in an interview with Jonah Raskin, "*Four-Gated City* is a prophetic novel. . . . I think that the 'iron heel' is going to come down. I believe the future is going to be cataclysmic."[3]

The whole point of *Children of Violence* is its enormous scope, its serious attempt to analyze the fragmentation of what Lessing sees as a mad society "hypnotized by the idea of Armageddon," as Mark put it in *The Four-Gated City*. Because of its subject and scope, in some ways this series might be considered a modern epic. In *The Orphic Voice*, Elizabeth Sewell attempts to define epic in a way that will give it contemporary possibilities:

> Epic, seen from the point of view of the working poet, is a dynamic instrument concerned with heroic achievement, advance, explora-

tion. The significance of these, in terms of man moving between earth and heaven, is inquired into in the person of the epic hero. . . . To represent epic as the high doings of one solitary figure of however superhuman proportions, a great cult of individualism, is to strike it dead, just as to represent the heroic age of such deeds and discoveries as primitive and left far behind us is to leave us all dead. Unprecedented deeds and explorations, with which epic deals, are lonely courses, and necessarily so. But the important thing from the beginning has been that the hero is identified with his people. He is his people in some sense. What are Gilgamesh or Beowulf or Dantë or Adam doing if they are not carrying us forward with them, exploring and struggling and suffering, out in advance of us but one with us still?[4]

At first glance Martha might not seem to be of epic stature; however, viewed from the standpoint of Sewell's definition, she gains significance. In the course of her life she manages to cut through all the mental and social constructs that trap every other character, and the result is an epic view of society and all its conventions and ills. Exploring her psyche, she descends into the underworld, and before her life is over she has seen both angels and devils. However, she is one of humanity; she is able merely to point the way, not follow it herself.

Children of Violence begins with fifteen-year-old Martha Quest at home on the family farm in "Zambesia." (In the author's notes at the end of *The Four-Gated City* Lessing says that she used the name of an imaginary country because she did not want it supposed that she was writing just about southern Rhodesia, where she spent her first twenty-five years. "My Zambesia is a composite of various white-dominated parts of Africa and, as I've since discovered, some of the characteristics of its people are those of any ruling minority anywhere whatever their colour, and some are those of white people anywhere—in Britain for instance.") The series ends with letters and reports from various characters who have survived catastrophic events in Britain and elsewhere, describing the worldwide pattern of events and the way new forms of power have become established. Thus, the original focus is small, the experience of a teen-age girl, and continues to widen as the novels progress.

Children of Violence is told chiefly from the point of view of Martha, and as she matures, her observations become increasingly profound. Lessing's handling of Martha's gradually deepening perceptions is one of the technical strengths of the series. Martha begins as an idealistic but critical adolescent, who only dimly perceives what she hopes to get from life but clearly sees what she rejects. Her important attributes are evident from the beginning. She is idealistic: she dreams about the ideal City where there will be equality and happiness for all. She has a mystical streak, shown in occasional, illuminating moments of unity. She is introspective and critical of her own faults when she is aware of them (for example, catching herself using the word *dago* in spite of her hatred of prejudice). But she is an inexperienced young girl who can not see far beyond her own discontents and the ideas she has picked up from her reading, and instead of trying to make intelligent decisions in regard to important actions, she tends to let events carry her along.

Martha Quest begins in 1935, but its significance goes back to the days before the First World War, when Martha's parents were still whole. The war has destroyed their lives, turning Mr. Quest into a defeated invalid and Mrs. Quest into his nurse. The novel begins when Martha is nearly old enough to leave home. She soon does so, taking an office job in town. There her scorn has new objects: the legal profession and its jargon, which she has to type, and the ineffectual members of the socialist political groups. She is soon swept into the role of "girl about town," spending nearly every evening at the Sports Club with Donovan, an asexual young man who is the son of Mrs. Quest's friend. She is swept into her first sexual experience with a man she does not care about. Then, when her feelings of social responsibility and feelings about her own dignity begin to reassert themselves, she repudiates the superficial life she has been leading only to be drawn into marriage with Douglas Knowell, a civil service employee.

A Proper Marriage takes place in an atmosphere of war, counterbalanced by a theme of fertility: for much of the novel dramatizes Martha's pregnancy and the birth of Caroline. Martha seems unconsciously determined to ignore that she is pregnant until it is too late for an abortion; this time she is trapped by biological rather than social forces. Douglas enlists, and when he returns (discharged because of an ulcer), Martha can not avoid seeing him objectively and realizing that it has been a grave mistake to marry him. Other illusions have been crushed as well; the ideal of motherhood must make room for the harsh reality of the day-to-day tensions between mother and child. Meanwhile the colony has been flooded with members of the R.A.F., who give impetus to the socialist groups. Martha becomes involved in politics, which stir up the old ideals that have become buried by her comfortable life as the feudal mistress of a prosperous household with many black servants. She finally leaves Douglas and also her young daughter, rationalizing that she is setting Caroline free from the sort of influence that Martha has had to endure from her own mother.

In *A Ripple From the Storm* Martha is part of a small but active communist group. In this novel Lessing dramatizes the tensions among people in politics with the same skill she has up to then applied to social situations. Martha is caught up, like her friends, with the idealism of their group. The whole spectrum of Zambesian political life is surveyed. Martha comes into contact with the Social Democrat Party and Mrs. Van der Bylt, Jack Dobie, and Johnny Lindsay. Judge and Mrs. Maynard represent the conservative group in power. The judge uses his in office; his wife drops hints in "the right places" when she wishes something done. Both of them exercise their influence, for example, when they wish to get servicemen posted from the colony because of political activities or for private reasons. In keeping with the main concerns of this novel, Martha marries again, but this time from a sense of camaradarie. Anton Hesse, a German refugee, and one of the leaders of the communist group, has claimed her half against her will after initiating an affair. Anton's employer then tells him that the C.I.D. frowns upon him, an "enemy alien," having an affair with a British girl. He is given three choices: legalize the relationship with marriage, end it, or face losing his job and being sent to an internment camp. Martha marries Anton, assuming that it will be a temporary arrangement. The communist group gradually breaks up as members leave the colony or take on other interests instead.

The metaphor that describes *Landlocked* is Martha's dream of the house in which different aspects of herself are assigned to different rooms. She feels fragmented, and she has duties toward a wide variety of people who would have little in common if they were to meet: her mother and dying father, her political friends, and her personal friends such as Maisie. To Martha's discomfort, Anton assumes that they have a real marriage. Martha continues to feel empty and waits for the man she has always envisioned as finally completing her being. She meets Thomas Stern and has an affair with him, the first experience in her life that has had any real significance for her. Thomas eventually leaves to fight the British in Israel. When he returns, he works for the government deep in the bush trying to educate the natives in matters of hygiene and agriculture. He dies of blackwater fever. Meanwhile Martha waits for the necessary papers to arrive concerning her and Anton's citizenship so that they can be divorced and she can leave for England.

The Four-Gated City begins in 1950, when Martha is twenty-five-years old. She is in London. For several months she drifts throughout the city, changing her personality and name, staying with different people—Olive and Jimmy, who run a little cafe, and Stella, who lives by the docks. She is reluctant to take a job that would effectively put her in a certain social niche. During this period she has an affair with a fellow African, Jack, whose serious interest in life is his women friends. During her sexual experiences with Jack, Martha begins to have intimations of a psychic life beneath the level of consciousness, a perception she also experiences in long walks through the city when she has not had sufficient food and sleep.

She accepts a job as secretary to Mark Coldridge, business man and writer. Intending to leave soon, determined to avoid responsibilities, Martha is nevertheless drawn into a series of events that prevent her from leaving. Mark's brother, Colin, defects to Russia, and since Mark refuses to repudiate his brother, he is considered to be a communist. Colin's wife, Sally-Sarah, a Jewish refugee, commits suicide, leaving her young son Paul in Mark's care. These events are a prelude to a five-year period called "the bad time," coinciding with the Cold War. Mark is married to Lynda, who is mentally ill; they have a son, Francis, who comes home from school for holidays. Lynda and a friend from the hospital, Dorothy, take up residence at the Coldfield house in a basement apartment. (Lynda can manage to stay at home as long as she is not pressured into too much proximity with Mark.)

Martha, Lynda, and Mark are the nucleus of this household, which spreads wide to a large number of family members and friends, and it is through this group that the reader watches the political and social trends of the fifties, sixties, and seventies. Some important members of the group are Margaret Patten, Mark's mother, a Tory, famous for her parties and always managing to be surrounded with the people who are important on the contemporary scene. Her stepson, Graham, also has a knack for being in step with the times, and when television dominates the culture, he hosts a popular talk show. Phoebe, the ex-wife of Mark's brother Arthur, is a hard-working member of the Labour Party. None of the children of the Coldridge family (Paul, Francis, and Phoebe's daughters Gwen and Jill) carry on any of the ideals of their parents' generation. Francis goes into the theater; Paul has many business ventures of unusual kinds; Jill has children by men she scarcely knows, although she lives with Francis.

While the fates of the Coldridge family members mirror the state of society, Martha's own personal growth continues. Her mother comes to visit, causing Martha to break down and go for psychiatric help. As pointed out earlier, she explores her psyche and finally brings to completion her ideas about the nature of personality and society. Finally, the Coldridge house is to be sold by force to the government, to be torn down or made into offices.

Before this event takes place, the reader leaves the scene entirely. The point of view of the last sections of the novel has been partly Martha's and partly that of an omniscient narrator, jumping from group to group. In the Appendix the novel takes the form of letters and reports, informing of a catastrophe; there has been an accident with radioactive weapons and perhaps nerve gas, and large portions of the world have been destroyed in what Francis later calls the *Epoch of Destruction*. A letter from Francis to his daughter Amanda describes the years before the catastrophe: the citizens of Britain grew increasingly violent; the entire country was apparently mad. Francis and a group of acquaintances formed a commune, which he describes. Finally he tells how Martha and his mother, Lynda, gradually overcame his repugnance for the occult and gradually persuaded him that a catastrophe was imminent, perceived in advance by psychics. The Appendix includes notes written by Mark describing the horrors of the refugee camp he is in charge of. Martha's letter to Francis describes her experiences during the

catastrophe and the life she has since led with a group of sur-
vivors on the island of Pharos. This postcatastrophe world is for
the most part ridden with wars and authoritarian controls, and
many people are crippled or mutated by radioactivity. Yet on
Pharos are a number of children who seem to be possessed of a
superior consciousness; it is related that they are the first of a
new kind of man and that eventually everyone will be like
them.

Like all Lessing's characters, those in *Children of Violence* are
fragmented and victimized by the collective psyche. While
Lessing was writing the series she said, "I want to explain what
it is like to be a human being in a century when you open your
eyes on war and on human beings disliking other human beings."[5] Most of the characters are archetypal, important not so
much for their personal histories as what they show about broad
social patterns that Lessing wishes to expose. For example,
Marjorie stands for all intelligent women who give up their own
development for the sake of husband and children. One of the
most ardent members of the communist group, Marjorie
specializes in the problem of women's rights. Nevertheless,
swept along by convention, she marries the rather stodgy Colin
and has several children. Immersed in domesticity, her "growing point" blunted, she recognizes ironically that she is close to
a nervous breakdown because something in her has conspired
to put her in the very position she once lectured against.

It is only with the greatest effort that Martha has extricated
herself from such a position in *A Proper Marriage*, since so large
a part of her being is pulled toward the unconscious enactment
of the woman's role: "One of those warm, large, delightful,
maternal, humorous females she would be; undemanding, un-
possessive. One never met them, but, if she put her mind to it,
no doubt she could become one. She would lapse into it as into
the sea and let everything go. . . ."[6] Her critical mind eventually is able to cut through the illusions of motherhood: "What

one did not see, what everyone conspired to prevent one seeing, was the middle-aged woman who had done nothing but produce two or three commonplace and tedious citizens in a world that was already too full of them" (p. 534). But to isolate the problem is not to solve it:

> If she was to leave Douglas, for what way of living was she to leave? There's something so damned *vieux jeu*, she thought gloomily, in leaving like Nora, to live differently! Because we're not such fools any longer. We don't imagine that rushing off to earn one's living as a typist is going to make any difference. One is bound to fall in love with the junior partner, and the whole thing will begin all over again. (p. 535)

A contrary situation is dramatized by the good-natured Maisie, whose story shows how simple, conventional lives are wrecked by the times. Athen, the Greek, member of the communist group, points out justly that Maisie is not concerned about women's rights, because she still belongs to a simpler past. She would have been happy as a housewife; however, the war has ended that possibility. She loses two husbands in the war and then becomes pregnant by Binkie Maynard, the madcap son of Judge Maynard. Mr. Maynard cruelly prevents a marriage, and Andrew McGrew, one of the leaders of the communist group, marries Maisie to give her child a name. However, when Binkie is due back on leave, Andrew begins to be bothered that Maisie's child is not his. In conventional possessiveness, his blossoming love for her withers. This series of events permanently ends Maisie's faith in men. Instead of finding a warm relationship with a husband, she ends in a sordid way of life—attracting customers to a bar because of her casual sexuality—because it is work that will allow her to be close to her child. At the end of *Landlocked* Martha is pained by the changes in Maisie, her expression of "simpering watchfulness," but her fragmentation is expressed poignantly; her face still retains "an innocence that was still her deepest quality," and her two "white capable hands" seem to have a life of their own: "The hands knew that they were in the right, that they were good, that there was no need for them to listen to criticism."

Mrs. Van der Bylt represents one more view of twentieth-century women: the outstanding achiever who is fragmented because of what she must give up. A leading socialist who works tirelessly for the underprivileged, Mrs. Van der Bylt does so at the cost of her health and emotional life. Her husband is unsympathetic, and even as a bride she realized that her only recourse was to cut off emotion toward him—or let him dictate to her. Yet feeling responsible for him and the children, she is always on call to them. She works too hard and has constant backaches.

Nearly every character in *Children of Violence* is crippled because of being split. Even Athen Gouliamis, so single-minded in his idealism as to be called by Martha "a flame-like conscience for others" (*Landlocked* p. 303) is tragically fragmented because of deep shame for his love of certain pleasures—good wine and his cream colored suit. In a different world he would never question a delight in beauty and pleasure. As it is, he chooses death as a guerrilla fighter in Greece rather than give in to what he considers his least admirable side. Anton Hesse, Martha's second husband and one of the leaders of the group, is Athen's opposite. Jewish, his family have all died during the war; only one aunt is found alive. Gradually his materialism grows stronger through his association with the prosperous Forsters. He stays in Zambesia and marries Bettina Forster, even though he has waited for years to return to Germany and begin a political career. For Anton, the events of the war years are too strong for his idealism. Athen's situation is tragic; Anton's is a farce, as Martha's friend Jasmine tersely comments.

In *The Four-Gated City* one learns that in the war Jack found out the body could be trained to do anything: after his ship was destroyed, he forced himself to hang on to a piece of debris, hour after hour, holding a flap of shoulder flesh closed so that he would not bleed to death. Therefore, all of Jack's knowledge is in his body. Unchecked by reason, he eventually turns into a sadistic exploiter of women. Lynda Coldridge began life whole as a sensitive and charming young girl who could read minds and who was in touch with an inner, kind voice, which guided her. She is assumed to be ill (because she is different) and is subjected to cruel psychiatric treatment that plunges her permanently into a psychic hell similar to the one that Martha explores only briefly.

In *Martha Quest* Martha is a critical and intolerant young girl. As a mature woman she comes to see that individuals are not responsible for their weaknesses; society is at fault. Yet people are not children and should be responsible for the ills of society. Nevertheless, there is something inherent in man that nullifies individual strength and insight. Society inevitably becomes the blind beast that attacks new ideas. Mark writes a novel in which men are the prisoners of events, a situation that prevails in *Children of Violence*. Since unconscious actions frequently lead to violence (as it does in *The Grass is Singing* and " 'Leopard' George") the whole of the human race is trapped in repetitious patterns of violent behavior. And since each individual at the deepest level is part of the collective, he can not avoid being shaped by it. The following passage speaks not just for *Children of Violence* but for Lessing's work as a whole:

> The soul of the human race, that part of the mind which has no name, is not called Thomas and Martha, which holds the human race as frogspawn is held in jelly—that part of Martha and of Thomas was twisted and warped, was part of a twist and a damage—she could no more disassociate herself from the violence done her, than a tadpole can live out of water. Forty-odd million human beings had been murdered, deliberately or from carelessness, from lack of imagination; these people had been killed yesterday, in the last dozen years, they were dying now, as she stood

under the tree, and these deaths were marked on her soul. (*Land-locked*, p. 463)

It is this mass shadow that looms behind every individual story in *Children of Violence*.

Lessing is quite specific about why mankind can not control events: society as a whole has the same responses as an individual. When part of the mass psyche is repressed, the result is dangerous neurosis and violence. For example, according to Jung, Nazi atrocities against the Jews were an expression of the German national shadow. In *The Four-Gated City* Francis echoes this idea when he describes England just before the catastrophe, with its combination of a smooth-talking establishment and continual eruptions of violence. It is "like a man making a speech about civic virtues to a well-dressed audience; but he turns to reach for a glass of water on the platform table, and he has exposed a monkey's flamingly indecent bottom" (p. 568).

The idea of the mass shadow as described by Jung and used by Lessing is classic hubris modernized, and it is the story of Milton's Adam and of Faust. Although Jung does not pretend to understand the psyche, he feels that it is essential to recognize that something does exist outside the small, lighted area of ego-consciousness. During the Age of Science, the psyche has become synonomous with "what I know," and the result is "an inflation of consciousness that can apparently be checked only by the most terrible catastrophes to civilization"—man's "God-almightiness" expressed by an entire society and calling forth inevitable destruction.

When the fate of Europe carried it into a four years' war of stupendous horror—a war that no one wanted—hardly anyone asked who had caused the war and its continuation. No one realized that European man was possessed by something that robbed him of free choice. This state of unconscious possession will, no doubt, continue unchecked until at last European man becomes 'afraid of his God-almightiness.' But this is a change that can begin

only with individuals, since masses—as we know only too well—
are blind beasts.[7]

The problem, then, is collective, but the solution must be
individual, since according to Jung only an expression of individuality can counteract the blind pull of collective forces.

In *The Four-Gated City* one archetypal character sums up this
modern hubris: Jimmy Wood. Like Conrad's Professor in *The
Secret Agent*, with his bombs and his dreams of blowing up the
entire world, Jimmy is two-dimensional, not so much a person
as a force. A mechanical genius, Jimmy appears to be "some
sort of machine himself" (p. 164). He has no normal emotional
resonance and no ethics about the uses to which his machines
will be put. He is a robot that operates on a certain type of
energy (Mark's conversation) and when he fails to get enough
of it, he can not work.

Martha is excited to discover the large body of mystical literature that has been ignored by modern society; she finds there
an authentic note of vitality that has been missing from her own
life and from Western culture as a whole. Jimmy, too, reads this
literature (ironically, it is from him that Martha first gets it), but
what he takes from it are ideas devoid of life and feeling that he
uses for his machines and his science fiction novels. In this way
Jimmy is an illustration of contemporary society as a whole,
which may give curious, intellectual interest to esoteric themes
but is unable to endow them with the serious attention that
Lessing appears to feel that they require and deserve. Finally,
Jimmy makes a machine that provides human beings with extrasensory perception but which "burns out" their brains. The
source of his idea is from esoteric literature. Jimmy Wood
epitomizes Lessing's view of a society that has inflated reason
and cleverness to a dangerous degree and that makes gods out
of machines instead of trying to discover with humility what in
man may be truly godlike.

When catastrophe strikes in *The Four-Gated City*, it seems to be the logical conclusion of the Jimmy Wood mentality: man's ingenuity, his inflated consciousness, overcomes humane emotion and humility, and the mass shadow engulfs society completely.

Although a deep psychic split is the central problem, *Children of Violence* shows that society is difficult to change because of the autonomy of collective convictions—what Jung calls "the brute force of collective consciousness and the mass psyche that goes with it." When a person identifies with one of the current isms, he releases a menacing power; most vulnerable are those who have least access to their instincts, their interior selves.[8] This mechanism of convention makes people like wild game automatically following their well-known runways. But when new conditions arise, "panic seizes the human being who has been held unconscious by routine, much as it seizes an animal, and with equally unpredictable results."[9]

Such is the society of *Children of Violence,* and one of Lessing's chief interests here is to dramatize the power of collective consciousness. One example is racism. Martha is deeply disturbed by the fate of the black man in Africa, but few white Africans question the situation. Mrs. Quest's treatment of Martha's servants in *A Proper Marriage* is typical of the white colonial. While Martha feels guilty about an arrangement that forces her household staff to take orders from her (especially her dignified cook, who is more than twice her age) and to work for ridiculously low wages, Mrs. Quest storms into the Knowell household at regular intervals to manage "properly." She warns Martha that the nursemaid may give Caroline diseases by sleeping in her room, rages against the child's sitting on the lap of the garden boy, accuses the cook of stealing, and points out all the evidences of poor housekeeping. Her attitude is that the blacks are filthy beasts who must be kept under control. This is the prevailing attitude among white people in Zambesia. It is not until *The Four-Gated City,* when Mrs. Quest is an old woman, that for the first time in her life she sees a black as a human being. The lonely old woman then strikes up a touching relationship with young Steven, who works in the home of friends she is visiting. Many of the colonials whom Lessing portrays live their entire lives without cutting through the collective passion of racism to reach an individual emotional response. [10]

Race prejudice divides the Social Democratic Party for which Mrs. Van der Bylt works so hard. Her group wishes to include the blacks; the white labor division does not. As a result, the party splits in two and the reactionary conservatives remain in power. Because they are caught in the collective emotion of racism, the liberals fail to make any social reforms. The old patterns of injustice go on.

Like the wild beasts of Jung's analogy, the white population panics when its feudal society is threatened even in small ways. In the memorable strike episode in *Landlocked*, the white males arm themselves in a foolish overreaction to the blacks' orderly move for higher wages. Mobs attack innocent lone natives. All the blacks (not just the strikers) are moved onto the location and kept there, ensuring, as Johnny Lindsay points out, that every black man, woman, and child gets a course in how to organize a strike, and if he tries to run away, is brought back to make sure he does not miss a lesson.

Some people make use of collective emotion in dealing with others. Martha goes to Dr. Stern when she begins thinking about leaving Douglas, and he soothes her with the belief that she is simply going through one of the moods that affect all women at certain times, "playing her like a fish on a line" (*A Proper Marriage*, p. 531). During her pregnancy and after childbirth, it is indeed the case that there are certain psychological and physiological stages that seem fixed; Alice has her baby shortly before Martha, who watches the two of them go through apparently inevitable phases. However, Martha is convinced

that to continue living as if every emotional reaction is a meaningless phase, is to ignore important truths:

> She could not bear to think of the *everyone*, the *we* and the *all*. So
> everyone had moods in which they ran off to the doctor, that
> archpriest, who gave them bottles of tonic and assured them they
> were exactly like everyone else? They went for a holiday, then
> they began another baby and were perfectly happy? All the same,
> she said to herself, it is the mood which is the truth, and the other a
> lie. (pp. 533–34)

The important thing is to distinguish between private and
collective emotion. Mrs. Quest with Steven is responding from
her own instincts, and so is Martha when she sees her marriage
and her life are dull. To be swept along by mass reactions
results in the monster: repetition. Only emotion from the heart
leads to correct relations, and only if that emotion has escaped
the "twist and damage" that Lessing sees at the heart of modern society.

The Four-Gated City dramatizes the collective emotions that
sweep through society from the fifties to the seventies: the
Cold War era with its suspicion, anarchy, and nihilism; the
protests and peace marches of the sixties, and the uncontrolla-
ble wars; later, the return to interest in the arts and food,
clothes, and decor—a superficial gaiety that masks a general
neurosis and corruption. The Coldridge household mirrors society's changing moods. The members are ostracized during
the Cold War because of Colin Coldridge's defection to Russia.
Later the house is a center for anyone with a social cause. After
1965, Lynda and Martha become hostesses, and Lynda is a
great success. Significantly, her bizarre behavior scarcely attracts attention, and the white gloves that conceal tortured,
chewed nails become a gay social joke. Finally, a new mood is
hinted. Margaret Patten, Mark's mother, who has an innate
sense of the cultural climate, can be counted on as a reliable
prophet of social trends, and the important people are always

on her guest lists. At the end of the novel, her guests all have a definite fascist leaning, sign of a new repressive government waiting in the wings.

However, the narrator informs that the futile cry for law and order will be only the shadow side of a completely disintegrated society, described in the Appendix by Francis: "The human race had driven itself mad" (p. 576). Lessing's image for the state of things is television, which blends pictures of people dying with food commercials, all in one bland unity, "yet composed of the extremes of nastiness in a frenzy of dislocation, disconnection" (p. 446). The Coldridge home, once a unity, becomes a metaphor for a disintegrating society:

> All the house was like this, nothing obviously breaking or peeling, but everywhere was shoddiness and shabbiness, and—this was the point—there seemed to be no centre in the house, nothing to hold it together (as there had been once when it was a real family house?). It was all a mass of small separate things, surfaces, shapes, all needing different attention, different kinds of repair. . . . This was the real truth of what went on not only here but everywhere: everything declined and frayed and came to pieces in one's hands . . . a mass of fragments, like a smashed mirror. (pp. 336–37)

The final disintegration is symbolized by the enforced sale of the house to the government. From this time the family will be scattered without even their home as a central focus.

In the Appendix the reader learns about a world that is divided almost to the point of extinction. Francis and Mark refer to wars and authoritarian controls. There is no communication between large areas of Asia. Although the centers of power have changed, old patterns exist more rigidly than before the catastrophe. Mark's refugee camp is hell on earth with its grotesque mutations and plagues, and it reflects conditions that exist all over. In Martha's letter is a vision of a world that is at one point hovering on the edge of final destruction, completely split into good and evil.

During that year we hit the depths of our fear, a lowering depression which made it hard for us not to simply walk into that deadly sea and let ourselves drown there. But it was also during that year when we became aware of a sweet high loveliness somewhere, like a flute played only just within hearing. We all felt it. We talked about it, thinking it was a sign that we must be dying. It was as if all the air was washed with a bright promise. Of what? Love? Joy? It was as if the face of the world's horror could be turned around to show the smile of an angel. (p. 604)

Society has headed into its tailspin because of the power of collective convictions and of the mass shadow, but at some point it is evident that there is an unconscious death wish at work. Martha observes that suddenly nothing seems to work any more. Dorothy, Lynda's friend, keeps a journal with long entries describing the incompetence of workmen who come to make repairs on the house. Martha notes that American astronauts died because of the failure of a piece of equipment no more complicated than an electrical switch. In the Appendix Francis picks up this motif again: "an electrician splicing a wire unconsciously cursed it out of a kind of hatred for what it stood for; it soon broke and burned out fuses and wiring. He did not know what he had done" (p. 569).

This idea of an unconscious suicidal force at work in society is expressed by George Steiner in his study of contemporary culture, *In Bluebeard's Castle*. Steiner claims that from 1830 onward, in response to the horrors of industrialization, a "counterdream" appears: "the vision of the city laid waste." It shows up, for example, in an odd school of painting in which Vandals and Huns overrun modern cities. London, Paris, and Berlin are depicted in ruins, "famous landmarks burnt, eviscerated, or located in a weird emptiness among charred stumps and dead water."[11] Steiner believes that there is a connection between these romantic fantasies and Warsaw and Dresden, that the horrors of World War II were partly a result of wish fulfillment. Such is the mad society of *The Four-Gated City*, racing toward its own half-willed destruction, borne along on the energy of collective thought that is multiplied in power by the unconscious psychic contents buried there.

Thomas Stern is one of Lessing's most important and memorable characters. Most of the characters in *Children of Violence* represent broad social forces. However, Thomas plays an even larger role: his life mirrors the fate of society as a whole. He is a prophetic character in two ways, foreshadowing both the coming fragmentation and death of established culture and also the possibility of rebirth.

In chapter two I have described the way Thomas is consumed by his shadow. Unlike Anna, who finally recognizes the violence within her and comes to terms with it, Thomas is unable to do so and is destroyed. In Thomas's "last testament" there is a significant fable: "Once there was a man who travelled to a distant country. When he got there, the enemy he had fled from was waiting for him. Although he had proved the usefulness of travelling, he went to yet another country. No, his enemy was *not* there. . . . So he killed himself" (*Landlocked*, p. 534).

This strange tale describes Thomas's own last years. In going to Israel to fight, Thomas is really trying to escape the sardonic anger and nihilism that, as Martha sees later, (*Four-Gated City*, p. 176) are his real enemies. They have surfaced because of the concentration camps and become enflamed by encountering Sergeant Tressel, his old rival from the war days, who epitomizes for Thomas the way carelessness and lack of imagination cause much of the misery in life. To get relief from his real emotions, Thomas becomes swept up in a collective one, the fight for Israel; but the Israeli cause is Thomas's leopard, a projection. As Martha wryly observes, "In Israel a British soldier would fall dead . . . in Sergeant Tressel's place" (p. 462). There are no Sergeant Tressels in the bush, where Thomas goes to help African natives; no longer buoyed up by collective emotion, he withdraws into himself and goes indifferently to his death. When Martha hears that he has died of blackwater fever, she thinks, "Well, of course! . . . what else had he been wanting but to die, futilely, away from his own people, and among strangers" (p. 512). Thomas, the peasant, like society itself, has been forced from rootedness; becomes embroiled in fragmentation and its inevitable result, violence; is consumed by his own shadow; and is finally destroyed, half-suicide, half-victim.

Nevertheless, Thomas is one of Lessing's few visionary characters. He gains stature partly by means of a dream in which Martha sees him going to his death. The Christian parallels are quite plain: Thomas is lean, dark, and Semitic. The atmosphere is medieval, and he is about to be hanged on a rough wooden scaffold by a group of churchmen. And as has been seen, Thomas's papers are his "last testament." Thomas is a prophet of a new age even as he is a victim of the old. The lessons of his Rabbi, which he repeats to Martha, outline the crucial problem for society, the need for a total change of consciousness. Before, mankind was rooted, was born, grew up, married, and died under one tree. But today the view of the universe has expanded, and humanity must see itself as part of a larger whole: "He said it was evolution, that the next thing for man was to feel the stars and their times and their spaces. Otherwise he was a maggot in dirt" (*Landlocked*, p. 460). Thomas's warnings look ahead to *The Four-Gated City:* Lynda Coldridge, born with unusual extrasensory powers, is an evolutionary advance, a forerunner of the children of Pharos, who will eventually transform the world.

"Vermin! Vermin! We are all vermin!" scrawls Thomas in crude red letters across his last testament. Able to see further than most, Thomas can not cope with his vision. Unlike Anna, who finally resurrects a saving idealism with which to combat joy-in-destruction, Thomas simply goes under. Martha eventually reaches the place Thomas has been, in the company of the self-hater, the mass shadow, who almost destroys her.

Most of Lessing's novels show their protagonists struggling to keep themselves together in a disintegrating world. Anna's story is played out against a fragmented society. *The Summer before the Dark* opens in sophisticated, contemporary London collapsed into the primitive: because of a power strike, Kate Brown is struggling to prepare afternoon tea over a twig fire. Jack Orkney discovers his son's friends in the attic cooking over a paraffin stove, the fuel heedlessly placed near the flame. This incident seems to be an analogy for society: at any moment the conflagration could begin. In all the novels, concerned citizens work to alleviate hunger, stop war, put an end to brutality—all to no avail. Everything and everybody is breaking up.

Speaking about the contemporary scene, Lessing could be describing *Children of Violence:* "I feel as if the Bomb has gone off inside myself, and in people around me. That's what I mean by the cracking up. It's as if the structure of the mind is being battered from inside. Some terrible new thing is happening. Maybe it'll be marvelous. Who knows? Today it's hard to distinguish between the marvelous and the terrible."[12]

Children of Violence, Lessing's epic view of society, most clearly dramatizes the rigid structure of twentieth-century culture and the upheavals that are breaking it up. Since Lessing believes that *The Four-Gated City* is prophetic, one can say that she believes mankind is in a period of transition; but the new is not to emerge naturally and peacefully from what has gone before. For Lessing, as for Yeats, the "rough beast" is inevitable. Although she experiments with the idea of conscious evolution, a willed mutation, it is the pattern of the phoenix that carries most authority in her work: the new rising from the ashes of the old.

5

The Ideal City

And the four gates of Los surround the universe within and
Without, & whatever is visible in the vegetable earth, the same
Is visible in the mundane shell (reversed in mountain and vale).
—William Blake, *Jerusalem* 72, 11. 45–47.

Although at first glance there would seem to be little connection between an apparently realistic modern novelist and one of
the great visionary poets, Doris Lessing and William Blake are
surprisingly similar in outlook, however different in expression.
And both, in their use of the image of the city, are part of a long
tradition, which includes Saint Augustine's civitas dei and
civitas terrena, the city of faith and the city of disbelief; Paul
Bunyon's Celestial City and City of Destruction in *Pilgrim's
Progress;* and of course the New Jerusalem of the Apocalypse.[1]
In the twentieth century both cities appear in the work of
Aldous Huxley: *Brave New World* pictures a civitas terrena of
the future, in which the spirit is completely in the service of a
totalitarian government; *Island* portrays his civitas dei; in Pala,
Western science and Eastern mysticism are grafted together to
form a new, whole society.

It will be evident that this tradition refers not to cities of
brick and stone, but of the spirit: mankind's hope—perhaps

potential—set off against the poverty of his reality; harmony as opposed to despair. It would seem that in her title *The Four-Gated City*, Lessing has deliberately invoked Blake, whose Jerusalem stands both for the integrated man and the perfected society—possible only when mankind is freed from the power of faulty reason and reunited with imagination. Blake's Albion—England—is sleeping, fallen man, comparable to the city of Lessing's fiction. Jerusalem—the City—is mankind's Emanation (part of the self then separated), inspiration, and "Divine Vision."[2] Los symbolizes poetic imagination, the powers of prophecy and creativity that can bring Jerusalem into being by reuniting Albion with his Emanation. But first mankind must be freed from his constricted vision, his specter:

> The spectre is the reasoning power in man, & when separated
> From imagination, and closing itself as in steel, in a ratio
> Of the things of memory, it thence frames laws & moralities
> To destroy Imagination, the Divine Body, by martyrdoms & Wars.[3]

Albion's final awakening is brought about by four flaming arrows that finally annihilate his specter. Afterward, harmony reigns: "And every man stood four-fold; each four faces had" (*Jerusalem*, 98, 1. 12). Both Lessing and Blake wish to annihilate the single vision of rational thought, waken mankind from its sleep, and bring into being the harmonious fourfold individual and the City. Jerusalem—city of Peace—is its symbol.

Although the tradition of the City stands behind all of Lessing's novels as a mute ideal of personal and social harmony, its image is most explicitly developed in *Children of Violence*, growing and changing with Martha's development, and with it, the nature of the creative imagination required to bring it into being, essentially a perception of the unity of all things.

Gradually, over the course of the series, Lessing reveals the two cities on increasingly deep levels. For example, Martha's early experiences are very similar to her mature ones; even in

Martha Quest is seen the shape of the warlike society with its martyred inhabitants, the mystical vision necessary to counteract it, and the ideal City that Martha longs for. Martha will return again and again to much the same experiences, understanding them better each time, like a muffled melody that becomes clearer with each playing. Lessing duplicates a familiar pattern of knowledge with this technique, since much wisdom is simply knowing better things one has always half-known. The principle is especially well known in psychiatry, when a good analyst essentially helps people understand more clearly problems they have sensed but not fully realized.

The motif of the City appears first in *Martha Quest*. Martha, inexperienced and idealistic, often dreams of a noble city, harmoniously designed, with "grave and beautiful" citizens of all colors. "She could have drawn a plan of that city, from the central marketplace to the four gates." Outside one of the gates stand her parents and almost everyone she knows, "forever excluded from the golden city because of their pettiness of vision and small understanding" (p. 21). There is both truth and irony in Martha's dreams. Humanity is indeed excluded from the City because of pettiness and limited understanding (a fact that is a central theme of the series); however, Martha herself shares these weaknesses, something she has no way of knowing. Her own intolerance is signified by the role she imagines for herself—sternly turning away even her own parents.

In its form, Martha's city has many of the same characteristics as her mature vision, years later; for example, she has hit on the mandala shape, symbol of wholeness, and on one level she recognizes that there should be no divisions among people—black, white, and brown will mingle happily. However, these similarities merely underscore the difference between a rational conception such as this and a vision based on true understanding, which taps deep levels of the psyche. Only when Martha approaches her own integration will she be able to perceive clearly the true nature of the City and what it requires.

Her first stirrings of nonrational perception, necessary to balance reason, occur spontaneously and are "the gift of her solitary childhood on the veld" (p. 210). They are intimately connected with the African landscape but move beyond it to a place outside of time and ordinary space, where there is some universal force that she fails to understand:

> There was certainly a definite point at which the thing began. It was not; then it was suddenly inescapable, and nothing could have frightened it away. There was a slow integration, during which she, and the little animals, and the moving grasses, and the sunwarmed trees, and the slopes of shivering silvery mealies, and the great dome of blue light overhead, and the stones of earth under her feet, became one, shuddering together in a dissolution of dancing atoms. She felt the rivers under the ground forcing themselves painfully along her veins, swelling them out in an unbearable pressure; her flesh was the earth, and suffered growth like a ferment; and her eyes stared, fixed like the eye of the sun. Not for one second longer (if the terms for time apply) could she have borne it; but then, with a sudden movement forwards and out, the whole process stopped; and *that* was "the moment" which it was impossible to remember afterwards. For during that space of time (which was timeless) she understood quite finally her smallness, the unimportance of humanity. In her ears was an inchoate grinding, the great wheels of movement, and it was inhuman, like the blundering rocking movement of a bullock cart; and no part of that sound was Martha's voice. Yet she was part of it, reluctantly allowed to participate, though on terms—but what terms? For that moment, while space and time . . . kneaded her flesh, she knew futility; that is, what was futile was her own idea of herself and her place in the chaos of matter. What was demanded of her was that she should accept something quite different; it was as if something new was demanding conception, with her flesh as host; as if there were a necessity, which she must bring herself to accept, that she should allow herself to dissolve and be formed by that necessity. (pp. 62–63)

Martha's illumination fits Evelyn Underhill's description of the basic mystical experience:

> In mysticism the will is united with the emotions in an impassioned desire to transcend the sense-world, in order that the self may be joined by love to the one eternal and ultimate Object of love;

whose existence is intuitively perceived by that which we called the soul, but now find it easier to refer to as the "cosmic" or "transcendental" sense. This is the poetic and religious temperament acting on the plane of reality.[4]

Although Martha does not understand these moments of mystical insight, she does take from them a sense of value in some obscure way. They provide her with an inner tuning fork; in her reading she is guided by what rings true with it. Later she sees that the moments on the veld have been "her lodestone, even her conscience" (p. 210). However, the outstanding emotion has been pain, being forced to admit her insignificance and at the same time make the enormous effort of a new understanding. These events foreshadow Thomas's "star-consciousness" in *Landlocked*, which insists that until man can understand his position in the scheme of things he is a "maggot in dirt." They also look ahead to the agonizing mental explorations that Martha will eventually make. But chiefly they signal to Martha a type of understanding different from rational perception, the specter that in Blake's philosophy, and also Lessing's, "frames laws & moralities/ To destroy Imagination, the Divine Body, by martyrdoms & Wars."

Martha's lodestone moments are appropriately named, for they exert a magnetic force, pushing her toward growth and understanding as she makes her way among the "laws and moralities" of Zambesian society. However, as a girl her desire for security and happiness always works against her integrity: "Draping myself like a silly, clinging vine on anything that sounds strong," she criticizes herself justly at one point (*Ripple from the Storm*, p. 101). Nevertheless, she has not the strength of vision to resist, but allies herself to one illusion after another: society's "official" view of marriage and motherhood, the illusion that communism will lead to justice and equality, the belief that England is without corruption, the romantic dream that a man can complete her and give her contentment.

In every case, Martha can not get beneath the illusion until she has thrown herself into the whole experience; and she can not escape it until some outstanding event sparks sufficient energy. For example, Martha is aware of her dissatisfaction with the shallow lives of the Sports Club crowd, but it takes a particularly offensive incident to finally break with it. Perry forces a native waiter to perform a shuffling war dance inside a circle of mocking young people, who have been singing, "Hold him *down*, the Zulu warrior." After a fight about racism with Donovan, who has been her constant escort at the club, Martha flounces into the house saying, "that's over. I'm finished with *that*" (*Martha Quest*, p. 218), meaning the Sports Club and its values.

However, nothing prevents her from becoming hypnotized by another illusion. Meeting Douglas Knowell, she sees him as a sober young man deeply concerned about social issues—all because he reads *The New Republic*. Impetuously she agrees to marry him, borne along on his assumption that because they have a sexual encounter, they have a claim on each other. At the point of changing her mind, Martha finds that all their friends are preparing to celebrate, and she does not have the courage to call off the wedding.

Characteristically, Martha finally has the courage to leave her safe, comfortable, and stultifying married life only because another illusion glimmers in the distance—the ideals of the active socialist groups, which have gained force from members of the R.A.F. who are stationed in the area. A romance with one of these young men provides the emotional spark necessary to bring Martha's relationship with Douglas to a crisis. When a communist group splits off from the main organization, Martha is part of it, certain that people like themselves, following in the path of Russia, will save the world. Martha's political activities engross her until their futility begins to become apparent. The final blow is word from Russia describing the truth of

Stalinism. However, by then Martha's group has disintegrated. At the end of *Landlocked* Martha, Marjorie, and Jasmine attend a meeting of a new group of communists. The illusions are the same that Martha and her friends once held; even the leaders are from the same mold as people they had known. The wheel of repetition continues to turn.

In the first three novels the focus of attention is predominantly on institutions and groups: marriage, the nuclear family, institutionalized childbearing, the social roles of women, the civil service of a white-dominated colonial country, and conservative, liberal, and radical political groups. When individuals are dramatized, they tend to be significant because of their connection to such collective forms, and Martha's experiences serve to dig beneath the superficial patterns toward an understanding of the reality beneath.

There is a subtle change of emphasis in *Landlocked*. From this point the focus is turned toward relationships that are independent of social groups or forms, dramatizing the inevitable failure of loving relationships in a world where everyone is twisted and damaged. When characters have a broad significance, they are attached to large philosophic trends rather than institutions. In this way, as pointed out earlier, Jimmy Wood epitomizes the machinelike mind of a technological society and Thomas dramatizes the fragmentation and suicide of an entire society.

In *Landlocked* is shown the twisted relationship between Maisie and the Maynards, who bully the girl, hoping to take away her daughter, Rita, their granddaughter. Ironically, Mr. Maynard has earlier callously prevented a marriage between Maisie and his son Binkie. And even though Maisie loves her daughter, the manner of her life keeps her from giving the child proper care.

Martha is sickened by events in her parents' home. The Quests have moved from the farm into town, and Mr. Quest has been slowly dying for two years. In one particularly terrible scene, Martha sees her father—who has never really lived—clutching greedily the arm of vivacious little Caroline. "It's my arm!" he insists, grasping not so much the child as life itself. Mrs. Quest cruelly forgets to tell Martha that her daughter is at the house, forcing Martha to come in contact with Caroline. On one occasion, the little girl realizes—perhaps unconsciously—that Martha is her real mother. She sticks out her tongue at "Aunt Matty" and runs from the room. Lessing implies through these unfortunate relationships that no individual has the strength to rise above the twisted society that molds every life. An anomaly is Johnny Lindsay of *Landlocked*. Mrs. Van der Bylt describes him as "naturally good" (p. 475). Despite ill health caused by the mines where he worked as a young man, he tirelessly devotes his life to others. Also, in their outstanding relationship, Martha and Thomas briefly rise above destructive forces, and with Thomas in the shed that they call their home, Martha temporarily finds a shelter and a center. In the entire five volumes, theirs is the only powerful, reciprocal loving relationship, and it is the turning point of Martha's life. However, it is a love that is doomed because of the violent forces that Lessing dramatizes at the heart of society.

In *The Four-Gated City* there is another shift of emphasis. Having analyzed institutions and personal relationships, Lessing turns her attention to society as the organism bent on its own destruction. Martha's growing perception allows her (and the reader) to witness the disintegration and clearly see the psychic forces that create such a situation. Significantly, Martha has outgrown her need to hang onto a social group or ideal or to look for completion in another person. In her first months in London she purposefully sheds her identity, trying on different roles and living with different social classes, unwilling to settle permanently in one place. When she does so, in the Coldridge household, it is because she is needed, not because she wishes security or is enticed by an ideal. She stays because events take such a turn when Colin defects and his wife commits suicide that only she can hold things together. It is a mature and realistic acceptance of responsibility, not imposed by some collective emotion or biological instinct but accepted freely.

Martha is able to pick her way through the "martyrdoms & Wars" of society because the fragmentation of the city is from time to time counter-balanced by her experiences of unity, similar to her early lodestone moments on the veld. Always they represent a freedom from structure that is impossible in daily life. Taking Douglas across the open veld to meet her parents, she is exhilarated by a fleeting sense of freedom: "How terrible that it must always be the town or the farm; how terrible this decision, always one thing or the other, and the exquisite flight between them so short, so fatally limited . . ." (*Martha Quest*, p. 240). And always these experiences imply the mystical union between the one and the many, the world in a grain of sand. In *Landlocked*, Martha and Jack Dobie drive to Thomas's farm: "And the empty space not only contained her and Jack, two tiny antlike figures, she contained the space—she was the great bell of space, and through it crawled little creatures, among them, herself" (p. 429).

During the incident in which Martha and Alice drive to the veld in the rain and immerse themselves in the red, muddy water of the potholes, Martha is exhilarated and temporarily armed against the inanity of her marriage, the life of the city. For a moment she actually has a place in the veld, the fertility of her own belly mirroring the fecundity around her. The creatures that come to her attention are amphibious: a water snake, a snail, and a frog. They live in two elements, and so for the moment does Martha—and not just water and air: she has slipped into the unified, nonrational element of nature. However, such moments can only be rare and transitory; when the blinding rainstorm stops, the two women are naked and unprotected, getting back to the car only moments before a gang of workmen files by—a sharp reminder that consciousness has evicted mankind from the unconscious Eden of nature.

If the veld teaches lessons of unity, it also imparts knowledge of separateness and struggle. Martha perceives it from the time she is young:

> it was as if the principle of separateness was bred from the very soil, the sky, the driving sun; as if the inchoate vastness of the universe, always insistent in the enormous unshrouded skies, the enormous mountain-girt horizons, so that one might never, not for a moment, forget the inhuman, relentless struggle of soil and water and light, bred a fever of self-assertion in its children, like a band of explorers lost in a desert, quarreling in an ecstasy of fear over their direction, when nothing but a sober mutual trust could save them. (*Martha Quest*, p. 57)

In later years Martha gets a clearer idea of this struggle and her part in it. In an important episode in *A Ripple from the Storm*, Martha has a series of dreams during an illness. In an old mine pit, dug by slaves under the whip of a white overseer, she sees what first appears to be a rock but is actually a giant lizard that has been imprisoned for "a thousand ages." It is alive, "steadily regarding her with a sullen and patient query. It was a scaly ancient eye, filmed over with mine dust, a sorrowful eye. It's alive, she thought. It's alive after so many centuries. And it will take centuries more to die. Perhaps I can dig it out" (p. 95). Next she dreams of the cold, misty shore of England, "the chilly shallow shores of nostalgia, where no responsibility existed" (p. 97). She senses that there is a danger in not connecting the two dreams. In a third one, Martha is responsible for stemming the flood of violence and terror in entire countries, but in carrying out her duty in one place she forgets it elsewhere.

These dreams are an economical picture of the themes of the city and the veld. The ancient lizard is somehow connected with slavery and brutality; nevertheless, he is thoroughly embedded in the age-old rock. Exposed by the gold mine, his eyes filmed with dust, he is not so much menacing as patient, sorrowful, and universal. The lizard seems to represent the state of nature that is embodied in the African veld: the unthinking violence and brutality enacted by instinctual nature for survival—and continued by man in his hatred and violence toward others. The lizard is the cold necessity that Charles Watkins perceives from the crystal.

Martha is torn by two feelings: it is right and natural that the lizard should be there, yet she would like to get him out. To dream of escape to England is a danger; she must face up to her responsibility. As the later novels show, this challenge is twofold—both to help others and to try to help form the all-encompassing consciousness that will free man from the repetitive, instinctive violence in which he is trapped. As part of creation, humanity is inevitably moved by the forces of necessity; however, he has the potential to stop enacting gratuitous violence on others.

The key to harmony lies with the expansion of consciousness. It is in *Landlocked* that Martha begins to show a more profound knowledge that reaches below the level of rational thought, something more than the spontaneous lodestone moments. It is evident partly in her increased powers of intuition and sensitivity to the messages of her body. A certain tightening of the flesh when Joss announces his departure from town signals to Martha her disappointment, her knowledge that unconsciously she is preparing to have an affair. When the first book about the truth of Stalin becomes available, Martha feels that it is true: "One has an instinct one trusts, yes . . . " (p. 486). When she begins her affair with Thomas, she learns from the reactions of her body that something within her opposes her infidelity to Anton, even if she has never considered theirs a real marriage. (Her stomach and bladder respond nervously, and she realizes from Anton's sexual advances to her that she is

unconsciously sending seductive messages to him out of guilt.)
Before beginning her relationship with Thomas, she intuits
that it will be "more serious than anything yet in her life,"
although she has no idea in what way (p. 353). In *The Four-
Gated City* this intuition develops into extrasensory perception,
which allows her to overhear some of the thoughts of people
around her. At the end, from Pharos, she is able to communicate through extrasensory means with certain people, such as a
Canadian trapper.

However, the turning point for Martha in her gradual development is her affair with Thomas. Like the moments on the
veld, it creates for her an ecstatic yet painful sense of unity. For
example, on one occasion they stand by an open window in their
shed during a storm, washed in orange and green light, splat-
tered by rain, surrounded by liquid birdsong:

> They laughed and rubbed the freezing water from the sky over
> each other's shoulders and breasts. They felt as if they might never
> see each other again after this afternoon, and that while they
> touched each other, kissed—they held in that moment everything
> the other was, had been, ever could be. They felt half savage with
> the pain of loss. (p. 372)

Sex with Thomas brings to Martha profound psychic knowledge. In *The Four-Gated City* Martha describes her sexual experiences with Jack as a channeling of energy, normally divided, that connects her to "the dynamo, the center of her
life," from where she has visions of good and evil. Sex with
Thomas appears to have a similar power:

> Perhaps, when Thomas and she touched each other, in the touch
> cried out the murdered flesh of the millions of Europe—the squan-
> dered flesh was having its revenge, it cried out through the two
> little creatures who were fitted for much smaller loves, the touch
> only of a hand on a shoulder, simple hungers, and the kindness of
> sleep. Instead—it was much too painful, and they had to separate.
> (*Landlocked*, p. 428)

The experience profoundly influences both Martha and Thomas. Consumed by the shadow side of this other world and his own nature, Thomas goes steadily to his death. Martha, aware after that of the hidden world of the psyche, never again longs for love and security as she has previously done. From that time, her chief goal is knowledge, which she achieves in *The Four-Gated City* on ever deeper levels.

The image of the ideal changed with Martha's new knowledge, reappears in part one of *The Four-Gated City* in a much more mature version than in *Martha Quest*. During "the bad time," Martha is drawn to the idea of the mythical city of legend and fable; Mark becomes interested and together they plan one. Excited by the idea, Mark turns it into a short story and then a novel, *A City in the Desert*. Beautiful and harmonious like the city of Martha's childhood dream, this city has two important new features. The first is its lack of categories: although everyone has a place and a function, there is nothing static about the pattern. The buildings are used for a variety of activities; there are no set functions for church or marketplace. Second, there is an undefined "lode-place or nodal point," perhaps embodied in the gardeners or perhaps in a place. An outer city grows up around the inner city, but it is riven by competition and has specific groups, such as a hierarchy of priests. No one here seems to have the secret that once led to harmony, order, and joy. When an envoy to the inner city asks to buy it, the answer is that "the secret could not be sold, or taken: it could only be earned, or accepted as a gift" (p. 135). Finally the inner city is destroyed by the outer one, and this is the beginning of written history.

Martha and Mark's story invites several interpretations. The inner city represents wholeness, innocence, harmony—not only in its beauty and order but in its mandala shape: four roads lead into it, intercepting a series of arc-shaped streets. Certainly this is a re-creation of the lost Golden Age; and its destruction by the warlike outer city suggests wholeness lost through the divisions of modern thought and the development of the alienated ego. The City can also be seen as a Utopia, a model for a time when the divisions of contemporary society may be overcome.

But as the story progresses, the secret that could not be sold or taken becomes increasingly important. In Martha's childhood dream, people are excluded from the City because they are not worthy; and she herself guards the door. Here, also, people are excluded, but because of their own inability. None of the outsiders is able to perceive the secret; looting and killing, the interlopers merely destroy the special quality of the original city, and the secret then becomes petrified into a branch of history held by priests.

This part of the story bears a strong imprint of Sufism, with its many stories of lost or hidden knowledge—held by superior gardeners or boat builders, for instance; lacking it, the citizens of town or country suffer various hardships. Speaking of Sufism as a contemporary mode of perception, Idries Shah in *The Sufis* frequently refers to the secret that protects itself—presumably because those who do perceive it have the wisdom not to adulterate or misinterpret it.

Keeping in mind these aspects of Sufism and the importance of it to Lessing's later work, one has the final impression that Martha and Mark's ideal City is not so much a Utopian dream as a state of mind, an interpretation reinforced by Mark's later addition—that the original city is built in the middle of the desert, the roads leading to it beginning in the sand, out of nowhere. The effect of this passage is a coming-to-consciousness, as the traveler moves from the sterility of the desert to the mandala-shaped city:

> Travellers coming in from the desert found it hard to say when the exact moment was when their feet found the right road. Then trees appeared, on either side; then in the distance, the first houses of the city. For leagues of hot dusty travelling, a silent yellow sand,

and then the white city, with its sharp black shadow and its shaded
gardens, and over it, a blue sky where birds wheeled, into which
rose domes and spires and the sounds of voices. (p. 135)

From intuition to sharp vision: the movement of this final
paragraph describing the City leaves one with the sense of a
completed pilgrimage, the same pattern to be found in the first
half of *Briefing for a Descent into Hell* and in *The Summer before the
Dark*, the two novels that most show the shift in mood evident
in Lessing's work since her study of Sufism. However, *A City in
the Desert* is a high point of vision in what is otherwise an almost
unrelievedly pessimistic work, since all attempts at Utopia,
either personal or social, are abortive.

It is characteristic that in imagining the City in the desert,
Martha comes spontaneously upon themes that she later
explores intellectually. The secret that can not be sold or taken
looks back to Martha's visionary moments on the veld and her
increasing powers of intuition. It looks ahead to her discovery
of mystical literature: yoga, Zoroastrianism, esoteric Christianity, tracts on the *I Ching*, Zen, witchcraft, magic, astrology,
vampirism, scholarly treatises on Sufism, Rosicrucianism, alchemy, Buddhism, the poems of Saint John of the Cross, and
the Upanishads (p. 486). There is something there that attracts
her, although she never puts into words exactly what it might
be. However, she notes that all are talking "about the same
processes, the same psychological truths" and share "gleams of
life, the authentic note or throb of vitality, the unmistakable
pulse" (p. 488). Also they represent "everything rejected by
official culture and scholarship" (p. 486). Lessing appears to
have used *The Sufis* as her source, since this list is nearly a
duplicate of Shah's examples of relics of Sufic thought or religions and cults that have been strongly affected by Sufism.[5] In
her review, Lessing singles out this information for special attention and repeats the list that she later uses in *The Four-Gated
City*.[6] Certainly there is a connection between these items and

the secret of the inner City in the desert that later becomes the history of a legend, in the hands of priests.

Although these items are very different from one another, they are all concerned in some way with the shadow side of existence, where reason is not a sufficient guide, and with the potential vision of unity that seems to be the chief interest of Sufism. The *I Ching*, witchcraft, magic, astrology, and vampirism in different ways all recognize a connection between mind and matter quite different from the separation between them that has held firm in the mainstream of thought since the growth of science. Rosicrucianism, Christian mysticism, Zoroastrianism, Buddhism, Zen, Hinduism, yoga, alchemy, and Sufism are all forms of mystical belief and therefore by definition are concerned with unity as opposed to the divisiveness of logical thought.

Martha seems to view esotericism as a source of knowledge that may have the power to infuse into Western culture a saving vision of wholeness. Joseph Strelka's comments on this theme are similar to Lessing's and illuminate her views. According to Strelka, for moderns esotericism does not represent a romantic return to a mythic wholeness, even though its inspiration comes from ancient forms of knowledge:

> Esotericism corresponds to a kind of sublimated form of myth at a time when wholeness is being sought again. . . . It is not a question of returning, but of advancing through all the sophistication of rational development without relinquishing an inch of intellectually attained splendor, proceeding stage by stage from the *purgatio* to the *illuminatio* to the attainment of that integration and wholeness which all great esoteric traditions describe as a kind of '*unio*.'[7]

Another word frequently used by the great esoteric traditions is love; Lessing makes the connection between it and the final vision of unity Martha strives for when she has the narrator of *The Four-Gated City* suggest that love is "the delicate but total acknowledgement of what is" (p. 10). Martha's interest in a mythical Golden Age and later absorption by mystical literature makes her intellectually aware of the possibility of a unified perception, and when she eventually explores her inner consciousness, she attempts to hold on to conscious awareness in an essentially nonrational experience. However, her attempt to combine two modes of perception fails because she is not strong enough to endure the "total acknowledgement of what is": the mass shadow, in the form of the self-hater, defeats her. At the furthest point of knowledge is indeed a sense of unity; one man is every man and every quality implies its opposite. However, the mass psyche is so twisted that it can not be borne by human beings in their present state of development. It remains for the seven children of Pharos to create a City of the imagination in their more highly developed minds.

Throughout *Children of Violence* until the end of part one of *The Four-Gated City*, Martha picks her way through established society, and her moments of vision are instinctive and spontaneous. Even Martha and Mark's most clearly expressed view of ideal unity, the City in the desert, has the familiar shape of a fable or myth. From this point on, however, traditional forms of all kind begin to disintegrate, both in the subject matter of the novel and its narrative structure. The turning point, as Martha realizes, is the suicide of Sally-Sarah: "to look back from the day after Sally's death, to even the day before it, it was as if a bomb had gone off" (p. 150). This event does more than usher in "the bad time"; from then on, the rigid patterns of the city begin to shift and crack.

Martha up to that time has jealously guarded her freedom. Unwilling to become involved with the Coldridges' many problems, she has made plans to leave. Sally's death changes that; Martha in effect adopts the family as her own. Doing so places her at the center of a group through which Lessing shows economically society's drift toward destruction; for the Coldridge family and its associates are a microcosm of society and mirror its fate.

The house itself expresses the solidity and apparent strength of the nineteenth century, when it was built. Martha remarks that it is all of a piece and lends a feeling of security to anyone raised there: "Nothing in this house believed in the possibility of destruction" (p. 102). The people connected with it represent almost the entire spectrum of middle-and upper-class thought and activity, making up a special unity, as Martha notes: "What an extraordinary household this was, after all, this entity, containing such a variety of attitudes, positions! A Whole. People in any sort of communion, link, connection, make up a whole" (p. 211).

The collective emotions that sweep through society buffet the Coldridge clan or carry it along. Then gradually the house begins to deteriorate, symbolizing the crumbling of all nineteenth-century values and the fabric of contemporary culture. Eventually there is a forced sale to the government, and the family is left homeless, without a center: the slender tie that has held this group together is broken.

However, for Lessing disintegration always opens up the possibility for something new—the blade of grass that grows in the rubble. Destruction of the city may possibly mean the creation of the City. As social and conceptual forms dissolve, the creation of new, less rigid forms is possible. For example, the crumbling of Martha's personality structure, described in chapter three, in a sense makes possible a new personality, free from ordinary needs and fears and with increased powers of perception.

In the same way, the breakdown of traditional social units makes possible new, experimental ones, partly in response to the times, partly through chance or intuition, and partly through conscious effort. Most detailed is the immediate Coldridge household, with Mark, Martha, and Lynda at its

center—one of several attempts to create the City. Its chief flaw
is that instead of being made up of individuals who are themselves whole, each member contributes his particular
strength—reason, intuition, or service—to a total unity that is
not entirely satisfactory and that suffers from outside forces. It
is Lynda who contributes the power of intuition, but her reason
and capability for service have been damaged. Enduring her
"silly" periods in the basement apartment, she epitomizes the
buried, unrecognized "secret" that Lessing feels could liberate
mankind. The damage done to Lynda by psychiatrists and
machines dramatizes Lessing's belief that most methods of
psychiatric treatment destroy the mind's spontaneous attempts
toward regeneration.

Mark represents well-meaning reason, but his fine qualities
are made impotent by his weaknesses. His unceasing yearning
for Lynda is perhaps a projection of his real need, acceptance of
the "secret" that first Lynda and then Martha intuitively accept. To the end Mark rails against the "nasty mixture of irony
and Saint John of the Cross and the *Arabian Nights* that they all
(Lynda, Marcha, Francis) went in for" (*Four-Gated City* p. 613).
And while Mark is a responsible person, he serves others in a
twisted, neurotic manner. As he is aware, his need to "save and
protect" is for him an emotional need. He fails because of his
lack of intuition. He can not understand Lynda; and when he
forms the plan of a rescue operation to save people from the
coming catastrophe, he has no way of heeding Lynda's innate
knowledge that the plan is doomed to failure. Because of
Mark's lack of intuition, his best impulses are warped and useless. Finally he lapses into complete cynicism.

Martha contributes responsibility to this little society. It is
she who holds things together, making possible whatever unity
and protection the household creates. The name with which
Lessing has endowed her appears to be particularly appropriate. Like the Martha of the Bible, she is "distracted with much

serving" and "careful and troubled about many things." Jesus tells Martha that she needs what Mary has chosen—to sit at His feet and hear His message. (Luke 10: 38–42). Similarly, Martha Hesse needs—and eventually finds—the knowledge that completes her nature; and like the Biblical Martha, she grows in patience and sympathy.

Besides incorporating all the qualities of the unified personality, the Coldridge household is without what Lessing sees as the rigidity of a traditional social framework. Family and friends are always curious about this ménage à trois that challenges the accepted norm of marriage. The group embraces anyone who needs a home: Phoebe's girls appear to spend most of their time there, and the dinner table always includes large numbers of family and friends. The house is a meeting ground for people of all races and beliefs.

Other embryonic versions of the City are Paul's houses, in which he installs outcasts of society, and Francis's commune, described in the Appendix. Both stand outside the ordinary framework of society. Of the two the commune is more important: Jill Coldridge's own brood, reminiscent of the "many-fathered children" of Martha's adolescent dream, are black and white and born out of wedlock. Francis, although he is Jill's cousin, lives with her and loves the children as his own. The commune provides a haven in an increasingly mad society, and it is made up of people who are groping tentatively for new social forms. However, the group disintegrates after it is publicized. Marauding groups damage the buildings, believing they are destroying a pernicious communist society. Worse (according to Francis) the members of the commune begin to intellectualize its raison d'être, resulting in internal divisions. The group finally falls apart, dramatizing Lessing's belief that any social structure organized around a rigid concept is doomed.

Finally, on the island of Pharos, the City is established in a primitive form. The original group displayed right feeling: they came to that particular ship at the time of the castastrophe "because of a personal trust or liking" of a leader or an intuition that "this was the right place" (p. 598). The group is mixed in color, but there is no prejudice. It is a cooperative community with equal rights, but members all share a special knowledge or feeling, especially heightened in the seven special children. When it is told that one of them, Joseph Batts, will be a gardener in the outside world, the connection is completed between this group and the gardeners of Mark's imaginary city. Knowledge of "the secret" is the birthright of the new children of Pharos, who represent a fragile beginning of a new race. However, this society is possible only at the expense of the old. The slate has been wiped clean: all amenities along with all previous ideas are gone, and the new has its beginning in a place that can just barely support life. And it must not be forgotten that, looking at the world at large, duality has not been overcome. East and West are separated by rigid political boundaries; and if the children of Pharos are new whole beings, one must not forget the grotesque mutations of the refugee camps. While it is suggested that eventually all humans will be like the Pharos children, one suspects that it will at best be a centuries-long process.

In contrast to Martha's rescue attempt, which ends with the society on Pharos, Mark has attempted to build a city in Tunisia with the funds of an American industrialist who "needed *to do good*" (p. 552). As Diane Smith has pointed out, Mark "wants to save everyone willy-nilly in an impersonal, bureaucratic way," and his plan includes a benevolent dictator. However, collective solutions are never successful. "There is no political solution out of the dangerous situation the world finds itself in. There are only individual solutions."[8] The outcome of Mark's way of thinking is imaged in the refugee camp that he supervises after the catastrophe. Earlier Mark had called himself an unwitting conspirator of Jimmy Wood (p. 506); Jimmy invents machines that ruin or at best supplant human potential, but Mark's factory produces them. Lessing seems to agree that Mark's assessment of himself is correct. However well-meaning and responsible a citizen he may be, Lessing shows that as long as he is ruled by logical constructs alone, he contributes to the kind of world he then administers: shattered by war and inhabited by war's victims.

The Four-Gated City gradually abolishes all the values that are ordinarily the stuff of literature, and as a result, traditional narrative structure breaks down as the novel progresses. In *The Golden Notebook* the contrast between art and life is depicted in Anna's preoccupation with the way conventional form excludes experience; so she writes a novel and the experience that went into it, then blends the two together to make a new, whole form. In *The Four-Gated City*, however, there is no reconciliation between art and experience. Lessing probes human motives and values like a searchlight—not to dramatize but to expose; therefore narrative forms dissolve. In this way, the structure of the novel parallels its vision.

In the first place, Martha's point of view becomes less important as her life blends into the general fate of humanity. Except for her important, final psychic exploration and the letter from Pharos, she fades into the background. Accordingly, the point of view becomes increasingly omniscient, telescoping events, such as the foundation of Mark's city in Tunisia, and observing events of which Martha would have no personal knowledge. For example, Maisie's daughter Rita, at that time fully grown, comes to London and eventually marries Mark. One of her conversations with Paul is offered, as well as an experience with a man who asked her out. Also, there is a good deal of narrative summary and analysis that corresponds to Martha's own mature vision. Neither her own psyche nor society hold any secrets for Martha; correspondingly, the narrative is no longer shaped by the unique point of view of a limited character.

The contrast is given emphasis in one passage in section two that is told through the point of view of Mrs. Quest. Here events are once again shaped in traditional narrative style, reflected by the old woman's loneliness, her mixed emotions about going to London to live with Martha, and her growing affection for the little black boy who works at the home where she is visiting. This method is used once again in the Appendix in Mark's emotional journal entries. Something about the state of the world is presented, but the reader particularly learns about Mark, the most limited in vision of the three who give long accounts of the events of and after the catastrophe.

The gradual change in point of view throughout the series is mirrored in the changing use of imagery. Throughout *Children of Violence* Lessing frequently uses imagery to dramatize knowledge that Martha has not yet grasped intellectually. For example, *Landlocked* opens with a long description of Martha sitting by the office window and the pattern on her back made by shade and sunshine. This passage symbolizes the fragmentation of personality that Martha only later begins fully to understand.

The climax of *Landlocked* is a dramatic episode full of significant imagery — the dance at the Parkland Hotel. Martha is married to Anton but in love with Thomas. Anton is dating Millicent, and Maisie is with Athen. The six of them drive out to the hotel for the evening, the events of which not only bring the action of the novel to a climax but also form a poem of unity and fragmentation. The evening begins badly, with many misunderstandings. Martha has put on a severe black dress, and Thomas dislikes her in it; he has been hoping to see her in a romantic dance dress. She changes for him, but Millicent has meanwhile gone home to change into a short dress like Martha's. She is forced to change again, and the evening begins under the shadow of irritations and disappointments. Martha wants to sit with Thomas in the car, but propriety reigns, putting her with Anton. The group sits on the veranda of the hotel where charcoal braziers make blazing patches of heat and light, forming a pattern that mirrors the fragmentation that characterizes the entire evening. Martha sees it within herself. In an alcoholic haze she glances down at her left hand. "It was monstrously, unbelievably ugly, like a weapon. . . . Her hand was like a pair of pincers, the claw of a lobster, something cold and predatory. She looked at her left hand, astounded by its cruelty. Meanwhile her right was in the depths of Thomas's hand, through which she received simple messages of warm health" (p. 420).

Yet at the same time Martha is swept up into a piercing sense of unity similar to her experiences on the veld. Thomas uses the word *love* for the first time, and their fusion—together, and with everything around them—seems so strong that nothing should be able to disturb it. However, when Sergeant Tressel appears, he brings a discord that will shape the future:

> Tonight, she and Thomas together, the six of them together—it was like the lift of a wave towards the sky before it breaks into a fragmented crest of flying white foam. She and Thomas would soon part, and soon this love . . . would have gone, been blown apart. Like a town in Europe, dark under a sky bursting with bits of flying flame and steel. And the Tressels, now sitting in a group of noisy friends at their table: their appearance this evening could have been foreseen. Martha felt as if she had known all her life that on this evening, this starry winter's evening, she would sit by a man she loved with her whole heart, and look past flaring braziers at a red-faced fattish man in a badly cut dinner suit, and know that he was an enemy too strong for her. (p. 415)

The emotion of this episode at the hotel comes from the familiar situation of doomed love, although it gains added importance by its suggestion of universality, that no such thing as simple romantic love can survive in such a world. Martha and Thomas's love has been a profound experience for both of them, but at the Parkland Hotel it takes the form of a romantic dream. Martha has wished only "to be conscious of herself as a pretty young woman in a romantic dark blue dress" (p. 414). With the help of wine, she and Thomas are able to forget the murderous hatred inspired in Thomas by Sergeant Tressel, and the two of them sit side by side in the guises of Martha and Thomas: pretty young woman and strong brown peasant. In other words, the experience bears little resemblance to Martha's usual hard analysis, which ordinarily gets beneath illusions of all kinds. On this particular evening their love is dramatized in a way directly analogous to art and literary romance. Its effect is heightened by Martha's painful emotions and the narrative device of imagery.

For the most part, this sort of episode simply does not exist in *Children of Violence* after *The Four-Gated City* is well under way. Gradually, rational analysis takes over both in narrative method and in the action itself, as Martha explores her psyche. Martha is no longer interested in romance or in such emotions as happiness; they are simply irrelevant. Except for the passage told from Mrs. Quest's point of view in section two, the reader is no longer swept up in the private emotions of the characters.

There is one exception: Mark's journal in the Appendix. Torn by cynicism and despair, his writing bears little resemblance to the even, objective reports of Martha and Francis. He is particularly emotional about Lynda. After she is dead (of bubonic plague), he sees her smile in many different people and suffers an agony of longing. Mark describes an incident in which he sends a young soldier on an errand so that he can once again see "Lynda's smile." These pages create a curious effect. The reader is reminded how long it has been since he has experienced in the series the emotions that are usually aroused in fiction—distress from the plight of a character, delight in his success, frustration from his failures. These emotions usually stem from certain assumptions: that traditional romantic love is important, that worldly success is to be desired, that sharply delineated personalities are the most worthy of interest.

In *Children of Violence* Lessing eventually eliminates these traditional values and the literary forms that ordinarily convey them. Martha, whose life has been the subject of five volumes, simply disappears as a recognizable character. One has known her mainly as a critical, idealistic, yearning young woman. With knowledge, she loses all these traits and recedes into the background. In time interest in her is not what she will do or what will happen to her but what she knows. When Martha reports that she will soon die, it becomes a matter of little importance, and the same is true for the deaths of the other characters, briefly reported. The usual values are then suspect. Traditional love has been exposed for the most part as neurotic longing or romantic illusion. The nuclear family has disintegrated and with it any interest in family relationships or marriage. The poetic dream of a return to the unified world of unconscious nature becomes nonsense; were it possible, it would lead only to blind, repetitive behavior. Worldly success is meaningless: money, talent, and power are associated with forces that are merely destructive. Self-knowledge can go only so far. Inevitably with such revelations traditional narrative breaks down. The symbol is no longer needed because discursive analysis takes its place. The dramatic scene or episode is impossible, because it dramatizes outmoded events—unless it is fanciful, like science fiction, and like the descriptions of the postcatastrophe world in the Appendix. Perhaps Lessing had ideas like these in mind when she said in an interview that she believes that science-fiction writers "have captured our culture's sense of the future."[9]

The question stands: at a certain pinnacle of awareness, where human conflicts are exposed as the results of clinging to illusions and where mankind is One, what place is there for art with its dramatizations, its simulations and symbols? When Kate Brown is in the middle of her most agonizingly perceptive state in *The Summer before the Dark*, she goes to a play,

Turgenev's *A Day in the Country*. About a woman who has been the center of attention but is then losing her position (Kate's own problem), the play has in former years moved and disturbed her. At this time it appears to her as an insane farce: "parody of something. Really they all ought to be falling about, roaring with laughter, instead of feeling intelligent sympathy at these ridiculous absurd meaningless problems."[10] It is "as if a parcel of well-born maniacs were conducting a private game or ritual, and no one had yet told them they were mad. It was a farce and not at all a high-class and sensitive comedy filled with truths about human nature. The fact was that the things happening in the world, the collapse of everything, was tugging at the shape of events in this play and those like them, and making them farcical. A joke. Like her own life. Farcical" (pp. 172–73).

In this passage Lessing restates the idea implicit in the evolving narrative form of *Children of Violence*. Mark's agony for Lynda stands out in the end almost like a pathetic farce when one looks at it against Martha's final knowledge. In a sense, Martha's deepest perception has her completely boxed in. On the one hand, she has explored inner consciousness as far as she can; on the other, she has dissected society and exposed as meaningless most ideals and values about which people organize their lives. Martha's best achievements are merely holding actions—first, at the Coldridge household, from where various abortive Cities are tried; second, on Pharos, where she is essentially a midwife and nurse for a new race. Had Lessing stayed with this particular view, there would have been little room for future novels, except perhaps science fiction.

Lessing's view of society does not change appreciably after *The Four-Gated City*; however, her view of consciousness does, and it is influenced more by Sufism than by Jung. Martha is blocked by the Jungian mass shadow. In *Briefing* this problem is no longer primary; in *Summer before the Dark*, it disappears altogether. Martha, Kate, and Watkins make the same pilgrimage; they go beneath the outer forms of personality to perceive the essential self and the vision possible to it. The problem of *Children of Violence* is the relation between the individual and the collective, and Lessing pursues this theme relentlessly to the end: the individual, though uniquely himself as the watcher, the one who observes, is also part of humanity. As such, he is inevitably twisted and warped, unable to go beyond a certain point of unity. The only Utopian city possible is a little community stripped bare of every amenity. The only inner City possible comes about through a Darwinian mutation: a new consciousness triggered by nuclear holocaust. *Briefing* and *Summer*, on the other hand, are both concerned with the nature of the observer, the watcher—not so much in its relation with the collective but with the cosmos.

The vision of *Briefing* is from a different vantage point; Lessing has in a sense stepped back in order to be more inclusive. Watkins, too, meets the collective unconscious, symbolized in the blood feasts of the women, and transcends it. In his view from the Crystal, cold necessity becomes part of a larger scheme. It is not the collective unconscious that defeats Watkins but the collective consciousness: the force of society, which pulls him back to so-called sanity, that is actually a one-dimensional view of life. The doctors, priests of society, insist that shock treatment will bring back his memory; and since Watkin's main concern is to remember something just out of reach, he submits. However, his judgment is faulty because he is fairly certain that he will regain his memory on his own terms. His urgency is to recall the memory of unity he experienced during his illness; however, shock treatment merely returns the structure of his former life, with its divisions. Approaching the City, he takes another path and arrives back at the city instead.

The "delicate but total acknowledgement of what is": this is how the narrator of *The Four-Gated City* describes love, which is another term for unity, the City of the spirit. In that novel the vision of unity is split into its opposites—the beautiful gardens that Martha once sees, and the self-hater. *Briefing* presents a vision of unity without such divisions. It is the clearest presentation in Lessing's work of the interior City; as such, it is appropriately connected to the stone city that figures in Watkins's pilgrimage.

Like the forgotten secret of the City in the desert and the myth of the Golden Age, an implicit theme throughout Lessing's work, Watkins's stone city symbolizes lost knowledge, some prelapsarian condition no longer completely understood. Watkins can not understand why the city has become deserted, since it has all the apparent necessities: good building material, completed buildings, pure water, and a beneficent climate. Also, it has a living quality, "as if this city was itself a person, or had a soul, or being" (p. 58), giving Watkins a sense of being among friends.

In this description Lessing is retelling the description of the City in the desert; some instinctive knowledge once existed, lost through faulty vision. Both cities have a similar fate, being overrun by inferior beings—in this case, the rat-dogs and their vicious wars. The City in the desert has a center, perhaps located in people, such as the gardeners, perhaps in a place, like the empty octagonal room beneath a library. The stone city has a quite definite center: the mandala-shaped central square. Watkins starts to clear it but is deflected by the pull of the moon (subjectivity, the pull of the ego) and the bloodfeasts of the women. Both cities are psychic states. Thus Watkins, with the help of the white bird (Hermes, messenger of the gods), finally clears the center and establishes, temporarily, the City of the mind: the delicate but total acknowledgment of what is.

The vision in the Crystal is a bold attempt to portray discursively a vision of unity generally attempted only by poets. It is the vision that lies behind *The Divine Comedy* and *The Tempest*. In modern literature it is glimpsed in Eliot's "Four Quartets" and the last section of *To the Lighthouse*. However, Lessing does not let poetic images speak for themselves, as Virginia Woolf does, for example, to create an ineffable experience of unity. Instead, she paints a precise picture intended to be grasped by the intellect. Although her method corresponds with her theme—the need for a heightened, unified consciousness—it sometimes results in dense and awkward passages. For example:

> No one knows what has existed and has vanished beyond recovery, evidence for the number of times Man has understood and has forgotten again that his mind and flesh and life and movements are made of star stuff, sun stuff, planet stuff; that the Sun's being is his, and what sort of events may be expected, because of the meshings of the planets—and how an intelligent husbanding of humanity's resources may be effected based on the most skilled and sensitive of forecasting, by those whose minds are instruments to record the celestial dance. (p. 130)

This is an important passage; it gives in capsule form the central meaning of Watkins's vision. However, as *Four-Gated City* does in another way, it simply bypasses ordinary literary values, moving from image to essay. Considering the broad range of Lessing's talent—she can write forceful poetic prose when she wishes—it is a mistake to assume that such passages are mere lapses in ability.

Lessing achieves clarity by this method. Watkins's cosmic vision is complex and is composed of various images and fables, but because of its discursive passages a central core of meaning can be easily abstracted from it. Essentially, it is a vision of harmony, "a pattern, bad and good, everything in turn, everything spiralling up" (p. 131). In *Landlocked* and *The Four-Gated City* Lessing has made brief references to the "forces" that lie outside normal human vision and that can "invade" people under certain circumstances. Here these forces are presented in the metaphor of planetary influences. The solar system is only part of a much larger whole, as an earthly atom is part of a larger system. But every atom—like earth—must follow the laws of unity.

Lessing describes the cosmos as a delicate, shining web enclosing the earth. It has a special, rare light shared by certain "strands" of humanity, who provide a link or bridge to the whole. Those sensitive to it are aware of being part of a "delicious pulse of joy and creation" (p. 112). In the solar system the source of light is the sun, "the controlling governor of them all," "sanity and simplicity," "the deep low organ note that underlies all being" (p. 117); "Humanity was a pulse in the life of the sun" (p. 116). Once again Lessing outlines the Golden Age, this time on a cosmic scale: at one time (perhaps in ages of which anthropologists have no knowledge), earth was part of the general harmony. However, planetary forces—specifically, a powerful comet ramming the earth—made the earth wobble and poisoned the air. The inhabitants were left "teased and tormented by a queer half-memory of the time before they became poisoned" (p. 121).

Because of this catastrophe the cold weight of necessity counterbalances joy. Necessity is part of the scheme of things, a result of the physicality of existence, but earth has been a particularly bad casualty because mankind has been captured by the "cold, hungry moon" whose tides impel everyone into saying *I-I-I* instead of *We*.[11] The result of this subjectivity has been the spread of hate and fear that is affecting the solar system as a whole, upsetting the balance. To stop its poisonous influence, it may have to be "lopped off" by the Celestial Gardener. At this point in history, there is a crisis. Cosmic necessity is putting earth under special and unavoidable stresses at that juncture, such as earthquakes, volcanic eruptions, and epidemics. When these forces are joined to those caused by human blindness, the result may be catastrophic. Unless men can be alerted to the whole scheme of things and "husband their resources," the entire planet may be destroyed.

Watkins's vision is an imaginative way of presenting the idea that the individual, all life on earth, and cosmic forces are intertwined in one whole. However, humanity—through inattendance to these links—is increasing its own cold necessity to a dangerous, if not fatal, degree. Although human beings can not completely sever themselves from various kinds of necessity, they can vastly improve their lot by becoming aware of the "rare light" that forms a divine pattern: the knowledge that the Sufis say is the heart of every religion. Creation is going somewhere; everything is "spiralling up." As part of this cosmic movement, humankind has the opportunity of evolving. The key is knowledge: in the crystal Watkins sees that having recognized his part in the blood-slaughter under the moon, he is somehow able to transcend it, and that it has been a necessary stage in his development. Like the boy in "A Sunrise on the Veld," a person must see his own share in collective guilt; only then is it possible to transcend it. Put into discursive terms, these ideas appear to be those which Lessing has dramatized over and over in her fiction.

During the "briefing," the party to descend to earth sees a film forecasting coming events. It will be a catastrophic era; a decade or two will be equivalent to centuries of evolution. However, out of the ruins will emerge a new, mutated race. Not much different in appearance from the old, it will have "increased powers of perception, a different mental structure." "This remnant of an old, or the beginnings of a new race" will have as heritage "all the accumulated experience of the human race, plus, this time, the mental equipment to use it" (p. 140). This description is of course a recounting of the new children of Pharos from a different perspective. It also casts light on the case of Charles Watkins. Instead of what could have been psychic regeneration, Watkins has achieved merely a temporary vision of all the accumulated experience of the race (including, presumably, the original Golden Age). However, he does not have "the mental equipment to use it"; he soon succumbs to the pressures of a "moon-crazed" society, accepting the advice of his doctors to have shock treatments, which destroy his vision.

The social pressures on Charles Watkins look ahead to "The Temptation of Jack Orkney" and *The Summer before the Dark*. In these realistic works, Lessing explores the pressures that she sees to be working against intelligent and responsible people in society and that keep them from psychic unity. Realism enables Lessing once again to dramatize people in society, and critics who have been uneasy about her experimental novels have shown whole-hearted admiration of these, which are more traditional in form.[12] Yet such realistic novels inevitably stop short of the frontiers of experience where Lessing has carried out her most provocative themes. Orkney and Kate Brown both sense the need to transcend the limits of their present lives, but neither sees with the clarity of Martha or Charles Watkins; one wishes to send them off to read *The Four-Gated City* and *Briefing for a Descent into Hell*.

Nevertheless, *The Summer before the Dark* is the most positive of Lessing's novels. Kate grasps intellectually the nature of personality and society and the roles they impose. However, the rest of her perception is nonanalytical. When Kate deposits her battered seal into the ocean, she captures a sense of her own divinity, as Watkins has seen that he is a tiny spark of light in a massive pattern. The novel is optimistic in the same way as traditional religious literature: though the world falls about one's ears, the soul, properly tended, will reach its proper home.

Doris Lessing's ethic comes down to this: everyone's duty is to learn as much as possible about himself and help other people as honestly as he can in this twisted world, without sacrificing integrity. Only an enlarged consciousness, a uniting of reason with knowledge and a perception that is not presently associated with reason, will help dig out the giant lizard of violence: such a consciousness will lift humankind above blind, instinctual behavior like the sun beetle's and prevent behavior like Mary Turner's, the result of suppressed knowledge. Until sufficient numbers of people achieve this largeness of mind, people and nations will continue to fight one "leopard" after another in the manner of "Leopard" George.

It does not work to impose an ideal or do a duty; rather, one should respond simply to simple needs. Mental constructs of any kind will always have a hidden flaw. Throughout Lessing's later works, the only correct actions are simple and loving, and they seldom have any connection with traditional morality. Maisie, despite her irregular life, raises her daughter Rita to be a fine person. Paul rescues homeless misfits and gives them a place to live. Francis is a father to Jill's children, and his commune holds together as long as it is free of ideology and selfish longings. Martha is effective when she looks after the Coldridge clan and the community on Pharos. The important relationships in *Briefing* are based not on role but a quality in being in tune: Charles and Violet; Rosemary Baines and Frederick Larson. Kate Brown's poignant situation, despite her spiritual enlightenment, is to discover that the loving relationships around which her life has been based have been fraudulent.

In every Lessing novel, society rolls on toward destruction, with most of its members suffering either from physical or spiritual hunger. An occasional character fights free from the general pattern but more than that is needed to make even a dent in things as they are. "It would be like a willed mutation," thinks Jack Orkney, dreaming of the possibility that a new generation really could transcend the preceding one. In the later work, the method for doing so becomes increasingly clear.

The burden is on the individual to clear his or her mandala center of its choking debris: limiting assumptions, fragmenting ideas, a false sense of the separate ego, the superficiality of unconscious role-playing. Only after doing so is it possible to glimpse what is eternal—which is not just the Other but is a spirit that also lies within. In *Briefing,* Watkins describes to Violet another level of living that beckons with a sense of urgency. He says that certain things in life are like shadows of it—coincidences and dreams, for example. "The important thing is this—to remember that some things reach out to us from that level of living, to here . . . but all these things, they have a meaning, they are reflections from that other part of ourselves, and that part of ourselves knows things we don't know" (p. 301).

This higher level is something discernible by those whose minds have cracked—Watkins in his illness, for example—but it is a vision not easily grasped by ordinary consciousness. After coming around from his plunge into the depths of the psyche, and before shock treatment, Watkins is left only with a sense of urgency, the need to remember some difficult knowledge that makes the knower as different from other men as men are from monkeys.

Kate Brown perceives it in her final seal dream. It also appears in quick glimpses in several short stories in *The Temptation of Jack Orkney.*[13] In "The Other Garden" the narrator walks through a hidden garden shaped like a man. It is miniature, a perfect analogue to the larger outer garden. Although the month is January, the narrator continually imagines the coming perfection of summer, when the garden will have been touched by the sun. Even then, it has an atmosphere of mystery and completion: "As you leave, the place draws itself in beyond you, is gathered in to itself, like water settling after a stone has disturbed it. There it is, whole, between its hedges, its bare trees, repeating and echoing like a descant, using every theme that is used in the great Park outside, but used there roughly, in crude form" (p. 230).

In "Out of the Fountain" the vision appears in a perfect pearl, given by old Ephraim, the diamond cutter, to lovely young Mihrène; he is stung because she cheapens herself by wearing false pearls. After the incident, for no discernible reason, Ephraim begins a collection of opals, moonstones, pearls, white jade, crystal, well-cut glass: any white or clear stone that catches and reflects light. Says the narrator, "their value related to some other good which had, arbitrarily and for a short time, the name Mihrène" (p. 7).

However, this idea of the good is not a separate, transcendent reality; it is not Platonic. It is indissolubly mixed with humanity and characterized by energy, movement, and change. In "Lions, Leaves, Roses . . ." the narrator walks through streets and parks, hoping to "catch a fragment of late summer in this clouded year" (p. 149). To do so, she must walk with senses open and mind empty of thoughts and words. She comes upon a woman who says gleefully that the sun always follows her, and the narrator is "envious of her whose cracked mind let the sunlight through" (p. 149). The bits of sunlight available to most are fleeting: the fur of a squirrel shining in the light, windows on fire with the setting sun, showers of gold leaves from the shovel of a gardener. Such details are an earthly reflection of the source of all things; but this final cause is not static, it is characterized by time and process. For example, at sunset, the narrator perceives that during her walk, "the sun had sped, dragging us with it, in an inconceivable curve towards . . ." (p. 154). Then she has a momentary vision of unity combined with energy, moving toward death and rebirth: "Leaves, words, people, shadows, whirled together towards autumn and the solstice" (p. 154).

Purification of the spirit, an eternal good that is reflected on earth, the ambivalence between creation and destruction, life and death: these of course have been the themes of myth, poetry, and religion from their beginning. However, Doris Lessing still lies firmly within the traditions of the humanistic novel in her dramatizations of human affairs, however esoteric her themes. Her unusual achievement is to combine both streams. She wishes to offer new potential for the enduring themes, to bring them out from between the covers of leather-bound books and into contemporary lives.

Although Lessing has expressed impatience with art and its limitations, this criticism does not include the artistic imagination. "An Unposted Love Letter" from *The Temptation of Jack Orkney* suggests a nearly divine role for the artist. An actress writes to a man she has loved from a distance. His warmth has inspired her work, a transformation she accomplishes through emotional and artistic control: ("the cool circle of my chastity, the circle of my discipline"). A passage from this unmailed letter conveys a sense of the artist as seer and maker in the highest possible sense—the alchemist who can indeed turn dross into gold, creating not just an artifact but a higher form of being:

> I am a great space that enlarges, that grows, that spreads with the steady lightening of the human soul, and in the space, squatting in the corner, is a thing, an object, a dark, slow, coiled, amorphous heaviness, embodied sleep, a cold stupid sleep, a heaviness like the dark in a stale room—this thing stirs in its sleep where it squats in my soul, and I put all my muscles, all my force, into defeating it. For this is what I was born for, to fight embodied sleep, putting around it a confining girdle of light, of intelligence, so that it cannot spread its slow stain of ugliness over the trees, over the stars, over you. (p. 146)

Afterword

The Memoirs of a Survivor was published after this book was completed, but I would like to add a few words on this, one of Lessing's best and most important novels. It is a product of her artistic and personal maturity and has a sureness of touch and perception not consistently present in her earlier work. The familiar themes are here too: the death throes of the city; an unresponsive social structure fatally strangling itself; the relationship between the individual and the collective; the unification of the unconscious with the conscious mind to create the City, the total self. As in *The Summer Before the Dark*, the final City is of the soul rather than society; however, in *Memoirs* Lessing takes a new step. In *Summer*, Kate wonders if she can somehow include others in her rebirth: she wishes that Maureen, too, can learn from the seal dream. Maureen's stubborn refusal to listen would indicate no, although the hair puppet she makes at the end of the novel hints that some part of her has indeed learned from Kate and that Maureen will not be in her fifties before she sheds her roles and her cynicism. In *Memoirs*, however, the main characters' fulfillment is for others as well.

The geographical limits of this novel are small, an indication of its economy. The action takes place in a city neighborhood and also a looking-glass house that the unnamed narrator periodically visits when a blank wall of her living room dissolves. This set of rooms and gardens is the inner space that for Anna, Martha, and Charles Watkins was vast and chaotic. The narrator lives in a comfortable flat in an unnamed city, but the wheels of society are creaking to a halt. Food is scarce, power undependable and expensive, all organizations broken down. Inexplicably, a man deposits at the apartment a young teenager, Emily, and her ugly pet, Hugo, a strange cross between a cat and dog. The man tells the narrator that the girl is now her responsibility and then disappears. Emily, unquestioning, settles in, and the narrator accepts the situation thinking that, after all, in such times nothing can be considered too strange.

The novel covers a period of about two years. Emily is eleven or twelve when she arrives and is about fourteen at the end. However, she matures with hothouse speed, going through all the traditional stages of adolescence and womanhood in that brief time, much as Martha does much more slowly in *Children of Violence*. There is a critical, clever, jeering phase, painful sensitivity to criticism, blossoming sexuality, mature sexual involvement, loss of sexuality, responsibility for others (as a house mother in a children's commune led by her lover, Gerald). At the end of the novel, Emily's eyes are those of a 35- to 40-year-old woman. She belongs to two worlds—the somewhat traditional one of the narrator, where she is looked after, and the new world of the street and commune, where all mores and survival tactics are new. At Emily's arrival, the narrator has to look after her. Later, the reverse is true, since Emily is quick to learn the ways of the new world and guides her former guardian, who is slow to notice changes and to adjust.

The city becomes increasingly difficult and dangerous, and its inhabitants pour out. As in Russia after the revolution, large gangs of children form, a new social unit. No word returns from those who leave, since communication has virtually stopped. At one point the narrator sees that it is as if they have dropped off the edge of a flat earth. Meanwhile, the filth builds, the air becomes increasingly heavy and unbreathable, and human life becomes less valuable. At the lowest point appear groups of parentless children like rats out of the underground tunnels where they have been living. They have lost all trace of human values and are more likely to murder someone they know than a stranger because it is more obvious to do so. All sense of love and loyalty is gone. Lessing's description of the city is extreme, but at the same time it is merely an intensification of trends in contemporary society. Even the ratlike children are not entirely imaginary in the light of "mouse gangs," groups of young children who have been known to assault defenseless individuals.

As the city spirals down, a countermovement upward takes place in the narrator's discovery of the house on the other side of the wall. The scenes there vary. Some are described as "personal," that is, having to do with individual history and emotion. The narrator sees many scenes of Emily as a child, but the era is Victorian, not recent, and clearly they dramatize universal patterns. Indeed, at one point the narrator searches for a crying Emily, only to find Emily's mother as a child. Through an unhappy, overbearing mother and a secretly prurient father Emily learns guilt, hypocrisy, lovelessness, and the neurotic need to please. Other, "impersonal," scenes are empty rooms, sometimes being cleaned and painted, other times in total disarray. Once a room has been destroyed by soldiers and contains a corpse, clearly a version of the wretched collective mind, the "sound barrier" of *The Four-Gated City*. The narrator carefully cleans and repairs one room and never sees it again, presumably a metaphor for working on, and through, a problem and freeing oneself from a destructive pattern. The gardens of *The Four-Gated City* and "The Other Garden" are here as well; the narrator discovers two gardens, one below the other, a paradise of flowers, vegetables, and clear mountain air and water. Always in this looking-glass world, however chaotic it is, the narrator is aware of an unseen presence, an elusive note of joy. That is, in inner space the Self may be discovered, with all the complexity it suggests.

Two scenes from this inner world are central to the novel, each representing one of the two worlds. In one, Emily frantically and futilely tries to sweep up a torrent of decaying leaves that sift down into a roofless house, just as in the city Emily (along with the narrator and Gerald) tries to deal with a dying society by helping look after the homeless children. The other scene is a room in which an old faded carpet is gradually being brought to color, life, and meaning through the work of many people, each finding a matching piece from a separate pile of bright-colored fabric and putting it in place, a metaphor for the creation of the City, and the only sign in this novel of others engaged in similar attempts to triumph over a failing world.

The final triumph is not in the world outside but behind the wall. When things are at their worst, and the rat children have gained complete control, the narrator, Emily, Gerald, and Hugo wait out an interminable winter inside the apartment. Suddenly a weak patch of sun on the wall brings a realization that something important is imminent. The wall opens and this time all of them enter. Finally the elusive presence has taken a form, a beautiful goddess figure, who leads them through a new door as the old world dissolves into glittering fragments. Gerald hesitates for a moment because the unregenerate children he has cared for are behind him, but at the last moment they run through also. This event, grace, represents a new step in Lessing's thought.

In *The Memoirs of a Survivor* the City is entirely of the spirit. There is nothing here comparable to the blade of grass after the holocaust spoken of in *The Golden Notebook* or the new children in *The Four-Gated City*, who will eventually create a new society. As in *The Summer before the Dark*, the physical world simply loses its hold as an inner, spiritual world develops.

Nevertheless, the City is created here, as in all the novels, by shedding the rigid layers of the persona, exploration of and unification with inner space, and responsibility for others. None of the four would have reached the City and helped others to get there except for their sense of duty and love. It is clear that Emily would have left—dropped off the edge of the earth—except for her attachment first to Hugo and then the children. The narrator stays because Emily does, and Gerald is entirely devoted to the children in his communes. Hugo is the symbol of duty and devotion: although miserable when he feels unloved, he nevertheless seems to believe that his one role in life is to look after Emily, and in his own way he does so. At the end, his ugliness is transformed into beauty and dignity.

The Memoirs of a Survivor reflects Lessing's consistent pessimism about society and her increasing perception of the need for and possibility of spiritual enlightenment. She has called it an autobiography and it should be seen as that: not a science-fiction tale but a pilgrim's progress, in which she shares with her readers her own experience of different and difficult ways of being, long forgotten by the city, both inside and outside the novel.

Appendix

Notebooks	Shadow of the Third	Free Women
Anna Wulf	Ella	Anna Wulf
Michael (lover)	Paul Tanner (source of name is perhaps Paul Blackenhurst of Africa)	Michael
Janet	Michael (son, named for Anna's lover)	————
Molly	Julia	Molly Jacobs
Richard	————	Richard
(unnamed wife)	————	Marion
Tommy (age 17)	————	Tommy (age 20)
Mrs. Marks (Mother Sugar)	————	Mrs. Marks (Mother Sugar)
In final blue notebook and golden notebook:		
Saul Green	————	Milt

Notes

Chapter 1

1. Quoted by William York Tindall, *The Literary Symbol* (1955; reprt. Bloomington, Ind.: Indiana University Press, 1965), p. 181.
2. Lessing, *Martha Quest* (1952; reprt. New York: Simon and Schuster, 1964), p. 21. Further references in the text will be to this edition.
3. Lessing, "The Small Personal Voice" (1957; reprt. in *A Small Personal Voice* [New York: Alfred A. Knopf, 1974]), pp. 9,7.
4. Drabble, "Doris Lessing: Cassandra in a World Under Siege," *Ramparts* 10 (February 1972): 54.
5. 1951; reprt. in *African Stories* (New York: Ballantine Books, 1966), pp. 64, 66, 68. Further references in the text will be to this edition.
6. C. G. Jung, *The Integration of the Personality*, trans. Stanley Dell (New York and London: Farrar and Rinehart, 1939), p. 71.
7. "Approaching the Unconscious," *Man and His Symbols* (1964; reprt. New York: Dell, 1968), p. 83.
8. 1951; reprt. in *African Stories*, pp. 204, 206, 217, 221.
9. Diane Smith in "Ant Imagery as Thematic Device in the *Children of Violence* series," unpublished paper for MLA Seminar 46: The Fiction of Doris Lessing (1971), lists many instances of Lessing's use of ants as a destructive force. I would add only that there is no value judgment accorded this destruction. It is simply a fact of nature.
10. 1953; reprt. in *African Stories*, p. 390.
11. Erich Neumann, *The Origins and History of Consciousness*, trans. R. F. C. Hull (1949; reprt. New York: Pantheon Books, 1954), p. 15.
12. C. G. Jung, "The Structure of the Psyche," *The Collected Works*, vol. 8, ed. G. Adler, M. Fordham, and H. Read; trans. R. F. C. Hull (Princeton, N. J.: Princeton University Press, 1960), para. 329.
13. "unbroken, continuous whole," Ernst Cassirer, *An Essay on Man* (New Haven, Conn.: Yale University Press, 1944), p. 81; "the deep . . . nature," *An Essay on Man*, p. 82.

14. "Whatever . . . Reality," Ernst Cassirer, *Language and Myth*, trans. Susanne K. Langer (New York: Harper Brothers, 1946), p. 56; "only . . . exists," *Language and Myth*, p. 57.

15. Cassirer, *An Essay on Man*, pp. 25–26.

16. Cassirer, *Language and Myth*, p. 3.

17. A. N. Whitehead, "Uses of Symbolism," in *Symbolism in Religion and Literature*, ed. Rollo May (New York: George Braziller, 1960), p. 241.

18. Lessing, *The Four-Gated City* (New York: Alfred A. Knopf, 1969), pp. 429, 430. Further references in the text will be to this edition.

19. Joseph Campbell, *The Masks of God: Primitive Mythology* (New York: Viking, 1959), p. 472.

20. Cassirer, *Essay*, p. 62.

21. Meyer Abrams, *The Mirror and the Lamp* (New York: Oxford University Press, 1953), p. 65. The quotation is from Coleridge to Wordsworth, 30 May 1815, *Letters*, 2: 648–49.

22. Sewell, *The Orphic Voice: Poetry and Natural History* (New Haven, Conn.: Yale University Press, 1960), p. 36.

23. William York Tindall, *Forces in Modern British Literature: 1885–1946* (New York: Alfred A. Knopf, 1947), p. 186.

24. Charles Feidelson, Jr., *Symbolism and American Literature*, 2d ed. (New York: Phoenix Books, 1959), p. 50.

25. Krishna, *The Biological Basis of Religion and Genius*, 2d ed. (New York: Harper and Row, 1972), pp. 42–43.

26. Ornstein, *The Psychology of Consciousness* (San Francisco: W. H. Freeman, 1972), pp. 12–13.

27. Werner Heisenberg, "The Representation of Nature in Contemporary Physics," trans. O. T. Bentley, *Year Book of the Bavarian Academy of Fine Arts* 3 (1954); reprinted in *Symbolism in Religion and Literature*, p. 232.

28. Ibid.

29. Cassirer, *Essay*, p. 25.

30. Jung, "Approaching the Unconscious," p. 45.

31. Lessing, *The Temptation of Jack Orkney and Other Stories* (New York: Alfred A. Knopf, 1972), p. 277.

32. Krishna, *The Biological Basis*, pp. 115–16.

Chapter 2

1. Whitehead, pp. 241, 243, 250.

2. This aspect of Lessing's work is one of her most important and obvious themes. It has received attention by Paul Schlueter, *The Novels of Doris Lessing* (Carbondale, Ill.: Southern Illinois Press, 1973) and also two dissertations: Alfred A. Carey, "Doris Lessing: The Search for Reality," Ph.D. diss., University of Wiscon-

Notes

sin, 1965; Diane E. Sherwood Smith, "A Thematic Study of Doris Lessing's *Children of Violence*," Ph.D. diss., Loyala University, 1971.

3. 1951; reprt. in *African Stories*, p. 49. Further references in the text will be to this edition.

4. (1962; reprt. New York: MeGraw-Hill, 1963), p. 142. Further references in the text will be to this edition.

5. Lessing, *Landlocked* (1965; reprt. New York: Simon and Schuster, 1966), p. 539. Further references in the text will be to this edition.

6. (New York: Alfred A. Knopf, 1972), pp. 274-75. Further references in the text will be to this edition.

7. Jung uses the same phrase to argue against a reductive theory in the views of Adler and Freud on neurosis: "They say to everything, 'You are nothing but . . . .' They explain to the sufferer that his symptoms come from here and from there and are nothing but this or that." *Collected Works*, vol. 8, "The Problem of the Attitude Type," para. 67.

8. (New York: Alfred A. Knopf, 1969), p. 420. Further references in the text are to this edition.

9. McDowell, "'The Devious Involutions of Human Character and Emotions': Reflections on Some Recent British Novels," *Wisconsin Studies in Contemporary Literature* 4, no. 3 (Autumn 1963): 348.

10. Cf. Alfred A. Carey: "Is there no such thing as the 'real' Julia Barr? 'We are all interchangeable,' she said earlier. Martha Quest felt this also. We are all creatures of forces outside our control which make us what we are. . . . The terrible truth may be that all men *are* interchangeable; only the systems allow them to seem independent." "Doris Lessing: The Search for Reality," p. 190.

11. Lessing, *Going Home* (London: Michael Joseph, 1957), p. 35.

12. Lessing, "A Mild Attack of Locusts" (1955); reprt. in *African Stories*, p. 573.

13. Lessing, "The Sun Between their Feet" (1963); reprt. in *African Stories*, p. 627. Cf. Anne M. Mulkeen, "Twentieth-Century Realism: The 'Grid' Structure of *The Golden Notebook*," *Studies in the Novel* 4 (Summer 1972): 273. Mulkeen notes that the beetle's lack of vision makes it impossible for him "to open himself to new possibilities."

14. Lessing, "A Letter from Home" (1963); reprt. in *African Stories*, pp. 633–34.

15. Lessing, "The Story of Two Dogs" (1963); reprt. in *African Stories*, p. 667.

16. Lessing, *Particularly Cats* (New York: Simon and Schuster, 1967), p. 15.

17. Lessing, "The Second Hut" (1951); reprt. in *African Stories*, pp. 97–98.

18. Lessing, "Plants and Girls" (1957); reprt. in *African Stories*, p. 613.

19. Abrams, pp. 171–72.

20. Lessing, "Dialogue," *A Man and Two Women* (New York: Simon and Schuster, 1963), p. 242. Further references in the text will be to this edition.

21. Langer, *Feeling and Form* (New York: Scribner, 1953), pp. 397, 409.

22. Cassirer, *Language and Myth*, p. 98.

23. Lessing, "The DeWets Come to Kloof Grange" (1951); reprt. in *African Stories*, p. 115.

1. Doris Lessing, quoted by Roy Newquist, Interview by Roy Newquist, 1964, reprt. in *A Small Personal Voice*, p. 60.

2. Lessing, *In Pursuit of the English* (London: MacGibbon and Kee, 1960), p. 1.

3. Lessing, *The Grass Is Singing* (1950; reprt. New York: Ballantine, 1964), p. 57. Further references in the text will be to this edition.

4. Ellen Brooks in "Fragmentation and Integration: A Study of Doris Lessing's Fiction," Ph.D. diss., New York University, 1971, pp. 331–32, shows how this novel may also be read in terms of Freud. Accordingly, Moses represents the id, while the conventional ethics of society constitute Mary's superego. Since Mary's repression is sexual, either a Freudian or Jungian reading of the novel is possible.

5. R. D. Laing, *The Politics of Experience* 1967; reprt. New York: Ballantine, 1968), pp. 141, 129. Further references in the text are to this edition.

6. The preceding paragraph is summarized from Laing, p. 129.

7. Both Brooks and Marchino have pointed out resemblances between Laing's and Lessing's views of mental illness. See "Fragmentation and Integration," p. 528, and Lois Marchino, "The Search for Self in the Novels of Doris Lessing," *Studies in the Novel* 4 (Summer 1972): 259. Marchino shows several resemblances between Charles Watkin's inner journey and Laing's chapter, "The Ten-Day Voyage."

8. Lessing, "On *The Golden Notebook*," *Partisan Review* 40, no. 1 (Winter 1973): 14.

9. Ibid., p. 15.

10. Ibid.

11. Yet this is sometimes the assumption. See, e.g., Schleuter, p. 111. However, as John L. Carey points out in "Art and Reality in *The Golden Notebook*," *Contemporary Literature* 14 (Autumn 1973): 440, "By making Anna her author, Lessing blurs almost totally the distinction between truth and fiction."

12. Jung, *Collected Works*, vol. 8, "On the Nature of the Psyche," para. 430.

13. Ibid., vol. 13, "Commentary on *The Secret of the Golden Flower*," para. 67.

14. Ibid., vol. 17, "The Development of Personality," para. 317.

15. Annis Pratt, "The Contrary Structure of Doris Lessing's *The Golden Notebook*," *World Literature Written in English* 12 (November 1973), has related these contrarieties to the myth of William Blake. Pratt finds three main dichotomies: naiveté or openness to experience opposed to close-minded cynicism; chaos versus partitions; and spiritual nakedness versus rigidity.

16. Cf. Annis Pratt in "The Contrary Structure," who sees the main theme of the red notebook to be Anna's struggle between wishing to keep her vision of communism and having to face such events as the McCarthy purges and the Prague executions of the 1950s.

17. Jung's research and conclusions are presented mainly in *Alchemical Studies*, *Collected Works*, vol. 13, and *Mysterium Coniunctionis*, ibid., vol. 14.

18. Jung, *Integration of the Personality*, p. 227.

19. *See* Shah, *The Sufis* (New York: Doubleday, 1964), pp. 194–95. Many of

Shah's arguments about the widespread influence of Sufism are based on the structure of Arabic with its cluster of words around a given root. As a result of the structure, a complex set of symbols could be built up to disguise the exact nature of Sufic ideas, which were frequently heretical. However, the abstruse meanings were often lost in translation.

20. Jung, *Integration of the Personality*, p. 227.

21. Jung, *Mysterium Coniunctionis*, para. 4.

22. In this list of meanings I am oversimplifying a very complex matter, since the symbols tend to overlap and vary. Alchemical texts are vague and abstruse, deliberately so, since the alchemists were indulging in a forbidden enterprise except insofar as their work blended with Christianity. Jung's *Mysterium Coniunctionis* traces the enormous complexity of alchemical symbols. Here I am following John Read, *The Alchemist in Life, Literature, and Art* (London: Thomas Nelson and Sons, 1947), p. 7, for the meanings of salt, for sulphur as sun, fire, soul, and air, and mercury as moon, water, and spirit. The other attributes are from Jung (who also touches on Read's meanings, but much less simply). Shah shows linguistically how the original meanings were sulphur, homonym for *kibirat* (greatness, nobility); salt, homonym of *milh* (goodness, learning), and mercury, sharing the root for "To open a lock, to break." Among the Sufis as well as the medieval alchemists, the meanings were complex and secret. Ibn el-Arabi gives another version, that sulphur stands for the divine and mercury for nature. "The interaction in correct proportion produces the Azoth, the ennobled essence." (These are closer to Jung's meanings.) *See* Shah, *The Sufis*, p. 195.

23. Read, *The Alchemist*, p. 7.

24. Quoted by Read, p. 7.

25. Read, p. 9.

26. Jung, *Mysterium Coniunctionis*, para. 137.

27. Ibid., para. 168.

28. Jaffé, "Symbolism in the Visual Arts," *Man and His Symbols*, pp. 277–78.

29. Neumann, *Origins*, p. 15.

30. Neumann cites for references: Helen Schoch-Bodmer, "Die Spirale als Symbol und als Strukturelement des Lebendigen," *Schweizerische Zeitschrift fur Psychologie und ihre Anwendungen (bern)*, vol. 4 (1945): 324 ff., and Hans Leisegang, "Das Mysterium der Schlange," *Eranos-Jahrbuck 1939* (Zurich, 1940), pp. 151–250.

31. von Franz, "The Process of Individuation," *Man and His Symbols*, p. 247.

32. (New York: Alfred A. Knopf, 1971), p. 131. Further references in the text will be to this edition.

33. Barnouw, "Disorderly Company: From *The Golden Notebook* to *The Four-Gated City*," *Contemporary Literature* 14 (Autumn 1973): 503, 493.

34. Jung, "Approaching the Unconscious," pp. 165–66.

35. Jung, "The Synthetic or Constructive Method," *Collected Works*, vol. 7, para. 113.

36. Jung, *Integration of the Personality*, p. 111.

37. Jung, "The Persona as a Segment of the Collective Psyche," *Collected Works*, vol. 7, para. 251.

38. Jung, "Paracelsus as a Spiritual Phenomenon," *Collected Works*, vol. 13, para. 210.

39. Jung, *Integration of the Personality*, p. 303. Cf. also a quotation in Laing (p. 134) from Karl Jaspers, *General Psychopathology* (Manchester, England: Manchester University Press, 1962), pp. 417–18. Jaspers recorded a patient's experience in his own words: "I believe I caused the illness myself. In my attempt to penetrate the other world I met its natural guardians, the embodiment of my own weaknesses and fault. I first thought these demons were lowly inhabitants of the other world who could play me like a ball because I went into these regions unprepared and lost my way. Later I thought they were split-off parts of my own mind (passions) which existed near me in free space and thrived on my feelings. I believed everyone else had these too but did not perceive them, thanks to the protective successful deceit of the feeling of personal existence." The patient then endures a life-and-death struggle against these demons. In the end, they shrivel and vanish. He forms a new persona of "conventional lies, shams, self-deceptions, memory images, a self just like that of other people" (a description resembling Lessing's view of the persona). But now behind it is a higher self that sounds much like the one described by Jung as the product of individuation, the superior personality that somehow stands above the joys and sorrows of everyday life and the part of the personality that is affected by them. In Lessing's novels, Anna Wulf, Martha Hesse, and Kate Brown all form such a personality.

40. Jung, *Integration of the Personality*, p. 41.

41. Ibid., p. 303.

42. Jung, "Basic Postulates of Analytical Psychology," *Collected Works*, vol. 8, para. 674.

43. Lessing, *The Temptation of Jack Orkney and Other Stories*, p. 280.

44. Cf. Marchino, p. 259. She points out a number of parallels between the two episodes.

45. Shah, p. 195.

46. The preceding information on the Hermetic tradition is summarized from Shah, pp. 194–98.

47. Titus Burckhardt, *Alchemy: Science of the Cosmos, Science of the Soul*, trans. William Stoddart (London: Stuart and Watkins, 1967), pp. 79–80.

48. (New York: Alfred A. Knopf, 1973), p. 77.

Chapter 4

1. Lessing, "On *The Golden Notebook*," p. 19.

2. Lessing, "The Small Personal Voice," p. 12.

3. Jonah Raskin, "Doris Lessing at Stony Brook: An Interview," 1970; reprt. in *A Small Personal Voice*, p. 70.

4. (New Haven, Conn.: Yale University Press, 1960), p. 304.

5. Newquist, p. 57.

6. (1952; reprt. New York: Simon and Schuster, 1964), p. 535. Further references in the text will be to this edition.

7. Jung, *Integration of the Personality*, p. 273.

8. Jung, "On the Nature of the Psyche," *Collected Works*, vol. 8, paras. 426, 405.

9. Jung, *Integration of the Personality*, p. 295.

10. However, "Little Tembi" in *African Stories* dramatizes that to do so in a corrupt society may do more harm than good. Singled out for attention, the child comes to expect more than society can grant him, and as a result his life ends tragically.

11. (New Haven, Conn.: Yale University Press, 1971), p. 19.

12. Raskin, "Doris Lessing at Stony Brook," pp. 65–66.

Chapter 5

1. Lessing's place in this tradition has been pointed out by Diane Smith, "A Thematic Study," p. 225.

2. S. Foster Damon, *A Blake Dictionary* (Providence, R.I.: Brown University Press, 1965), p. 206.

3. Blake, "Jerusalem" (74, 1. 10), *The Poems of William Blake*, ed. W. H. Stevenson (London: Longman, 1971), p. 788. Further references in the text are to this edition.

4. Underhill, *Mysticism* (1911; reprt. and rev. ed., London: Methuen, 1949), p. 71.

5. Shah, p. 25.

6. Lessing, "An Elephant in the Dark," *Spectator* 213 (18 September 1964): 373.

7. Joseph Strelka, "Comparative Criticism and Literary Symbolism," in *Perspectives in Literary Symbolism*, ed. Joseph Strelka, *Yearbook of Comparative Criticism* (University Park, Pa.: Pennsylvania State University Press, 1968): 17–18.

8. Smith, pp. 242, 161.

9. Raskin, "Doris Lessing at Stony Brook," p. 70.

10. (New York: Alfred A. Knopf, 1973), p. 174. Further references in the text are to this edition.

11. Clarence W. Richey has shown that the image of the cold, hungry moon that is fed by energy "from a state of consciousness known as sleep" may be found in the G. I. Gurdjieff-P. D. Ouspensky system of esoteric psychology. "Professor Watkin's 'Sleep of Necessity': A Note on the Parallel between Doris Lessing's Briefing for a Descent into Hell and the G. I. Gurdjieff-P. D. Ouspensky System of Esoteric Psychology," *Notes on Contemporary Literature 2*, no. 2 (March 1972): 9–10.

12. See, e.g., John Leonard, "The Last Word," *New York Times Book Review*, 13 May 1973, p. 47.

13. See Nancy Shields Hardin, "Doris Lessing and the Sufi Way," *Contemporary Literature* 14 (Autumn 1973), for a discussion of Sufism and its relation to "The Other Garden" and "Out of the Fountain."

Selected Bibliography

Primary Works

Lessing, Doris. *African Stories*. 1964. Reprint. New York: Ballantine Books, 1966.

_____. *Briefing for a Descent into Hell*. New York: Alfred A. Knopf, 1971.

_____. "An Elephant in the Dark." *Spectator* 213 (18 September 1964): 373.

_____. *The Four-Gated City*. New York: Alfred A. Knopf, 1969.

_____. *Going Home*. London: Michael Joseph, 1957.

_____. *The Golden Notebook*. 1962. Reprint. New York: McGraw-Hill, 1963.

_____. *The Grass Is Singing*. 1950. Reprint. New York: Ballantine Books, 1964.

_____. *The Habit of Loving*. New York: MacGibbon and Kee, 1957.

_____. *In Pursuit of the English*. London: MacGibbon and Kee, 1960.

_____. *Landlocked*. 1965. Reprinted in *Children of Violence*. New York: Simon and Schuster, 1966.

_____. *A Man and Two Women*. New York: Simon and Schuster, 1963.

_____. *Martha Quest*. 1952. Reprinted in *Children of Violence*. New York: Simon and Schuster, 1967.

———. "On *The Golden Notebook*." Partisan Review 40, no. 1 (Winter 1973): 15–30.

———. *Particularly Cats*. New York: Simon and Schuster, 1967.

———. *A Proper Marriage*. 1954. Reprinted in *Children of Violence*. New York: Simon and Schuster, 1964.

———. *Retreat to Innocence*. London: Michael Joseph, 1954.

———. *A Ripple from the Storm*. 1958. Reprinted in *Children of Violence*. New York: Simon and Schuster, 1964.

———. *A Small Personal Voice*. New York: Alfred A. Knopf, 1974.

———. "The Small Personal Voice." In *Declaration*, edited by Tom Maschler. London: MacGibbon and Kee, 1957, pp. 12–27. Reprinted in Lessing, Doris. *A Small Personal Voice*. New York: Alfred A. Knopf, 1974, pp. 61–76.

———. *The Summer Before the Dark*. New York: Alfred A. Knopf, 1973.

———. *The Temptation of Jack Orkney and Other Stories*. New York: Alfred A. Knopf, 1972.

Interviews

Newquist, Roy. "Interview by Roy Newquist." *Counterpoint*. New York: Rand McNally, 1964. Reprinted in Lessing, Doris. *A Small Personal Voice*. New York: Alfred A. Knopf, 1974, pp. 45–60.

Raskin, Jonah. "Doris Lessing at Stony Brook: An Interview." *North American Review* 8 (June 1970): 172–84. Reprinted in Lessing, Doris. *A Small Personal Voice*. New York: Alfred A. Knopf, 1974, pp. 61–76.

Critical Studies

Barnouw, Dagmar. "Disorderly Company: From *The Golden Notebook* to *The Four-Gated City*." *Contemporary Literature* 14 (Autumn 1973): 491–514.

Brooks, Ellen W. "Fragmentation and Integration: A Study of Doris Lessing's Fiction. " Ph.D. dissertation, New York University, 1971.

Carey, Alfred A. "Doris Lessing: The Search for Reality." Ph.D. dissertation, University of Wisconsin, 1965.

Carey, John. "Art and Reality in *The Golden Notebook.*" *Contemporary Literature* 14 (Autumn 1973): 437–56.

Drabble, Margaret. "Doris Lessing: Cassandra in a World Under Siege." *Ramparts* 10 (February 1972): 50–54.

Hardin, Nancy Shields. "Doris Lessing and the Sufi Way." *Contemporary Literature* 14 (Autumn 1973): 565–81.

Leonard, John. "The Last Word." *New York Times Book Review*, 13 May 1973, p. 47.

McDowell, Frederick P. W. " 'The Devious Involutions of Human Character and Emotions': Reflections on Some Modern British Novels." *Wisconsin Studies in Contemporary Literature* 4, no. 3 (Autumn 1963): 339–66. (Discusses Lessing pp. 346–50.)

————. "The Fiction of Doris Lessing: An Interim View," *Arizona Quarterly* 21 (Winter 1965): 315–45.

Marchino, Lois A. "The Search for Self in the Novels of Doris Lessing." *Studies in the Novel* 4 (Summer 1972): 252–61.

Mulkeen, Anne M. "Twentieth-Century Realism: The 'Grid' Structure of *The Golden Notebook.*" *Studies in the Novel* 4 (Summer 1972): 262–74.

Pratt, Annis. "The Contrary Structure of Doris Lessing's *The Golden Notebook.*" *World Literature Written in English* 12 (November 1973): pp. 150–60.

Richey, Clarence W. "Professor Watkins's 'Sleep of Necessity': A Note on the Parallel between Doris Lessing's *Briefing for a Descent into Hell* and the G. I. Gurdjieff-P. D. Ouspensky System of Esoteric Psychology." *Notes on Contemporary Literature* 2, no. 2 (March 1972): 9–11.

Schlueter, Paul. *The Novels of Doris Lessing.* Carbondale, Ill.: Southern Illinois Press, 1973.

Smith, Diane E. Sherwood. "Ant Imagery as Thematic Device in the *Children of Violence* Series. Unpublished paper for MLA Seminar 46: The Fiction of Doris Lessing (1971).

_____. "A Thematic Study of Doris Lessing's *Children of Violence*. Ph.D. dissertation, Loyola University, 1971.

General Works

Abrams, Meyer. *The Mirror and the Lamp*. New York: Oxford University Press, 1953.

Blake, William. *The Poems of William Blake*. Edited by W. H. Stevenson. London: Longman, 1971.

Burckhardt, Titus. *Alchemy: Science of the Cosmos, Science of the Soul*. Translated by William Stoddart. London: Stuart and Watkins, 1967.

Campbell, Joseph. *The Masks of God: Primitive Mythology*. New York: Viking Press, 1959.

Cassirer, Ernst. *An Essay on Man*. New Haven, Conn.: Yale University Press, 1944.

_____. *Language and Myth*. Translated by Susanne Langer. New York: Harper Brothers, 1946.

Damon, Foster S. *A Blake Dictionary*. Providence, R. I.: Brown University Press, 1965.

Feidelson, Charles, Jr. *Symbolism in American Literature*. 2d ed. 1953. Reprt. New York: Phoenix Books, 1959.

Heisenberg, Werner. "The Representation of Nature in Contemporary Physics." Translated by O. T. Bentley. In *Year Book of the Bavarian Academy of Fine Arts* 3 (1954). Reprinted in *Symbolism in Religion and Literature*. Edited by Rollo May. New York: George Braziller, 1960, pp. 215–32.

Jaffé, Aniela. "Symbolism in the Visual Arts. In *Man and His Symbols*. Edited by C. G. Jung. 1964. Reprt. New York: Dell, 1968, pp. 255–322.

Jaspers, Karl. *General Psychopathology*. Manchester, England: Manchester University Press, 1962.

Jung, Carl G. "Approaching the Unconscious." In *Man and His Symbols*. Edited by C. G. Jung. 1964. Reprt. New York: Dell, 1968, pp. 1–94.

_____. *The Collected Works*. 17 vols. Edited by G. Adler, M. Fordham, and H. Read. Translated (except for vol. 3) by R. F. C. Hull. London: Routledge and Kegan Paul, Ltd. and Bollingen Series. Princeton, N. J.: Princeton University Press, 1944–1967.

―――. *The Integration of the Personality.* Translated by Stanley Dell. New York and London: Farrar and Rinehart, 1939.

Krishna, Gopi. *The Scientific Basis for Religion and Genius.* 2d ed. New York: Harper and Row, 1972.

Laing, R. D. *The Politics of Experience.* 1967. Reprt. New York: Ballantine Books, 1968.

Langer, Susanne. *Feeling and Form.* New York: Scribner, 1953.

Neumann, Erich. *The Origins and History of Consciousness.* Translated by R. F. C. Hull. 1949. Reprt. New York: Pantheon Books, 1954.

Ornstein, Robert. *The Psychology of Consciousness.* San Francisco: W. H. Freeman, 1972.

Read, John. *The Alchemist in Life, Literature, and Art.* London: Thomas Nelson and Sons, 1947.

Sewell, Elizabeth. *The Orphic Voice: Poetry and Natural History.* New Haven, Conn.: Yale University Press, 1960.

Shah, Idries. *The Sufis.* New York: Doubleday, 1964.

Steiner, George. *In Bluebeard's Castle: Some Notes Toward the Redefinition of Culture.* New Haven, Conn.: Yale University Press, 1961.

Strelka, Joseph. "Comparative Criticism and Literary Symbolism." In *Perspectives in Literary Symbolism.* Edited by Joseph Strelka. *Yearbook of Comparative Criticism* 1 (University Park, Pa.: Pennsylvania State University Press, 1968): 1–28.

Tindall, William York. *Forces in Modern British Literature: 1885–1946.* New York: Alfred A. Knopf, 1947.

―――. *The Literary Symbol.* 1955. Reprt. Bloomington, Ind.: Indiana University Press, 1965.

Underhill, Evelyn. *Mysticism.* 1911. Reprt. and rev. London: Methuen, 1949.

von Franz, M.-L. "The Process of Individuation." In *Man and His Symbols.* Edited by C. G. Jung. 1964. Reprt. New York: Dell, 1968, pp. 157–254.

Whitehead, Alfred N. "Uses of Symbolism." In *Symbolism in Religion and Literature.* Edited by Rollo May. New York: George Braziller, 1960, pp. 233–50.

Index

[241]